THE ARCHITECTS OF TOXIC POLITICS IN AMERICA

The Architects of Toxic Politics in America: Venom and Vitriol explains the history of poison politics in America by profiling some of the key political "attack dogs" who have shaped the modern landscape.

Comparing and contrasting the Trump and Biden presidencies with administrations of the past, the book explains the unique character of the current toxic political moment and the forces that have created it. The book also focuses quite extensively on "non-presidential" architects of toxic politics: other politicians, campaign strategists, activists, and media figures (and a few key figures that have fulfilled two or more of these roles). Drawing on his long career as a journalist specializing in presidential coverage, Kenneth T. Walsh argues that due to the complex, often conflicting nature of American government, the angriest, most decisive voices can command media, voter, and legislative attention and thereby maintain and consolidate power. This results in frustration, alienation, and cynicism—and ultimately, a diminishment of voter participation that can reinforce the vicious cycle and lead to electoral disaster.

For anyone interested in politics, media, and the culture of "gotcha" journalism, this book will also be a valuable addition to undergraduate and graduate courses on politics, the presidency, political and media ethics, campaign history, and government.

Kenneth T. Walsh is a journalist, historian, and author. He covered the White House for more than 30 years for *U.S. News & World Report* and he is former president of the White House Correspondents' Association. He is an adjunct professorial lecturer at the American University School of Communication in Washington, D.C.

THE ARCHITECTS OF TOXIC POLITICS IN AMERICA

Venom and Vitriol

Kenneth T. Walsh

Routledge
Taylor & Francis Group
NEW YORK AND LONDON

Designed cover image: Getty/ tirc83

First published 2024
by Routledge
605 Third Avenue, New York, NY 10158

and by Routledge
4 Park Square, Milton Park, Abingdon, Oxon, OX14 4RN

Routledge is an imprint of the Taylor & Francis Group, an informa business

ISBN: 9780367710507 (hbk)
ISBN: 9780367710477 (pbk)
ISBN: 9781003149095 (ebk)

DOI: 10.4324/9781003149095

Typeset in Sabon
by Deanta Global Publishing Services, Chennai, India

For Barclay

CONTENTS

ABOUT THE AUTHOR

Kenneth T. Walsh is a journalist, historian, and author. He covered the White House for more than 30 years for *U.S. News & World Report*, including the presidencies of Ronald Reagan, George H.W. Bush, Bill Clinton, George W. Bush, Barack Obama, Donald Trump, and Joe Biden. He was one of the longest-serving White House correspondents in history. Walsh has won the most prestigious awards for White House coverage and he is former president of the White House Correspondents' Association. He is an adjunct professorial lecturer at the American University School of Communication in Washington, D.C. Walsh remains active as a commentator for various publications and media platforms, is a frequent TV and radio analyst on national affairs, and he gives many speeches in the United States and abroad. This is his tenth book about the U.S. presidency. His other titles include *Presidential Leadership in Crisis: Defining Moments of the Modern Presidents from Franklin Roosevelt to Donald Trump*, *Air Force One: A History of the Presidents and Their Planes*, and *Celebrity in Chief: A History of the Presidents and the Culture of Stardom*.

ACKNOWLEDGMENTS

I'd like to express my appreciation to the many individuals who provided support and assistance in writing this book and who helped to shape my thinking about toxic politics and its impact on American life.

They include five of the presidents whom I covered since I began as a White House correspondent in 1986: Ronald Reagan, George H.W. Bush, Bill Clinton, George W. Bush, and Barack Obama. I interviewed all of them during the course of my three-decade career as a White House correspondent and got to know them well.

Among the others I'd like to thank are the scholars and political strategists who for many years offered invaluable insights, such as Roger Ailes, Lee Atwater, David Axelrod, Howard Baker, Ross Baker, Dan Bartlett, Cornell Belcher, Doug Brinkley, James Carville, Bob Dallek, Dave Demarest, Frank Donatelli, Matthew Dowd, Ken Duberstein, Rahm Emanuel, Al Felzenberg, Marlin Fitzwater, Don Foley, Al From, Bill Galston, Geoff Garin, David Gergen, Ed Gillespie, Ed Goeas, Stan Greenberg, Steve Hadley, Jane Hall, Peter Hart, Karen Hughes, Bill Kristol, Joe Lockhart, Frank Luntz, Kevin Madden, Mary Matalin, Mike McCurry, Bill McInturff, Mack McLarty, Leon Panetta, Dana Perino, Roman Popadiuk, Colin Powell, Jen Psaki, Karl Rove, Bob Rubin, Larry Sabato, Brent Scowcroft, Leonard Steinhorn, Larry Summers, Sheila Tate, Tevi Troy, and Mark Updegrove.

Thanks to the staff at the presidential libraries and the White House Historical Association, wonderful resources for scholars and anyone who wants to learn more about America's presidents and the institution of the presidency.

And thanks to my children, Jean Walsh and Chris Walsh, for their unstinting support for their father and for their pursuit of their own visions of public service.

Most of all, I would like to thank Barclay Walsh, my wife and life partner, for all her support and assistance. Barclay used her talents as a professional researcher to improve this book in many ways, including shaping my thoughts about the topic.

I want to give a special acknowledgment to my parents, Tom and Gloria Walsh. My father, who died at age 82 in 2002, showed me the importance of strength, perseverance, and the work ethic. My mother, who died at age 95 in 2020 while I was writing this book, was a beacon of character, intelligence, and candor. My parents instilled in me the attitudes and values to succeed as a journalist, an author, and a person.

Kenneth T. Walsh
Bethesda, Maryland

PREFACE

This book stems from my growing distress about the negativity in politics that is poisoning our discourse as a nation, undermining civil society, and casting doubt on the legitimacy of democratic government.

After covering the presidency and national campaigns for more than three decades and studying politics and the presidency as a university teacher and author, it has become increasingly clear to me that our politics has become particularly toxic and unhealthy. The consequences have been profound.

Americans, distrustful and suspicious, now separate themselves into distinct social compartments in many ways. They frequently refuse to associate with people who seem "different," don't listen to people with opposing viewpoints, and increasingly consider their version of the truth and policy choices as holy writ. Having an open mind is no longer a core value. Truth itself is under attack, propelled by lies and deceptions, often by former President Donald Trump and his followers. American democracy is in trouble.

One of my main goals in writing this book is to explain the history and causes of this perilous state of affairs. It turns out that toxic politics, while particularly strong these days, is nothing new. It is part of our political DNA, and has a permanency that will make it all the more difficult to reduce.

This book will show that presidents, who have vast influence on the tone and substance of American politics, have frequently been promoters of discord, resentment, fear, and anger. In addition, a range of political operatives, conflict entrepreneurs, and provocateurs, including media figures and campaign strategists along with social media "influencers," have risen to prominence by spreading rancor.

I hope this book not only shows the depth of the problem but provides some ways to extract us from our current predicament. Perhaps most important is encouraging Americans to relearn the importance of trusting, respecting, and listening to each other.

Kenneth T. Walsh
Bethesda, Maryland

INTRODUCTION

The Reckoning

Venom and vitriol pervade American politics and government today, splintering the nation. Personal attacks and demonization crowd out respectful and productive discourse. Compromise is becoming a dirty word. Leaders spend more time spreading malice than promoting comity. Individual Americans and their representatives in Congress and other offices increasingly dismiss and deride those who don't share their worldview. Language is weaponized as never before to demean people and exploit fear, resentment, and grievance. Many Americans are losing their sense of responsibility, their tolerance, and their respect for others.

An apocalyptic mentality and growing divisions in our political culture are spreading to other areas of national life. They are straining everyday social interactions and damaging confidence in basic institutions such as government, science, schools, the military, law enforcement, and the media, fostering a willingness to label as enemies fellow Americans with differing lifestyles and views. Journalist Amanda Ripley says today's American politics has contaminated many other spheres of national life. "American politics now operate a lot like gang warfare, trapped in recurring cycles of blame, humiliation and revenge, punctuated by acts of violence," Ripley has written. "These kinds of feuds, sometimes known as high conflicts, function like perpetual-motion machines, engaging and frustrating people and never seeming to disappear."[1]

The poisonous culture is undermining our common values and the importance of truth itself as more Americans cling to conspiracy theories, refuse to accept facts, and seek confirmation of their biases rather than considering information that would test their judgments. And the

DOI: 10.4324/9781003149095-1

toxic culture sometimes emboldens domestic extremists to commit acts of violence, even murder. This occurred in Buffalo, New York on May 14, 2022, when a racist white teenager opened fire on people in a grocery store frequented by African Americans, killing ten, police said. It also occurred in Uvalde, Texas on May 24, 2022, when an 18-year-old gunman, seeking notoriety, killed 19 children and two teachers at an elementary school.

The venom even reached the home of then-House Speaker Nancy Pelosi, D-Calif., in the fall of 2022. A conspiracy theorist invaded her San Francisco residence aiming to harm the liberal leader and found her husband Paul Pelosi there alone. The intruder broke his skull with a hammer. Luckily for her, Nancy Pelosi was in Washington, D.C. at the time.

Some Americans may be surprised to learn that the slash-and-burn ethos has been with us for a very long time. It's just more immediate and compelling now because it is spread so effectively by presidents, political operatives, the traditional news media, and social media and individual "influencers" through Twitter or "X," Facebook, Instagram, and other information platforms. There is rising speculation that the United States is heading for more conflict and violence because the negativity is so profound.

Political scientists Nathan P. Kalmoe and Lilliana Mason have written that the nation's two major political parties are increasingly organized "into nearly warring factions with radically opposed visions for America."[2] Unable to find common ground, the parties' hard-line factions have battled each other to a near stalemate in Congress. In fact, there is shrinking room for compromise throughout the political system and a growing sense that confrontation is the only course for those who feel left out of the political system. And the voices are becoming increasingly angry and hostile.

Some legislators such as Rep. Marjorie Taylor Greene, R-Ga., call for a national "divorce"—almost a civil war—in which conservatives go their separate way in setting policy based on a right-wing agenda that includes more availability of guns, less government help for the needy, lower spending, reduced voting rights, and less support for democracy abroad and less opposition to authoritarian regimes, including Vladimir Putin's in Russia.

Commentator Ron Brownstein argues that Republicans are attempting to create their own country in states where they control the legislature and the governorship. In the process, they often shut the Democrats down and don't listen to the opposition's ideas.

Several examples of the caustic culture erupted during a single week during April 2023. *Washington Post* columnist Dan Balz wrote that these cases "highlighted the raging battle underway over the direction of the country."[3]

In a particularly egregious case, majority Republicans in the Tennessee House of Representatives expelled two African American legislators in April 2023 for breaking decorum when the pair participated in a boisterous demonstration in the legislative chamber to protest inaction on gun control. The protest came after a shooter in March killed six people including three children at a Nashville school.[4]

During that same month, two judges, one conservative in Texas and one liberal in Washington State, issued contradictory rulings on access to mifepristone, an abortion drug, in the aftermath of the Supreme Court's decision that overturned the national right to choose abortion. The Texas judge sided with antiabortion forces and the Washington judge sided with pro-abortion advocates. The dueling rulings, which were being adjudicated as this book was being written, show the depth of polarization on this crucial issue. "It seemed to be a metaphor for the conflicts and conflicting viewpoints that drive the opposing forces in the country," Balz wrote.[5]

Gov. Ron DeSantis of Florida continued his war against the Disney corporation over giving prominence to transgender individuals at Disney World and across Florida, which DeSantis opposed.

And former President Donald Trump, true to form, inflamed all sides when he complained bitterly about being indicted by a Manhattan grand jury in March 2023 for paying hush money to porn star Stormy Daniels in 2016 in order to keep her quiet about having sex with him. Trump had been worried that her allegations would damage his 2016 campaign for president, which he won despite Daniels's allegations. The grand jury decided there was sufficient evidence of Trump's guilt, including the charge that he broke campaign-finance laws. Calling it a "witch hunt," Trump denied wrongdoing in the case, which was still working its way through the judicial system as this book was being written. Trump is the first former or current president to face criminal charges.[6]

Trump savaged Manhattan District Attorney Alvin Bragg for persuading the grand jury to indict him. Trump also attacked New York Supreme Court Justice Juan Merchan, who was presiding over the case.[7] This undermined faith in the judicial system, especially among Trump's most loyal followers. And it showed that Trump, as he runs for president again in 2024, will use the same divisive, bullying, grievance- and fear-based tactics he used when he ran successfully in 2016 and when he governed for four years.

In June 2023, Trump also savagely attacked federal special counsel Jack Smith for persuading a grand jury to indict him on 37 charges involving Trump's mishandling, hiding, and refusing to return important government documents when he left office. They included secret files that described the nuclear capabilities of the United States and a foreign government, a foreign country's support for terrorist activities, and a potential U.S. attack on a foreign country. The charges included obstruction of justice, making false statements, and endangering national security.[8]

The former president called prosecutor Smith "a deranged psycho" who wanted to destroy Trump politically and prevent him from being elected president again in 2024.[9]

The cases were being argued in court when this book went to press, but Trump's behavior in these and other cases had already further undermined public faith in governing institutions including the presidency, law enforcement, the Justice Department, the judiciary, the Defense Department, and the media.

As this book will show, the presidents, their operatives and supporters have been most responsible for creating the caustic culture, and Trump is a prime example. Presidents have the loudest megaphone in American life and are vastly influential. They set the tone for public discourse and, unfortunately, many have played a key role in intensifying the toxic environment.

Also instrumental in shaping today's toxic culture are a range of influencers who have become combatants in the culture wars. They range from media personalities who peddle extreme views to independent operatives who are increasingly taking the roles of political provocateurs, merchants of malice, dirty tricksters, and character assassins. "Every high conflict is fueled by conflict entrepreneurs—people who exploit and inflame conflict for their own end," journalist Amanda Ripley says.[10]

Many of the historical threads of recent years, it turns out, lead directly to Donald Trump, the most negative president of all. He used supremely noxious tactics in his successful bid for the presidency in 2016 and while he held power. These included bullying and insulting adversaries, the creation of a near-fanatical cult of personality with himself at its core, and the willingness and ability to stir up grievances, resentments, and fears that have repeatedly emerged in the past, especially among white voters, but erupted with unusual ferocity at Trump's instigation. Trump followed in the footsteps of other authoritarians who were expert showmen.

"Trump has turned Republican politics on its head," long-time GOP pollster Frank Luntz told the *Washington Post* in March 2023. "We were so much more positive and hopeful, and it was Republicans who looked to the future with excitement and energy, but those days are long gone." Now, Luntz added, "Pessimism and negativity breeds more pessimism and negativity. You get darker and darker and go deeper and deeper into a hole, and you cannot emerge."[11]

Luntz was prescient. After Trump declared his candidacy for the presidency in 2024, he again spoke to the dark side of American life and promised his supporters that he would be their "warrior" and their "justice," adding: "And to those who have been wronged and betrayed, I am your retribution." This attitude is central to our problem with toxic politics, since retribution leads to more retribution, with no end in sight. Trump also said he was eager to be a dictator on "Day One" if we were elected again, showing his disdain for democratic norms and embracing authoritarianism. Pressed by critics to defend his approach, Trump said he wanted to use presidential power to close the nation's southern border to illegal immigrants and facilitate drilling for oil to provide more supplies and reduce prices.[12]

Despite his indictment and Trump's defeat in the 2020 election, as of late 2023 he remained a strong force in American politics and many conservatives still imitated his methods. Polls showed that he retained a firm hold on the Republican party as the 2024 campaign began, and GOP voters often backed the candidates he endorsed in 2022 Republican primaries even though a number of the Trumpsters went on to lose general elections.

Ominously, the contaminated atmosphere has led to insurrection. On January 6, 2021, rioters marched on the U.S. Capitol and broke in as they tried unsuccessfully to invalidate the fair and free election of 2020 that ousted Trump and installed Joe Biden as the U.S. president. "Now that we have injected poison into the atmosphere, you have people who don't believe the president [Biden] was legitimately elected," historian Alvin S. Felzenberg told me in an interview for this book. "This has never happened in our history before."[13]

But it is important to remember that the toxic tide, while at tsunami level now and threatening civil society at its core, always has been part of the nation's DNA, ebbing and flowing as Americans' anger, resentment, and sense of grievance waxed and waned.

In some cases, attack politics has been based on the truth, such as when a candidate condemns a mistake by an opponent or an accurately described position on issues. I consider these attacks justifiable as ways to inform voters about candidates seeking office. In other cases, attacks have been out of bounds, based on distortions and lies, such as spreading false rumors about personal matters or fabricating issue positions that aren't real. These are never acceptable and are a major concern of this book.

At a fundamental level, the lure of negativity is part of human nature. As researchers Stuart Soroka, Patrick Fournier, and Lilach Nir have pointed out, people seem drawn to negativity in gathering and assessing information in virtually every sphere, including information about politics and government. Soroka, Fournier, and Nir noted that "News coverage of current affairs is predominantly negative" and

> negativity in news is a product of a human tendency to be more attentive to negative news content. Just how widespread is this tendency? Our evidence suggests that, all around the world, the average human is more physiologically activated by negative than by positive news stories.[14]

"What explains the apparently widespread preference for negative information?" the authors asked.

> One account is rooted in evolutionary theory. Attention to negativity may have been advantageous for survival. Negative information alerts to potential dangers; it has special value in terms of "diagnosticity," or the "vigilance" that is required to avoid negative outcomes. This account of the negativity bias is evident in literatures in psychology, neurology, and, particularly, work on the importance of "orienting responses" in evolutionary biology. This account leads to the expectation of a negativity bias present across all human populations.[15]

"There is no message more powerful, primal, or primitive than the evocation of the need to protect the family and 'tribe,'" social scientist Stevan E. Hobfoll wrote.

> We are genetically primed and culturally shaped to alert, defend, and aggress and even to sacrifice the self in the service of that protection. In fact, the alert, defend, and aggress system is primary and fundamental to how humans are biologically built, emotionally primed, and cognitively programmed. This extends to the protection of our way of life and the fundamental elements of those things we hold most dear—the protective response against threats to our freedom, our nation, our land.[16]

Hobfoll added:

> The most effective way to add fervor, strength, and resolve to any political or social argument is to invoke the specter of loss and doom. The hyperbole of threat, and particularly existential threat, is the most powerful fuel of action. Framing in black and white, not shades of gray, is both the means and the terminus for attracting any audience's attention, whether at the doctor's clinic, in the courtroom, or in the world of politics. Reasonableness and carefully weighed argument does not sell newspapers, does not keep the viewer from the remote control, and does not attract donors' dollars.[17]

Hobfoll said, "Repeated fear messaging produces fear, and if it comes repeatedly from believed sources, be they parents or talk radio, they become reality. This was the Nazi's chief propagandist Joseph Goebbels' brilliant insight."[18]

The social critic H.L. Mencken, known for his savage hyperbole, showed that he understood a basic goal of negative politics when he wrote in 1918, "The whole aim of practical politics is to keep the populace alarmed (and hence clamorous to be led to safety) by menacing it with an endless series of hobgoblins, all of them imaginary."[19]

Offering a more nuanced and contemporary view was Frank Donatelli, a savvy analyst and former White House political director for President Ronald Reagan. "Politics used to be about coalitions," Donatelli told me.

> Now politics is more about money and repetition, Politics now is about reaching people further and further down in your base, and that requires much more negativity and stridency. That's how you get these people to show up at the polls. ... You've got to have people in a constant state of turmoil or those people won't turn out to vote.[20]

And staying popular with core supporters means continuing stridency and fear mongering after a politician is elected.

Political scientist R. Michael Alvarez has written that political attacks can have opposite impacts in different situations. Sometimes, attacks depress voter participation because they turn off citizens to politics and reduce their sense of civic duty. At other times, attacks increase participation because they provide important information to voters and move them to show up at the polls.[21]

Toxic politics was not a problem for the United States initially. The revered George Washington, hero of the Revolutionary War, was elected twice in 1788 and 1792 without an opposing candidate. Washington was a unique figure, considered the country's indispensable man, and few were willing to criticize him.

But in the competitive elections of 1796 and 1800, immediately after Washington retired, politics quickly became incendiary. The atmosphere of U.S. campaigns at the time, Lord Bryce wrote, was frequently "thick with charges, defences, recriminations, 'till the voter knows not what to believe."

The 1800 campaign between Thomas Jefferson and John Adams was particularly vicious, as was the caustic 1828 contest between Andrew Jackson and John Quincy Adams. Their rematch in 1832 was even more nasty. All of these campaigns are analyzed extensively in the next chapter of this book.

And of course the toxicity of American politics intensified in the years prior to the Civil War and sparked violence among members of Congress in the Capitol. I discuss these cases in more detail later in this book and show how the negative methods of the past have become firmly rooted in the practices of today.

The negativity of American politics got a huge boost from the presidents as their office gained extraordinary influence. "During the [20th] Century, particularly since World War II, the presidency went through a sweeping transformation: national politics now hinge on assertive presidential leadership that draws its strength from direct links with the public," wrote political scientists Norman C. Thomas and Joseph A. Pika.

> Changes in the presidency and its role in the larger political system accompanied several long-term developments, including a shift in responsibility for public action from state governments to the federal government, the political mobilization of citizens, and the emergence of the United States as a world power.[22]

Thomas and Pika added:

> Presidents could overcome the weakness of their office through the exercise of leadership skills, primarily the power to persuade. In the American system of fragmented power [divided among the presidency, Congress, the judiciary and the states], presidents had to function as the preeminent bargainer. Governing rested on acts of persuasion, not commands. Presidents could help themselves by consciously making choices that maximized their power to persuade. ... The president has three resources for bargaining: vantage points, which are the formal powers of the office; his reputation among Washington insiders; and popular prestige, which is based on public approval of his performance.[23]

"To be sure, free elections in a two-party system inevitably encourage polarization; voters who like some things about liberals or Democrats and some things about conservatives or Republicans end up having to choose one package or the other," newspaper columnist E.J. Dionne, Jr. has written. "In free elections, each side will always try to polarize the electorate in a way that will leave a majority standing on its side."[24]

The flow of our political system and our society toward negativity regained strong momentum after the end of the cold war consensus about fighting international communism. Victory in the cold war which became clear in the early 1990s removed a strong sense of unity within the United States. At the same time, millions of Americans lost faith in major institutions, such as the presidency, Congress, the Supreme Court, organized religion, banks, the police, and the media.

Intensifying the caustic environment over the years was a parade of political and ideological operatives who gained fame and influence from peddling their political toxins and exploiting the news media which often cannot resist giving a megaphone to the most extreme, loudest, and most outrageous voices. These operatives went a long way toward further contaminating the entire political system. As I will discuss, the rogues' gallery of these operatives and ideologues included the Rev. Charles Coughlin, the notorious right-wing "radio priest" who built up a large following during the 1930s and 1940s; Sen. Joe McCarthy, R-Wis., who led anti-communist witch hunts that increased the nation's paranoia in the 1950s; Lee Atwater, the master of negative politics who worked for Presidents Ronald Reagan and George H.W. Bush in the 1980s; Rush Limbaugh, the famous conservative radio partisan of the early 2000s; and Tucker Carlson, the right-wing Fox News television host who has specialized in slash-and-burn commentary and in recent years gained a large following among the aggrieved and the resentful.

"The history texts will note that by 2016, a leaderless Republican Party was primed for a hostile takeover," journalist Matt Bai wrote.

> Into that breach stepped an accomplished huckster and TV celebrity playing the role of garish billionaire and anti-immigrant populist. ... Trump was a skillful entertainer who terrified the political and media elite, and that was enough. ... But then there's the more alarming version of the free-standing, celebrity president—a demagogue who preys on divisions, an aspiring autocrat whose self-gratification eclipses all public good.[25]

Trump combined many techniques of toxicity from the past to make himself the king of negative politics. The Republican Party, led by Trump, has of late been increasingly dominated by politicians who believed their best hope to gain or hold onto power was to intensify resentments, expand grievances, and rip apart the other side any way they could. For congressional Republicans, this meant relentless attacks on the agenda of leading Democrats, including President Barack Obama, President Joe Biden, and House Speaker Nancy Pelosi, D-Calif., and obstruction of their proposals rather than attempting to find compromise.

The GOP in the House of Representatives, frustrated by being in the minority, even ousted their No. 3 leader, Rep. Liz Cheney, R-Wyo., in May 2021 because she dared to vote for Trump's impeachment for inciting the insurrection. Her removal from her leadership position was an act of vengeance typical of the toxic times. In October 2023, House Republicans led by conservative hard-liners ousted Kevin McCarthy, R-Calif., as House speaker, the chamber's No. 1 leader, after he began cooperating with Democrats.

GOP leaders portrayed the status quo, with the White House and Congress under Democratic control, in apocalyptic terms. They argued that enactment of the Democratic agenda would mean the destruction of liberty, free enterprise, and prosperity and the end of a status quo in which whites dominated politics and culture. Some operators of the Republican fear machine, again led by Trump, had previously made the false claim that Obama, the first African American president, was not born in the United States and was not a legitimate president.

The uses of conspiracy theories, falsehoods, and fear spread exponentially. The toxic atmosphere got so bad that in the spring of 2021, Republicans in several states made clear that they still did not accept the election outcome and wanted to overturn the results and give the presidency back to Trump. This proved impossible, but GOP activists turned their attention to strengthening their position for the 2024 election and taking actions that would suppress the potential Democratic vote. Republicans approved voter suppression bills in Texas, Florida, Georgia, and other places in an effort to minimize the anti-Trump vote in the future. And there was a recount of the 2020 result in Arizona staged by Republicans. It didn't lead to a change in Biden's Arizona victory but did further undermine the integrity of the system among Trump voters. They would not be shaken from their belief in the former president's bogus claims that the 2020 election was "rigged" against him.

"The truth could use more friends in 21st Century America, where a great many citizens have embraced large quantities of hooey—palpable nonsense, especially of the kind promoted by our recently departed president," journalist Robert G. Kaiser wrote in the *Washington Post*.

> The spectacle of Donald Trump's chronic fabricating—more than 30,500 whoppers in a single term in office, according to the *Washington Post*'s fact-checkers—is unique in American history. All those lies and inventions debased our public life. They made everyday lying normal for a great many public figures.[26]

Despite the attempts to deny him the White House, President Biden pledged to reduce the negativity which had marked the Trump administration. Biden had gone negative during his 2020 campaign against Trump, responding to the incumbent's attacks and mockery, but his criticisms were not nearly as harsh or personal as Trump's. After the balloting, Biden promised to be a unifier and reject Trump's brand of incendiary politics. And he did attempt to do this.[27]

However, Trump left a noxious legacy that was very difficult to overcome. Even though Biden, nine days after being sworn in, told Americans that "every disagreement doesn't have to be cause for total war," he eventually concluded that the distrust and cynicism that Trump spread had contaminated politics more than he ever dreamed possible. Americans increasingly live in separate cultural and political compartments, seeking to avoid people who disagree with them or who don't live as they do.

Describing America's caustic environment, scholars Emmett H. Buell and Lee Sigelman have written:

> Although democracies rely on a free, fair, and peaceful process of elections to determine who governs, campaigns typically are described in ways suggestive of warfare. Consider some of the many metaphors of military origin that have a long dominated campaign discourse, beginning with campaign itself. Verbs regularly borrowed from the battlefield include attack, target, invade ... and finish off. One hears countless references to air wars and ground wars, strategies, skirmishes, strongholds, enemy camps, troops on the ground, battleground states, and war rooms. Ground zero came into vogue even before the terrorist attacks of September 11, 2001. Rhetorically at least, presidential aspirants also dodge bullets, take no prisoners, dig in, or otherwise prepare for trench warfare. Occasionally, someone strings such terms together in memorable fashion, as did Patrick Buchanan immediately after winning the New Hampshire primary in 1996: "Mount up everybody and ride to the sound of the guns."[28]

The violent language of pugilism also permeates discussions of politics and government, creating an aura of anger and promoting metaphors of violence. The boxing metaphors include phrases such as putting on the gloves, taking off the gloves, fighting, coming out swinging, going toe to toe, throwing a punch, countering a punch, going for a knockout, down for the count, and throwing in the towel.[29]

"The tonal quality of politics has over time moved in a much more negative direction," said Mike McCurry, a longtime Democratic strategist and former White House press secretary for President Bill Clinton. He recalled how as a young aide in Congress he once suggested that a senator blast a legislative opponent for "stretching the truth to the breaking point." The senator's chief of staff admonished the young McCurry and said such language—in effect calling a fellow legislator a liar—had no place in the Senate and if had been actually issued in a press release, McCurry would have been fired. Today, all this seems quaint. Calling someone a liar is common—at all levels of politics.[30]

McCurry provided an interesting and valid explanation for why harsh negativity is more common among Republicans than Democrats. "Democrats are the party that believes in government," he told me, "and negative politics erodes the capacity for compromise. If you damage the opposition it hurts the ability to govern. Without compromise, you don't pass legislation."[31]

As I will explain later in this book, the partisan or quasi-partisan political media also have been growing in importance and power. The outlets include Fox News on the right and MSNBC on the left. They seek to divide and demonize. The mainstream news media add to the negativity with their long-term attraction to conflict and negativity. The rise of social media further polarizes the nation and creates fact-free or biased zones of information that too many Americans rely on.

The polarization extends to the devaluing of facts. In the growing phenomenon of confirmation bias, Americans increasingly seek reinforcement of their views in the media, such as the internet, television, newspapers, radio, and books, rather than open-mindedly assessing contrarian information or broadening their search for truth. Americans are increasingly hostile to each other, and finding unity is far more difficult. The result is a weakened democracy.

Notes

1 Amanda Ripley, "Help Tucker Carlson Help Himself," *Washington Post*, June 13, 2023, A19.

2 Quoted in Brandon Tensley, "Just How Close Is the US to Breaking Down into Conflict?" CNN Race Deconstructed, June 9, 2022. https://www.cnn.com/2022/06/09/politics/partisanship-january-6-race-deconstructed-newsletter/index.html.
See also Nathan P. Kalmoe and Lilliana Mason, *Radical American Partisanship: Mapping Violent Hostility, Its Causes, and the Consequences for Democracy*. Chicago, IL: University of Chicago Press, 2022.

3 Dan Balz, "A Dizzying Week Shows U.S. Roiled by Division," *Washington Post*, April 9, 2023, A1.

4 Justine McDaniel. "What Happens Next after Tennessee House Expelled Two Democrats," *Washington Post*. Last updated April 9, 2023. https://www.washingtonpost.com/politics/2023/04/07/tennessee-house-expulsions/.

5 Balz, A1.

6 "Trump Indicted in New York: Donald Trump Is Indicted in New York," *New York Times*. Last updated April 4, 2023. https://www.nytimes.com/live/2023/03/30/nyregion/trump-indictment-news.

7 Shayna Jacobs, Dylan Wells, David Nakamura, and Jacqueline Alemany, "Trump Pleads Not Guilty to 34 Counts," *Washington Post*, April 5, 2023, A1.

8 *New York Times* Editorial Board, "The Justice Department Had No Choice," *New York Times* Sunday Review, June 11, 2023, SR 11.

9 Maureen Dowd "Trump Is a Victim of His Own Sleaze," *New York Times* Sunday Review, June 11, 2023, SR 4.

10 Ripley, A19.

11 Quoted in Ashley Parker, "As Trump Vows 'Retribution,' GOP Hopefuls Also Descend into Darker Rhetoric," *Washington Post*, March 17, 2023, A9.

12 Michael Gold, "Trump Says He Wouldn't Be a Dictator 'Except for Day 1,'" New York Times, December 5, 2023, downloaded December 18, 2023.

13 Author's interview with Alvin S. Felzenberg, June 9, 2021.

14 Stuart Soroka, Patrick Fournier, and Lilach Nir, "Cross-National Evidence of a Negativity Bias in Psychophysiological Reactions to News," PNAS (Proceedings of the National Academy of Sciences of the United States of America), September 17, 2019, https://www.pnas.org/content/116/38/18888. The study is based on more than 1,000 respondents in 17 countries and six continents and focuses on "video news content."
15 ibid.
16 Stevan E. Hobfoll, *Tribalism: The Evolutionary Origins of Fear Politics*. London: Palgrave Macmillan, 2018, 1.
17 ibid., 4.
18 ibid.,58.
19 Quoted in Ralph Benko, "Threatened 'Global Catastrophes' Keeping You Up At Night? Rest Easy." *Forbes*, June 19, 2014. https://www.forbes.com/sites/ralphbenko/2014/06/09/threatened-global-catastrophes-keeping-you-up-at-night-rest-easy/?sh=16cb554c4aa3.
20 Author's interview with Frank Donatelli, September. 3, 2021.
21 R. Michael Alvarez, "Why Do Politicians Always Attack Each Other?" *Psychology Today*, November 22, 2011, https://www.psychologytoday.com/intl/blog/the-psychology-behind-political-debate/201111/why-do-politicians-always-attack-each-other?collection=82402.
Also see Emmett H. Buell, Jr. and Lee Sigelman, *Attack Politics: Negativity in Presidential Campaigns since 1960*. Lawrence, KS: University Press of Kansas, 2009, 5–6.
22 Norman C. Thomas and Joseph A. Pika, *The Politics of the Presidency*. Washington, D.C.: CQ Press, 1997, 444.
23 ibid., 445.
24 E.J. Dionne, Jr., *Why Americans Hate Politics*. New York: Touchstone, 1991, 15.
25 Matt Bai, "What Will History Say about Trump?" *Washington Post*, November 19, 2020, A23.
26 Robert G. Kaiser, "Can Reality Prevail Once Again in an Age of Information Warfare?" *Washington Post*, July 25, 2021, B1.
27 See Chapter 6.
28 Emmett H. Buell and Lee Sigelman, *Attack Politics: Negativity in Presidential Campaigns since 1960*. Lawrence, KS: University Press of Kansas, 2009, 4–5.
29 ibid., 5.
30 Author's interview with Mike McCurry, October 30, 2020.
31 Author's interview with Mike McCurry, June 30, 2021.

PART I

The Presidents

1

THE EARLY PRESIDENTS AND THE RISE OF NEGATIVITY

George Washington, the hero of the Revolution and a charismatic leader, was elected the first U.S. president in 1788 and re-elected in 1792 without opposition in the Electoral College. He was considered above reproach by most of his fellow citizens, essential to the success of the new nation, and few criticized him. But the elections of 1796 and 1800 were filled with vitriol, setting a pattern of negativity for the rest of U.S. history.[1]

John Adams vs. Thomas Jefferson

Caustic politics erupted immediately after Washington announced that he wasn't running for a third term. The presidential contest of 1796 between John Adams and Thomas Jefferson was a harsh and vicious episode, won by Adams, and their rematch in 1800, won by Jefferson, was even worse. The campaign of 1800, in fact, was one of the most negative in U.S. history partly because there were very large issues at stake and the nation's leaders were reluctant to compromise. Adams and the Federalists wanted a strong central government. Jefferson, Adams' leading rival and a member of the Democratic-Republican Party known simply as Republicans, favored more power for state governments.

The campaigning of 1796 and 1800 overflowed with venom. "It reached a level of personal animosity that almost tore apart the young republic and has rarely been equaled in two hundred years of presidential politics," political scientist Kerwin Swint wrote. "Jefferson was said to have financially cheated his creditors, obtained his property by fraud, robbed a widow of an estate worth ten thousand pounds, and behaved

DOI: 10.4324/9781003149095-3

in a cowardly fashion as governor of Virginia during the revolution."[2] Federalists claimed Jefferson had fled like a jackrabbit when the British raided Charlottesville in 1781.[3]

A newspaper supporting Adams in 1800 argued that a Jefferson victory would mean that "[M]urder, robbery, rape, adultery, and incest will be openly taught and practiced, the air will be rent with the cries of the distressed, the soil will be soaked with blood, and the nation black with crimes."[4] Jefferson was portrayed elsewhere as a sinner who "writes against the truths of God's words; who makes not even a profession of Christianity; who is without Sabbaths; without the sanctuary, and without so much as a decent external respect for the faith and worship of Christians."[5] Federalists branded Jefferson a "howling atheist."[6]

Jefferson backers were very negative, too. One Jefferson supporter warned fellow Republicans that the re-election of Adams would mean "chains, dungeons, transportation, and perhaps the gibbet."[7] Supporters of Jefferson called Adams a monarchist and accused him of turning his back on republicanism. The 1800 campaign also featured Jefferson's forces deriding Adams for being a hermaphrodite.[8]

Jefferson Republicans also called Adams "a fool, a hypocrite, a criminal, and a tyrant" and said his presidency was "one continued tempest of malignant passions." They claimed that Adams was planning to marry one of his sons to one of King George III's daughters, start an American dynasty, and reunite America with Britain. According to some Republicans, Adams dropped his schemes only when confronted by a "sword-wielding George Washington."[9]

The race in 1800 also was "colored by Federalist prosecutions of political opponents under the Alien and Sedition Acts."[10]

Fear of a French invasion of the United States caused the Adams administration to begin preparations for war, and the Adams forces won congressional approval of the Alien and Sedition Acts during June and July of 1798 to root out French support. Adams quickly signed them into law. Most important and far-reaching was the Sedition Act which prohibited "false, scandalous and malicious writing" against Congress or the president and made it illegal to conspire to "oppose any measure or measures of the government." It was unconstitutional in that it limited freedom of speech and freedom of the press, but its proponents said the country's survival was at stake and drastic measures were needed.

Among the many people prosecuted under the Sedition Act was James Callender, a supporter of Jefferson. He was sentenced to nine months in prison for "false, scandalous and malicious writing against the said president of the United States," John Adams.

After Jefferson defeated Adams in 1800, Callender demanded a government job, but Jefferson refused to give him one. Callender turned against

Jefferson and went public by printing in pamphlets and newspapers allegations that Jefferson had an affair with Sally Hemings, one of the slaves at his plantation at Monticello, Virginia, and fathered at least one of her children. Callender was the first character assassin in American politics, but his efforts didn't pay off as Jefferson won his bid for re-election in 1804 against Federalist Charles C. Pinckney.[11]

As for John Adams, the Alien and Sedition Acts turned out to be a blot on the Adams administration and the Federalists, and were a major reason for Jefferson's victory in 1800. By 1802, three of the acts had expired or were repealed except for the Alien Enemies Act which allowed the government to arrest and deport all male citizens of an enemy nation during a war. This remained in effect for many years.[12]

The race showed how effective negative politics could be, and many candidates have been following the 1800 example of negativity ever since. Personal assaults on the dignity and character of candidates have become staples of presidential campaigns.

Because the 1800 campaign had been so bitter and the country so divided, the outcome of the election was thrown into doubt. Under the Constitution at the time, each state allocated its votes in the Electoral College through the decision of its legislature which met during the period from May to December 1800. Neither Jefferson nor Adams received a majority of electoral votes, pushing the decision to the U.S. House of Representatives. Each state was entitled to one vote, as determined by a majority of each state's House delegation. At first, neither Adams nor Jefferson could reach the required number of nine states in order to be elected president. After 39 ballots and no resolution, Jefferson finally won.

Jefferson's defeat of Adams marked the first time power was transferred in the United States from one political party, Adams' Federalists, to another, Jefferson's Democratic-Republicans. Fortunately, the nation held firm as a constitutional republic despite the bitterness and negativity of the campaign.[13]

Andrew Jackson vs. John Quincy Adams

In 1828, supporters of both Andrew Jackson and John Quincy Adams used every negative line of attack they could think of and employed many dirty tricks and falsehoods to undermine the opposition. Each side attacked the personal life, character, values, experience, and policies of the other candidate. This campaign pushed caustic politics to new lows.

Jackson, a hero and former general during the War of 1812, dominated a tumultuous era of polarization during the mid-1800s. He became an attack politician in his own right, and he was both ruthless and effective. Jackson was the target of many other U.S. leaders because he supported a strong central government and seemed eager to push executive authority as far as he could. His opponents argued that he was an arrogant know-it-all with no government experience and a ferocious temper that was inappropriate for a president. Adams and his supporters favored government by benign, educated elites, people such as Adams, instead of rough-hewn, blunt-spoken, activist leaders such as Jackson.[14]

Jackson and John Quincy Adams (the son of John Adams who had won the presidency in 1796) ran against each other for the first time in 1824 along with candidates Henry Clay and William Crawford. No candidate received a majority in the Electoral College and the election was decided by the House of Representatives (as had happened in 1800 when Jefferson defeated John Adams). In the 1824 showdown, Clay announced his support for Adams, which gave the election to John Quincy. Immediately afterward, Adams named Clay as his secretary of state, and Jackson said it was a corrupt bargain—the trading of electoral support for a high-level federal appointment. His bitterness ran deep and injected special vitriol into the 1828 rematch.

"This was no mere political campaign; it was a four-year-long struggle between two political factions, two different regions of the country, and two radically different views of life and of governing," wrote political scientist Kerwin Swint of the campaign of 1828. "This may be the only presidential campaign that led directly to someone's death"[15]—Rachel Jackson, Andrew's wife who suffered from a heart condition and became depressed and ill during the campaign. She died of a heart attack several weeks after her husband was elected president.

Historian Lynn Hudson Parsons has observed:

> In the presidential election campaign of 1828 can be found the elements, sometimes rudimentary, of most elections to come: coordinated media, fund-raising, organized rallies, opinion polling, campaign paraphernalia, ethnic voting blocs, image making, even opposition research, smear tactics, and dirty tricks.[16]

Most, but not all, of these innovations were introduced by the Jacksonians, who time and again proved that they had grasped the significance of the shifting tectonic plates that lay beneath the political landscape better than their opponents. They recognized that the expanding electorate needed to be handled in new ways. They accepted, and for the most part embraced, the role of organized political parties in a republic. They understood, too, what effective political operatives in future elections would also come to understand: that although particular issues can be important, nothing in a presidential election is more important than the image of the candidate. In the end it was the image of Andrew Jackson, the Hero of [the battle of] New Orleans, the outsider untouched by "intrigue and corruption" in Washington, the defender of true republicanism in the face of its "aristocratic" enemies, that would prevail. It was one of the most powerful presidential images in American political history. Combined with the campaign put together on his behalf and the lack of an effective response by his opponents, it proved to be unbeatable.[17]

For his part, Jackson's temper always seemed on the verge of erupting. As the 1828 campaign began, his health fluctuated between fair to poor, partly because of painful wounds from dueling earlier in his life, and his sight and hearing were fading. All this made him more irascible. He took mercury-based medicines which caused intestinal problems, hurt his gums, and made his teeth blue. His mood worsened. "Left to himself, he nursed grudges and dreamed of violence against his enemies," wrote historians David S. Heidler and Jeanne T. Heidler.[18]

> Jackson told John Coffee "how hard it is to keep the cowhide from some of these villains." Old Hickory's increasing irritability so concerned his handlers that their repeated cautions about keeping quiet had become a rote drill, tiresome but necessary, for they knew a show of temper would only encourage the administration's operatives to more provocations.[19]

Kerwin Swint wrote,

> Much of the pro-Adams case revolved around vicious personal attacks against Jackson, his wife, and the rest of his family.[20]

Presidential historian Paul Boller says Jackson wept when he read in a newspaper that "General Jackson's mother was a common prostitute, brought to this country by the British soldiers. She afterward married a mulatto man, with whom she had several children, of which number General Jackson is one!"[21]

When Rachel Jackson discovered her husband crying in his office, she asked what was wrong. "Myself I can defend; you I can defend; but now they have assailed even the memory of my mother," he replied.[22] Yet it was the series of attacks on his wife that became more than he could bear.

Jackson and the former Rachel Donelson had been married since 1791. But Jackson's opponents found out that when she married Jackson she had not been legally divorced from her first husband Lewis Robards. Andrew and Rachel thought the divorce had been approved by the Virginia courts in 1791 but the couple was mistaken. Robards actually finalized the divorce in 1793. When the Jacksons learned that their marriage was not legal, they were married officially by a justice of the peace.[23]

According to Swint,

> So although the facts were not quite what they seemed, the mudslinging about the incident in the 1824 and 1828 elections was unforgiving ... The partisan publications backing Adams screamed headlines such as "Adultress" and "Bigamist." One pro-Adams pamphlet read, "Anyone approving of Andrew Jackson must therefore declare in favor of the philosophy that any man wanting anyone else's pretty wife has nothing to do but take his pistol in one hand, a horsewhip in another and possess her."[24]

Years earlier, Jackson had challenged a man named Charles Dickinson to a duel after Dickinson accused Rachel of being an adulteress. Jackson killed Dickinson.[25] Obviously, Jackson took slurs against his wife very seriously.

During the 1828 campaign, the Adams forces portrayed Jackson as ignorant on national and international issues and reckless in his personal conduct such as his history of dueling.[26] A political pamphlet sponsored by Adams' backers criticized him as

> no jurist, no statesman, no politician. ... he is destitute of historical, political or statistical knowledge; that he is a man of no labor, no patience, no investigation; in short that his whole recommendation is animal fierceness and organic energy; he is wholly unqualified by education, habit, and temper for the station of president.[27]

Adams's backers said Jackson had ordered the murder of six of his soldiers. Actually, the situation was murkier: six militiamen under Jackson's command had been executed after they were tried and convicted for desertion.[28]

A damaging version of this incident was described in "the coffin handbill," a document featuring depictions of coffins and denouncing the executions of six militiamen under Jackson's command at the end of the War of 1812. Jackson allies, pointing out that the six had deserted, defended the executions as justified. But the accusations stung the former general and damaged his reputation among some voters.[29]

For their part, Jackson and his supporters were very negative toward Adams. They reminded Americans of the "corrupt bargain" between Adams and Clay in 1824 as an example of the incumbent's lack of ethics and hunger for power and they said Adams stole the election. They attacked Adams for having a profligate lifestyle, buying personal items at taxpayer expense. They claimed he had premarital sex with his future wife. They accused Adams of procuring an American girl for Czar

Alexander I while Adams was minister to Russia. On the level of policy, Adams' opponents in Congress opposed many of his ideas, such as those on tariffs and building roads. They said Adams was a monarchist who distrusted everyday Americans and favored rule by elitists such as himself.[30]

When Jackson won, he ushered in a new era built upon populism and slash-and-burn politics.

Historian James M. McPherson wrote, "The presidential election of 1828 generated unprecedented excitement among the electorate. The percentage of eligible voters who cast their ballots jumped from 27 percent in 1824 to 57 percent in 1828,"[31] in part because the cult of personality surrounding Jackson stimulated massive turnout among his followers.

Ulysses S. Grant vs. Horace Greeley

The 1872 campaign between President Ulysses S. Grant, a Republican, and Democrat Horace Greeley was another low point in American politics.

Grant was elected in 1868 as the fighting general who had won the Civil War. But he named several corrupt officials to his administration (although he didn't profit personally from their trespasses) and lacked political skills such as the ability to build bridges with his opponents. News of the particularly damaging Credit Mobilier scandal broke late during Grant's re-election campaign in 1872. It was only partially revealed before the election and it didn't cost Grant his job. But it turned out to be a huge blemish on Grant's record. The scandal centered on the fact that the Credit Mobilier construction company, created by leaders of the federally supported Union Pacific Railroad, padded construction budgets and improperly charged Union Pacific vast fees. Members of Congress and other government officials in the Grant administration, including Vice President Schuyler Colfax, were implicated. Colfax was dropped by Grant from the ticket.

Grant's Republican Party was split over his leadership. Many considered him too passive and out of touch with the country. These Republicans wanted to end the spoils system, reform the civil service, withdraw federal troops from the South, and lower tariffs. These people split off from the regular GOP and formed the Liberal Republicans. This third party nominated newspaperman Horace Greeley as their presidential candidate in 1872. The Democratic Party also endorsed Greeley as their nominee.

Both Grant and Greeley were viciously attacked by their opponents. Grant was blasted as a drunk and a tyrant, and Greeley was dismissed as a traitor and outside the cultural mainstream.

Cartoonists intensified the negativity, a role they have regularly played ever since as will be described in Chapter 9. Throughout 1872, Thomas

Nast mocked Greeley in *Harper's Weekly* and Matt Morgan ridiculed Grant in *Frank Leslie's Illustrated Newspaper.*

"Greeley had urged reconciliation between North and South after the Civil War, and in his acceptance of the presidential nomination," political scientist Swint noted.

> *Harper's* ridiculed this appeal with a series of sickening cartoons of Greeley shaking hands with a rebel who had just shot a Union soldier, stretching out his hand to John Wilkes Booth across Abraham Lincoln's grave; and turning a defenseless black man over to a member of the Ku Klux Klan, who had just lynched a black man and knifed a black mother and her child.[32]

On the other side, Swint added,

> Greeley's supporters circulated a pamphlet called "The Grant Government: A Cage of Unclean Birds," written by Lyman DeWolf. Calling Grant's administration the "crowning point of governmental wickedness," it accused Grant of bringing forth a "burning lava of seething corruption, a foul despotism."[33]

Grant won re-election but American politics had again fallen deeply into the gutter.

Rutherford B. Hayes vs. Samuel Tilden

The campaign of 1876 featured a particularly vicious presidential contest between Samuel Tilden and Rutherford B. Hayes. "It involved a constitutional crisis lasting several months, which was not settled until literally days before the scheduled inauguration of the new president in March 1877," Swint wrote.[34]

Both candidates started off with strong credentials. Hayes, the Republican nominee, was a hero of the Civil War and had a strong base as governor of Ohio, a post he won in 1875 in part because of his reputation for integrity. Tilden, the Democratic nominee, was elected governor of New York in 1874 and had a reputation as a reformer.

> But both candidates and their supporters turned very negative during the heat of their campaign. Republicans accused Democrat Tilden for allegedly evading taxes, backing slavery, corruption, and planning to relieve the debts of the old Confederacy if he became president. Democrats accused Republican Hayes of corruption, stealing the pay of dead soldiers in his regiment during the Civil War, and "shooting his mother in a fit of insanity."[35]

Tilden received 250,000 votes more than Hayes nationwide as of election day. Of the states that certified their votes as of that day, Tilden had 184 electoral votes, one short of the 185 needed for victory. Twenty electoral votes in four states—Florida, Louisiana, Oregon, and South Carolina—remained in doubt.

After ferocious jockeying in which both sides accused the other of voter fraud, Democrats and Republicans in each of the three southern states submitted their own separate electoral vote counts to Congress. The Republican governors found that Hayes had won in their states but the legislatures there, controlled by Democrats, found that Tilden had won. One electoral vote was in dispute in Oregon, and this was also the subject of a fierce argument between Democrats and Republicans as to whether Hayes or Tilden should receive it.

Congress was divided, too, with the Democrats controlling the House and Republicans controlling the Senate. In January 1877, Congress passed a law creating a 15-member Electoral Commission to decide the next president. This commission gave all 20 disputed electors to Hayes and he was declared the president in a very messy end to the race.

But many Democrats were bitter. They were convinced the election had been stolen from Tilden and they derided Hayes as "His Fraudulency," "Rutherfraud Hayes," and "The Usurper."[36]

Overall, it was a time of rancor. "The 1870s and the 1880s gave us some of the most bitter and hateful political campaigns ever," Swint wrote. "The 1884 presidential contest between the Democrat, Grover Cleveland, and his Republican opponent, James G. Blaine, was one of the nastiest, more intensely personal campaigns ever."[37]

Grover Cleveland vs. James G. Blaine

In 1884, Democrat Grover Cleveland's presidential campaign and his reputation were shaken by the character issue. He was pressured to admit philandering in his youth but he won the presidency anyway, in part by attacking his opponents.

James G. Blaine, a former speaker of the House of Representatives and also a Republican U.S. senator from Maine, became secretary of state for GOP President James Garfield. Blaine certainly had a wealth of governing experience but he was also plagued by accusations of corruption such as bribery and conflicts of interest. Still, he won the Republican presidential nomination in 1884, marking the third time he ran for the presidency after failed campaigns to win the GOP nomination in 1876 and 1880.[38]

The Democrats chose New York Governor Cleveland, known as a reformer since his state election in 1882. But Cleveland's reputation for probity was badly damaged when the *Buffalo Evening Telegraph* printed an expose, "A Terrible Tale," on July 21, 1884, accusing Cleveland of having had an affair, as a young Buffalo lawyer, with a widow named Maria Halpin and fathering her child, Oscar Folsom Cleveland. It turned out that Cleveland, although he said he wasn't sure he was the father, paid for the boy's support for many years.

The story caused a sensation and was used by the Republicans against Cleveland, arguing that it showed immorality and depravity.

Cleveland supporters hit back by insisting that Republican nominee Blaine had what they called an embarrassing proclivity of his own—being attracted to men. One Democratic newspaper bluntly accused Blaine of being overly fond of fellow Republicans, noting: "But this thing of his kissing men – or pressing his bearded lips upon bearded lips – is too aggressive!"[39]

More damaging to Blaine were accusations published by the *Indianapolis Sentinel* in August 1884 that as a young man he got a woman pregnant and married her after being pressured by her father. Cleveland refused to use the allegations against Blaine, saying it was an improper tactic, and of course using these allegations would have made Cleveland look hypocritical because of the Maria Halpin accusations against him. "The other side can have a monopoly of all the dirt in this campaign," he told an aide.[40]

Not quite. Cleveland's campaign hit Blaine hard for being corrupt, greedy, arrogant and too cozy with big corporations and alien to everyday Americans.

Blaine also made a big mistake late in the campaign by failing to denounce a Presbyterian minister who told pro-Blaine clergymen in New York City that Cleveland's Democrats were "the party whose antecedents have been rum, Romanism and rebellion." Many Roman Catholic Irish Americans, a key voting bloc, were offended. The Cleveland forces spread the remark and newspapers carried it widely. Blaine waited too long to disavow the comments and they damaged him among many Irish American voters in New York. Cleveland narrowly won the state and with it the presidency.[41]

Cleveland had the last laugh on the character issue. Blaine supporters would chant at their rallies, "Ma! Ma! Where's my Pa?" After Cleveland won, his supporters chanted a reply in delight: "Ma! Ma! Where's my Pa? Gone to the White House, ha ha ha!"

> Although sorely provoked, presidential candidates of the nineteenth century generally adhered to a powerful, if unwritten, code that militated against them making their own case on the campaign trail. This taboo against "cadging," or directly soliciting votes, had obvious consequences for going negative. Surrogates made the case against the opposing party while standard-bearers remained seemingly aloof. Behind the

scenes, however, some nominees formulated strategy and/or wrote correspondence intended for publication in friendly newspapers.[42]

> By the end of the century the attack role of non-incumbent candidates for president had become more transparent. William Jennings Bryan stumped tirelessly in his 1896 bid to defeat William McKinley, and he may well have used the occasion to inaugurate the "trickle-down" argument that countless Democrats since have uttered against the economy under Republicans.[43]

This was the deeply negative contention that the GOP wanted to increase the wealth of the already-rich and was content to let tax breaks and other benefits for the well-to-do and big corporations "trickle down" to the middle class and the less fortunate. This argument has been a staple of anti-Republican campaigns ever since.

Theodore Roosevelt vs. the Plutocrats

As president from 1901 to 1909, Theodore Roosevelt relished political combat to achieve his goals and believed his harsh attacks against corporations and plutocrats were justified as the only way to rally public and congressional support for his populist objectives. (Political combat was part of his philosophy of fighting for the greater good. He believed actual combat in wartime was a character-builder for young men and strengthened the nation.)

In particular, Roosevelt delighted in condemning the very rich as "malefactors of great wealth," one of his most memorable phrases. The slogan shocked conservative business leaders but succeeded in "riling up the populist element, the most left-leaning cohort, among the progressives," historian Aida D. Donald has written.[44] This was his intention as a way to generate support for his legislative and regulatory approaches, which included higher taxes on the very rich and on big business, restraining the power of the railroads, new laws to regulate the stock market, providing for an eight-hour day for laborers, and workers' compensation for those injured on the job. Especially during the end of his presidency in 1907 and 1908 Roosevelt sought to limit the excesses of capitalism and side with the working class and the middle class. He had mixed success but many of his ideas eventually became widely accepted in the country, especially when his distant cousin Franklin D. Roosevelt popularized them during his presidency from 1933 to 1945.

TR was among the most pugnacious of presidents. But he rarely used his venom in a personal sense to demean and ridicule his opponents in petty and vindictive ways. Still, his war against trusts and excessive corporate power generated fierce hatred against him among business leaders and many wealthy Americans. They accused him of meddling in the business world by trying to break up big corporations and increase taxes, and seizing too much power by strengthening regulations on big business and intervening in labor-management disputes. But TR was proud of his combative style and argued that he was more even-handed than his corporate critics charged.

He wrote in a letter to an English friend:

> Here at home I am engaged in the pleasing task of trying to prevent the plutocracy on the one hand and the anarchistic labor group on the other from traveling exactly the same path that in Russia [has] made the autocracy and the wild-eyed radicals almost equally impossible, almost equally dangerous to the future of the country.[45]

He also told supporters that "the super-rich" opposed him "because they no longer ran the national government" and because he was imposing regulations on them. He added: "The owners of predatory wealth hate me … [and] they have no moral scruples of any kind whatsoever."[46]

Roosevelt generated fury on another score—race. He faced a wicked backlash from the South after he welcomed Booker T. Washington, the famous African American educator, to dine with him at the White House early in his administration. Roosevelt wanted to get to know Washington and solicit his advice on appointees and on policy questions. But much of the reaction to the invitation was virulently racist, and the dinner invitation became one of the most polarizing moments of Roosevelt's presidency.

"The most damnable outrage which has ever been perpetrated by any citizen of the United States was committed yesterday by the President when he invited a nigger[47] to dine with him at the White House," wrote the *Memphis Scimitar* on October 16, 1901.[48]

Senator Benjamin R. Tillman of South Carolina warned in a horrendously racist rant that "a thousand niggers in the South would have to be killed to teach them 'their place' again.'"[49]

Roosevelt was offended by the insults and the racist language. He privately praised Washington as "a good citizen and good American," and condemned "that idiot or vicious Bourbon element in the South."[50]

Roosevelt continued to seek advice from African Americans and to host them at the White House along with groups of whites, and he invited them privately to stay over at his home in New York. But never again did Roosevelt dine at the White House with an African American. "Roosevelt always maintained that he did nothing wrong, in any sense, as indeed he had not, but he bowed to the racists," wrote historian Aida D. Donald.[51]

This failure to confront the reality of racism was a historic blot on his record.

Woodrow Wilson vs. Anti-War Dissenters and African Americans

Woodrow Wilson, as president from 1913 to 1921, helped to create a toxic environment when he decided to push the United States into World War I. It wasn't so much the rhetoric he used or the attacks he levied that set the country back, it was the series of actions that Wilson and his administration took.

Wilson had campaigned against U.S. entry into World War I when he ran for re-election in 1916. But he reversed course after he won and went to great lengths to demolish dissent. As author Adam Hochschild pointed out in his 2002 book *American Midnight: The Great War, A Violent Peace, and Democracy's Forgotten Crisis*, which covers 1917 to 1921, the federal government under Wilson threw people in prison for opposing Wilson's war policies, censured various publications, and failed to investigate white riots against Black communities. Wilson's administration also moved to deport many immigrants and created much unfair anti-immigrant animosity.[52]

Hochschild told NPR:

> Press censorship operated on a huge scale in the United States. Some 75 newspapers and magazines were forced to shut down. There was a nationwide vigilante group with 250,000 members that was chartered by the Justice Department that went around making citizen's arrests, roughing people up in a very violent way. And during that period, there was roughly a thousand Americans sent to prison for a year or more, and a far larger number for shorter periods of time solely for things that they wrote or said.

Further, surveillance of American citizens for supposed anti-war activities grew immensely.[53]

Wilson also filled his administration with fellow segregationists and created an atmosphere where advancement for Black Americans was nearly impossible.[54]

"He was an unapologetic racist whose administration rolled back the gains that African-Americans achieved just after the Civil War, purged black workers from influential jobs and transformed the government into an instrument of white supremacy," the *New York Times* wrote in a 2015 editorial supporting the removal of Wilson's name from the Woodrow Wilson School of Public and International Affairs at Princeton University, where he had been president.[55] (Princeton eventually agreed and removed Wilson's name.)

In the late 19th and early 20th centuries, thousands of African Americans passed Civil Service exams or were given political appointments for good jobs in the government. But Wilson objected to Black people supervising white workers. "This was anathema to Wilson," the *Times* wrote,

> who believed that black Americans were unworthy of full citizenship and admired the Ku Klux Klan for the role it had in terrorizing African-Americans to restrict their political power. As the historian Eric Yellen shows in "Racism in the Nation's Service," Wilson stocked his government with segregationists who shared his point of view. … It was a premeditated attempt to impoverish and disempower a small but growing class of black middle-class professionals. This subversion was not limited to Washington. In a few short years, Mr. Yellin writes, the Wilson administration had established federal discrimination as a national norm.[56]

Notes

1 George Washington: Emmett H. Buell, Jr., and Lee Sigelman, *Attack Politics: Negativity in Presidential Campaigns since 1960*. Lawrence, KS: University Press of Kansas, 2009, 6.
2 Kerwin Swint, *Mudslinging: The Twenty-Five Dirtiest Political Campaigns of All Time*. New York: Union Square Press, 2008, 183–4. See also https://constitutioncenter.org/blog/on-this-day-the-first-bitter-contested-presidential-election-takes-place.
3 Emmett H. Buell, Jr. and Lee Sigelman, *Attack Politics: Negativity in Presidential Campaigns since 1960*. Lawrence, KS: University Press of Kansas, 2009, 5.
4 Quoted in Swint, 184.
5 Paul Boller, *Presidential Campaigns*. New York: Oxford University Press, 2004, 11.
6 Quoted in Buell and Sigelman, 5.
7 Quoted in Buell and Sigelman, 5.
8 Swint, 184–5.
9 Swint, 184–5.
10 Quoted in Buell and Sigelman, 5.
11 See Chapter 7.
12 "Alien and Sedition Acts," March 5, 2020. www.history.com/topics//early-us/alien-and-sedition-acts.
13 Swint, 189–90.
14 David S. Heidler and Jeanne T. Heidler, *The Rise of Andrew Jackson: Myth, Manipulation, and the Making of Modern Politics*. New York: Basic Books, 2018, 1–11.
15 Swint, 213.
16 Lynn Hudson Parsons, *The Birth of Modern Politics: Andrew Jackson, John Quincy Adams, and the Election of 1828*. New York: Oxford University Press, 2009, 133–4.
17 ibid.

18 David S. Heidler and Jeanne T. Heidler, *The Rise of Andrew Jackson: Myth, Manipulation, and the Making of Modern Politics*. New York: Basic Books, 2018, 333.
19 ibid.
20 ibid., 215.
21 Paul Boller, *Presidential Campaigns*. New York: Oxford University Press, 2004, 44.
22 Quoted in Boller, 44.
23 Swint, 215.
24 Swint, 215–16.
25 ibid., 216.
26 Swint, 217.
27 Quoted in Boller, 46.
28 ibid.
29 Heidler and. Heidler, 349–53.
30 Swint, 219–20.
31 James M. McPherson's Editor's Note, Lynn Hudson Parsons, *The Birth of Modern Politics: Andrew Jackson, John Quincy Adams, and the Election of 1828*. New York; Oxford University Press, 2009, x.
32 Swint, 178–9.
33 ibid., 179.
34 Swint, xiii.
35 Swint, 82.
36 This account is based largely on Swint, 82–6.
37 Swint, 203.
38 Swint, 204.
39 ibid.
40 Quoted in Swint, 209.
41 Swint, 210.
42 Buell and Sigelman, 6.
43 ibid.
44 Aida D. Donald, *Lion in the White House: A Life of Theodore Roosevelt*. New York: MJF Books, 2007, 222.
45 Donald, 206.
46 Quoted in Donald, 206.
47 The author has decided to quote the critics' exact and highly offensive language, including the "n-word," in this section to give a full sense of how virulently racist the response was.
48 Quoted in Donald, 138.
49 Quoted in Donald, 138–9.
50 Quoted in Donald, 138.
51 Donald, 140.
52 Dave Davies, "Woodrow Wilson Led the U.S. into WWI. He Also Waged War on Democracy at Home," "Fresh Air," *NPR*, December 13, 2022, downloaded July 15, 2023.
53 ibid.
54 "The Case Against Woodrow Wilson at Princeton," *The New York Times*. November 24, 2015. https://www.nytimes.com/2015/11/25/opinion/the-case-against-woodrow-wilson-at-princeton.html.
55 ibid.
56 ibid.

2

HOW PRESIDENTS OF THE MODERN ERA FOMENTED ATTACK POLITICS

Most of the modern-day presidents used the politics of attack to varying degrees. They include Harry Truman, Lyndon Johnson, Richard Nixon, Ronald Reagan, George H.W. Bush, Bill Clinton, George W. Bush, and particularly Donald Trump (as will be discussed later in this book). Some were responding to harsh attacks from opponents and were not the initiators of the harsh exchanges, nor did they get as personal as their adversaries. But several presidents went too far in their negativity by using distortion, exaggeration, outright falsehoods, or unfair personal attacks. These presidents made negative campaigning more pervasive and corrosive because they deftly used the bully pulpit of the nation's most powerful and visible office to magnify the toxicity.

Harry Truman

Harry Truman had experienced negative campaigns even before he ran for president in 1948. As President Franklin D. Roosevelt's vice-presidential running mate in 1944, he was falsely called a former member of the Ku Klux Klan, mocked for having undistinguished political and business careers, and savaged in other ways.[1] Critics also mocked Mrs. Truman as "Payroll Bess" for taking a paid job in her husband's Senate committee office, branding it as nepotism.[2]

The attacks on FDR, at the top of the ticket, particularly offended Truman. "Most of the newspapers didn't hesitate to lie, and there was a whispering campaign—I've always thought it was organized—that Roosevelt—well, that his mind was gone and he was senile and I don't

DOI: 10.4324/9781003149095-4

know what all," Truman told a biographer. "That about his mind was a damn lie. He wasn't well, but his mind—his mind was just as sharp as ever it had been, and that was the case whenever I saw him right up to the end."[3]

In 1948, three years after Truman had succeeded to the president following FDR's death, critics dismissed Truman as a political lightweight who could never be an effective national leader and who was too weak to confront the growing challenge of international communism. As he entered the campaign as the incumbent, Truman believed he had to go negative or he would be defined harshly by his opponents, and he did it with relish.

The 1948 campaign between Democrat Truman and Republican nominee Thomas Dewey showed what can happen when one candidate refuses to fight back against a tough, caustic opponent. And it was Truman, lagging in the polls, who took the offensive while the over-confident Dewey held back.

Heavily favored, Dewey, who was governor of New York, acted as if he were the incumbent rather than the challenger. He rested on his laurels and mostly ignored Truman's attacks. His passivity as a candidate and his overall aloofness drew a memorable remark by Alice Roosevelt Longworth, daughter of former President Theodore Roosevelt. She mocked Dewey, who came across as stiff and officious, as the "little man on the wedding cake," and the derisive description stuck.

Truman blasted Dewey as often as possible, attempting to portray his main opponent as out of touch. "He said something about how maybe he ought to have the engineer [of his campaign train] shot at sunrise because he backed up the train too far," Truman said later.

> We managed to get that news around the country, and it didn't help him much with the working people. The trouble was he'd forgot what it was like to have to work for a living, and it showed on him, which is why he lost the election.[4]

As political scientists Emmett H. Buell and Lee Sigelman have pointed out, Dewey refused to engage with Truman on a day-to-day basis. His vice presidential running mate, Gov. Earl Warren of California, was similarly inclined to stay positive, surrendering more ground to Truman. Their refusal to hit back continued even when it appeared that Dewey's lead might be shrinking. Dewey simply could not believe that Truman would beat him.[5]

"In any case, Truman presented himself as the underdog and proceeded to give the Republicans 'hell' in speech after speech," Buell and Sigelman note.

> He finally provoked a response from Dewey by claiming that Communists and Fascists alike hoped for a Republican victory. (Earlier, Dewey had drawn what he said was a contrast with the Democrats by vowing that his administration would not hire communists and fellow travelers.) Because he refused to single Truman out, Dewey's rebuke lacked much of a punch: "They have scattered reckless abuse on the entire right of way coast to coast, and now, I am sorry to say, reached a new low in mudslinging. This is the kind of campaign I refuse to wage."[6]

Truman didn't just go after Dewey. He famously went on fiery attacks against what he called the "do-nothing Congress" controlled by Republicans who refused to approve Truman's programs. He pointed out how the GOP majority wouldn't "pass laws to halt rising prices, to meet the housing crisis ... [approve] aid to education ... a national health program...civil rights legislation...an increase in the minimum wage...extension of the Social Security coverage and increased benefits"[7] and many other programs.

His combativeness and tireless campaigning made him seem like a man of the people vs. the conservative establishment—a modern-day tale of David vs. Goliath. It was a very appealing image.

He was so outraged and so often on the attack that he got the nickname "Give 'Em Hell, Harry," which he loved.[8] Truman won in a huge upset.

During his presidency, Truman was particularly incensed by conservatives such as Sen. Joe McCarthy, R-Wis., who accused Truman of allowing communists to infiltrate the State Department and other parts of the government. Bowing to the pressure, Truman began a "loyalty program" to identify communists in government and force them to resign, and he directed the Justice Department to compile a list of subversive organizations. But this wasn't enough for the critics, including McCarthy who said Truman's administration was still allowing "traitorous" communists to work for the government.

An angry Truman hit back, telling reporters that McCarthy's attacks were sabotaging the nation's bipartisan foreign policy and aiding the Soviet Union. "I think the greatest asset that the Kremlin has is Senator McCarthy," Truman declared.[9]

McCarthy in many ways poisoned the political system. "McCarthy legitimized conspiracy theories and brought an anti-communist and anti-intellectual message to the country," wrote historian Randall J. Stephens. "Fears of communist infiltration and racial integration fueled the ultra-conservative drive to take back control from supposedly compromised elites."[10]

Truman's temper flashed on many occasions and for reasons having nothing to do with Joe McCarthy, adding to the decline in civil discourse. One of the most famous cases came when *Washington Post* music critic Paul Hume published a harsh review of the singing skills of the president's daughter Margaret Truman after her performance as a soprano at Constitution Hall in Washington on December 6, 1950. "She is flat a good deal of the time—more last night than at any time we have heard her in past years," Hume wrote. "There are few moments during her recital when one can relax and feel confident that she will make her goal, which is the end of the song."[11]

The next day, Hume received a note on White House stationary from President Truman that said,

> I've just read your lousy review of Margaret's concert. ... It seems to me that you are a frustrated old man who wishes he could have been successful. ... Some day I hope to meet you. When that happens you'll need a new nose, a lot of beefsteak for black eyes, and perhaps a supporter below![12]

Truman's pugnacity manifested itself in other ways. During the 1960 campaign, long after he had left office in 1953, he expressed doubt whether Sen. John F. Kennedy, D-Mass., was ready for the presidency. Some outreach and fence-mending by Kennedy won Truman over before Election Day, but Truman's initial criticism showed that his willingness to speak his mind had not declined with age.

While he strayed into invective sometimes, Truman is admired by many to this day for plain speaking, confronting his adversaries, and fighting for his beliefs.

Lyndon B. Johnson

Lyndon B. Johnson followed John F. Kennedy into office after JFK's murder. Johnson, a tough competitor as a senator from Texas, always had an instinct for attacking. His 1964 Democratic presidential campaign created the most effective negative TV ad ever, which has served as a model for harsh campaign commercials ever since by stirring up voters' fears and emotions.

The 60-second "Daisy Ad" was a benchmark of negative politics. It was run by President Johnson's campaign on September 7, 1964 and portrayed Republican challenger Barry Goldwater, a senator from Arizona, as a dangerous nuclear warrior.

The ad was created by Tony Schwartz and other admen of the Doyle Dane Bernbach advertising agency in New York. It captured all the fears about Goldwater—fears fed by rumors spread by Johnson and his team that Goldwater was mentally unstable—and wrapped them into a single commercial.

The commercial was devastating but Goldwater's reckless, apparently off-the-cuff comments already had created doubts about his judgment and set the stage for the ad. One of his most damaging remarks was Goldwater's joke, referring to nuclear missiles, that he wanted to "lob one into the men's room at the Kremlin." It scared many voters and made the Daisy Ad even more powerful because it reinforced many Americans' suspicions that Goldwater was too bellicose.

At the GOP national convention where he was nominated in 1964, Goldwater shook up moderates when he declared, "I would remind you that extremism in the defense of liberty is no vice; and I would also remind you that moderation in the pursuit of justice is no virtue."[13] His embrace of extremism was deemed too dangerous by many voters.

The ad stirred up the deepest anxiety of the time—worry about nuclear war—and did so in the most dramatic way.

The ad begins with a three-year-old girl sitting in a field, picking the petals off a daisy. Sweet and innocent, she miscounts—"1, 2, 3, 4, 5, 7, 6, 6, 8, 9." At the count of "9," an announcer intrudes with the then-familiar reverse countdown of a missile launch, starting at "10," as the camera shows the girl's face, seeming surprised, then puzzled as she looks up. At zero, the camera focuses on one of her eyes as she sees a horrific nuclear explosion complete with the menacing mushroom cloud. Lyndon Johnson's familiar voice is heard declaring: "These are the stakes—to make a world in which all of God's children can live, or to go into the dark. We must either love each other, or we must die." An announcer concludes: "Vote for President Johnson on November 3. The stakes are too high for you to stay home."[14] Johnson is never shown in the commercial, and Goldwater is never mentioned by name.

But the 60-second ad tapped into the public consciousness, especially the worries about nuclear holocaust, international confrontations with communism, and Goldwater's apparent reckless and belligerent attitudes. Ad creator Schwartz recalled:

> it was like the woman who goes to the psychiatrist and is shown a Rorschach Daisy and the Dirty Pictures pattern and says, "Doctor, I didn't come here to be shown dirty pictures!" The Daisy commercial evoked Mr. Goldwater's probomb statements. They were the dirty pictures in the public's mind.[15]

The ad ran only once, during the film *David and Bathsheba* on CBS's "Monday Night at the Movies" on September 7, 1964. Complaining phone calls flooded the White House, and the Johnson campaign, concerned at first about a backlash, never ran the commercial again. But it quickly became the talk of the country. The three TV networks at the time—ABC, CBS, and NBC—broadcast it in full during their evening newscasts the next day, increasing its impact. And the networks continued to replay it as analysts and reporters assessed its importance. The newspapers also covered the ad extensively. Goldwater protested that the commercial was misleading and unfair, but his complaints called more attention to it.[16] "The homes of America are horrified and the intelligence of Americans is insulted by weird television advertising by which this administration threatens the end of the world unless all-wise Lyndon is given the nation for his very own," Goldwater said on September 29.[17]

The Daisy Ad was part of a larger negative approach developed by Johnson and his advisers. As reported by the website Conelrad,

> In addition to the higher-minded strategy meetings ... there was also a secret White House campaign apparatus known informally as "the Department of Dirty Tricks," "the anti-campaign," or "the 5 o'clock Club." It was a sixteen-man team that was headed by Johnson aides Myer "Mike" Feldman and Fred Dutton. Feldman reported directly to Johnson on the team's activities.

"This group—which met twice a day—monitored Goldwater's statements and positions and prepared various 'books' that captured all of his ripe material," according to Conelrad. "The 5 o'clockers also engaged in other more questionable activity such as feeding hostile questions to reporters covering Goldwater and otherwise trying to manipulate the mainstream media treatment of the senator."[18]

LBJ and the Democrats attacked Goldwater for his desire to change Social Security to make it voluntary and, he argued, less expensive for the taxpayers. The Johnson team claimed Goldwater was trying to eliminate the popular program entirely.[19]

But the Daisy Ad did the most damage. "Half a century later, we live in the world of negative political advertising that Daisy Girl pioneered," wrote historian Robert Mann. "For better or worse, the Daisy ad made emotions a much more potent weapon in our political campaigns, employing techniques that had previously only been applied to selling cars and soap."[20]

Goldwater, already in deep political trouble when the ad ran, never recovered politically. His campaign slogan, "In Your Heart You Know He's Right," was transformed into "In Your Guts You Know He's Nuts," a twist used by Goldwater critics. The Daisy Ad had done its job in completing the devastation of Goldwater's reputation. He lost to Johnson in a historic landslide.

In addition, the doubts about Goldwater highlighted a larger problem for conservatives at the time—right-wing groups and hard-line donors were regularly and harshly attacking Democrats and liberals. This damaged the conservative cause by making it easy to stereotype conservatives as overly zealous, extreme, and ignorant. For example, the ultraconservative John Birch Society condemned the civil rights movement as part of a communist conspiracy to damage the United States and pave the way for a communist takeover. Birch Society leaders such as Robert Welch also said local school boards were becoming too liberal and ignoring parents' wishes in developing teaching plans, blasted the press for being too liberal, and called for the impeachment of Chief Justice Earl Warren.[21]

Some conservative strategists, such as William F. Buckley, blamed the Birch Society in part for making Goldwater seem too extreme because many voters associated him with the Birch Society's ultraconservatism.[22]

After LBJ's smashing victory in 1964, toxic politics got worse. Millions of Americans turned against him because he was escalating the Vietnam War and because he was constantly expanding the power and intrusiveness of the federal government. As his term advanced, he was the target of widespread derision and sometimes violent protests. The animosity toward Johnson grew so intense that anti-war protesters would chant at anti-LBJ rallies, "Hey, hey LBJ, how many kids did you kill today?"

Ronald Reagan

During the later years of his career, President Ronald Reagan wanted to be known as a decent, courteous leader who was not divisive. But he did have a polarizing, negative streak that emerged during the early part of his political life.

Reagan attacked liberals, anti-war protesters, and members of the counter-culture during the late 1960s and mid-1970s when he was the Republican governor of California for eight years. He did the same as a presidential candidate in 1976, '80, and '84. Reagan's popularity soared, especially among conservatives.

As a presidential candidate in 1980, Reagan used the race-tinged image of a "welfare queen" to undermine support for social programs that helped the poor. He told the story of an anonymous Black woman, described by Reagan as having "80 names, 30 addresses, 12 Social Security cards," who managed to collect a tax-free income of $150,000. "In doing so," political scientist Angie Maxwell has observed,

> he portrayed racial minorities as undeserving "takers." ... The message to Southern white voters was both that African Americans were

to blame for their own standing in society and that government programs aimed at alleviating racial inequities would disadvantage white Americans.[23]

In seeking the presidency, Reagan issued what he called the 11th Commandment: "Thou shalt not speak ill of a fellow Republican."[24] But he violated his own commandment when he challenged Republican President Gerald Ford for the GOP presidential nomination in 1976. After a shaky start in that campaign, Reagan found his voice and ran up a string of victories in state nominating contests after he mercilessly attacked Ford for weak leadership. At the top of his target list was Ford's endorsement of transferring ownership of the Panama Canal from the United States to Panama. Reagan's gambit didn't succeed in winning him the nomination but it weakened Ford for the general election which he lost to Democrat Jimmy Carter, who used Reagan's weak leadership charge against Ford.

In 1980, Reagan again turned negative by faulting then-President Carter for failed leadership and unworkable policies. But Reagan didn't attack Carter personally or question his character, unlike so many candidates who go negative today.

After he won in 1980 and throughout his eight-year presidency, Reagan rarely criticized his opponents personally. He had an amiable private relationship with House Speaker Tip O'Neill, D-Mass., his main adversary on Capitol Hill, even though they clashed publicly on policy. And he didn't demonize O'Neill or his other political opponents in public or private.

With his soothing voice, bright smile, and easygoing demeanor, Reagan seemed more the benevolent grandfather than the conservative firebrand. Critics mocked him as lazy, ignorant, too old for the job, mentally unfit, and an "amiable dunce," but Reagan didn't respond with comparable insults. Reagan criticized his political foes, but he didn't try to demean them. And his sense of humor increased his popularity, especially his self deprecation. When he felt his work ethic was called into question, he joked that hard work never hurt anyone, but why take the chance? When opponents suggested he was too old for his job during the 1984 re-election campaign against former Vice President Walter Mondale, Reagan used a debate with Mondale to declare that he wouldn't make his opponent's youth and inexperience an issue in the campaign. This twist on the age issue won Reagan more admirers and softened the issue against the septuagenarian president.

As historian H.W. Brands has observed,

> Reagan could get righteously angry, as when the Soviets shot down a Korean airliner in 1983. "Words can scarcely express our revulsion at this horrifying act of violence," he declared.

> But anger wasn't Reagan's natural mode. He was an optimist at heart, and in every speech he conveyed his belief that America's best days were ahead. Goldwater frowned and warned; Reagan smiled and invited ... Reagan refused to demonize his foes. Instead, he charmed them, with a few exceptions. ... He didn't point fingers; he told jokes. He understood, from years on the lecture circuit, the disarming value of humor: that getting people to laugh with you is halfway to getting them to agree with you. He used humor more effectively than any president since Abraham Lincoln. Reagan was not an especially warm person, but he *appeared* to be. Many people disliked his policies, but almost no one disliked *him*.[25]

George H.W. Bush

George H.W. Bush called for a "kinder and gentler" presidency after eight years of Ronald Reagan, during which Bush was vice president. But Bush concluded that he needed to wage a harsh, negative campaign in 1988 and he stooped to conquer.

Bush didn't like to do political dirty work himself, so he gave the mudslinging role to tough hardball practitioners led by campaign manager Lee Atwater and media consultant Roger Ailes.[26]

During the 1988 Republican presidential nominating contests, Bush suffered an unexpected loss in the Iowa caucuses when he finished third, behind Sen. Bob Dole of Kansas and the Rev. Pat Robertson, a television preacher. Bush decided he had to undermine Dole, his main opponent, which he did in the next contest, the New Hampshire primary. "His one negative advertisement attacked Dole for straddling on the issues—on defense, on an oil import fee, and most importantly on tax increases," reported columnist E.J. Dionne, Jr.[27] The tough anti-Dole ad did the trick, and Bush finished first in New Hampshire and went on to win the nomination.

As the nominee, Bush and his team were eager to wage a negative campaign against Massachusetts Gov. Michael Dukakis as soon as Dukakis became the frontrunner for the Democratic nomination in 1988, and they found plenty of ammunition. The general-election campaign quickly became "brutish, backward-looking, divisive," according to Dionne.[28]

The attack strategy, which Bush preferred to call, euphemistically, "comparative politics," focused on Dukakis's long public record of liberal positions "and a train of enemies ready to quote it chapter and verse," wrote journalists Peter Goldman and Tom Mathews.[29] Among the targets were Dukakis's membership in the American Civil Liberties Union, a cardinal sin for conservatives, his opposition to requiring Massachusetts schoolchildren to salute the flag and say the Pledge of Allegiance, and the pollution of Boston Harbor during Dukakis's governorship.

"And there was, downstage center, Willie Horton, a black convict who had stabbed a white man and raped a white woman in Maryland while on furlough from a life sentence for murder in Massachusetts," Goldman and Mathews wrote.

> Jim Pinkerton—Pink, to his corps of fresh-faced young Duke-busters on Fifteenth Street [in Washington, D.C. where Bush had his campaign headquarters] had been poring over their findings one day in April when an exchange between Dukakis and [fellow Democratic presidential candidate Al] Gore caught his eye. Gore had made an issue of the Massachusetts furlough program. Most states had one and so did the Federal government but, as Gore noted, only Massachusetts permitted "weekend passes" for murderers doing life without parole; eleven, he said, had fled, and two had killed again. Dukakis, as it happened, had inherited the program from a Republican predecessor. Still, he had defended it until after the Horton scandal and his sniffish response to Gore never really addressed the question.[30]

Bush, a genteel Brahmin from a respected family and the best schools, didn't like the issue at first. It seemed too negative and unpresidential. But his hard-charging staff, especially campaign manager Atwater, Pinkerton's boss and mentor, thought, correctly, that the Willie Horton connection would hurt Dukakis badly. Atwater publicly suggested mischievously that Dukakis might put Horton on the Democratic ticket, and Atwater wouldn't let the issue go in his conversations with reporters. By the end of the campaign, which Bush won overwhelmingly, Willie Horton was a household name, and not in a good way.

"Bush's men would insist afterward that there was no racial undertone to the story, no conscious design to inflame white fears of black crime," Goldman and Mathews wrote.

> Their evidence was that the campaign's official advertising never showed Horton's face or alluded to his color; the story, in the official line, was a metaphor for Dukakis's peculiar values, and the race of its protagonist had nothing to do with it. But Horton's mug shot would appear in some independently produced commercials and fliers, and the men on Fifteenth Street sometimes made careless use of his story.[31]

Actually, Bush's high command saw the Horton scandal as a paradigm for all that was wrong with Dukakis and his candidacy. They considered him a tax-and-spend liberal, unpatriotic, an elitist, and weak on foreign policy. Their goal was to savage Dukakis and give people a reason to vote against him rather than find ways to persuade people to support Bush, considered a harder sell.[32]

Partly because of their use of the Willie Horton issue, Bush's general-election bid "would be one of the meanest national campaigns since the McCarthy era—so mean, in its worst moments, as to invite the suspicion that George Bush would say nearly anything to win," Goldman and Mathews wrote.[33]

The campaign also cemented Atwater's reputation as the nation's premier practitioner of negative politics at the time, described by one historian as "*l'enfant terrible* of Washington political consultants."[34]

President Bush, after his election, named Atwater the chairman of the Republican National Committee, drawing more attention to the young political streetfighter and enabling him to inspire many younger political operatives to imitate his slash-and-burn approach[35]

By this time, Atwater had expanded his influence within the Bush family by bonding with presidential son George W. Bush. Both of them were brash, irreverent, fun-loving, and ruthless in advancing George H.W. Bush—and Atwater taught George W. his negative tactics and strategies. Even though Atwater died in 1991, long before Dubya ran successfully for president in 2000, his influence on the younger Bush was profound.[36] And Atwater's influence manifested itself in another way—Dubya would hire Karl Rove, an Atwater acolyte, to be his chief strategist in the 2000 campaign and later made Rove deputy White House chief of staff.

The negativity also infected the elder Bush's presidency in fundamental ways, such as during the battle over Clarence Thomas as Bush's nominee for the Supreme Court. This struggle devolved into a debate over the truthfulness and character of Thomas, who was accused of sexual harassment by his former employee Anita Hill, versus the truthfulness and character of Hill. It played out in nationally televised hearings that riveted much of the nation. As Dionne noted,

> But the real struggle involved the nation's extended moral civil war over its cultural soul and over issues involving race and feminism. It was a fight in which the various sides were so utterly convinced of their moral righteousness that they were willing to flout all the rules in order to win.[37]

It was one of the most caustic Supreme Court fights in history, with Thomas eventually winning Senate confirmation.

Bill Clinton

During his 1992 campaign, Bill Clinton was hit with allegations of smoking marijuana, draft dodging, and what were seen as other personal failings. He quickly created a "war room" to immediately respond to rumors and innuendo in equally harsh terms during the 1992 campaign. It became an engine of negativity directed against his political adversaries. He replicated this approach by creating a war room during his presidency to win passage for a big health-care reform bill, which failed. But the very creation of a war room showed how much negativity and combativeness had taken over politics and governing.

The willingness to demean one's adversaries was a key tactic during Clinton's second term as his defenders derided women who accused him of sexual improprieties. The women's reputations were sullied but a number of their accusations later proved true, such as the claim by former White House intern Monica Lewinsky that President Clinton had an inappropriate sexual relationship with her.

Bill and Hillary Clinton had complained, accurately, of repeated efforts to derail his political career going back to his years as Arkansas governor by using unproven allegations against him. Eventually they came up with a phrase to describe it—"the politics of personal destruction."[38]

So the attacks on the Clintons that he endured from the start of his first presidential campaign in 1992 and throughout his eight-year presidency were nothing new for them. But the attacks grew more intense the longer his presidency lasted as his critics did all they could to hobble and embarrass him.

Pro-Clinton authors Joe Conason and Gene Lyons point out that the harsh tactics used by rivals against Clinton resulted in "the coarsening and debasement of democratic discourse; the abuse of criminal prosecution to resolve political disputes; and the diminishment of popular respect for the presidency, the Congress, the federal judiciary, the news media, and other vital institutions."[39]

During his sex scandals, Clinton used supporters to take on and undermine his accusers, such as Lewinsky and Gennifer Flowers, who said Clinton had committed adultery with her. Hillary Clinton, Bill Clinton's wife, also played a role in demeaning the accusers.

Several other women accused him of making crass and unwanted advances, which they considered sexual harassment. They included Paula Jones, Kathleen Willey, and Juanita Broaddrick. They were also dismissed and attacked.

Conservative strategist Peter Wehner condemned

> the degree to which Democrats including feminists, overlooked or accepted Bill Clinton's sexually predatory behavior—including his campaign's effort to smear his accusers and its use of a private investigator to destroy Gennifer Flowers's reputation "beyond all recognition" ... So Flowers was branded a "bimbo" and a "pathological liar,"

> even though Clinton later, under oath, admitted to having an affair with her.[40]

In 1994, Paula Jones said Bill Clinton

> had summoned her to a hotel room and exposed himself when he was the governor of Arkansas and she was a state employee. (Clinton denied the charges from Jones, Willey and Broaddrick.) Later she brought suit against him for sexual harassment. Her story was seized upon by a Republican operative, who urged her to go public at a conservative political action conference, the right's annual activist spectacle.[41]

Clinton's advisers trashed Jones in the media after she got attention for claiming that Clinton sexually harassed her. Clinton political strategist James Carville was particularly disparaging; "if you drag a $100 bill through a trailer park, you never know what you'll find," he said. Carville and other Clinton defenders said Jones was seeking cash for telling a tabloid tale. The negative assessment of Jones lingered for years.[42]

In addition, "Lewinsky has always been cast as the central female character of Bill Clinton scandals, and while that has been hell for her, it has been rather convenient for him," journalist Amanda Hess observed.

> Over two decades, it was easy to forget that the reporting on Clinton's consensual affair with an intern arose out of an even more damning context: Jones's harassment suit. (It was Lewinsky and Clinton denying their affair under oath in the Jones case that gave [independent counsel Kenneth] Starr the material to pounce.) Paula Jones spoke out against the most powerful man in the world, and when his lawyers argued that a sitting president couldn't be subject to a civil suit, she took them all the way to the Supreme Court and won. In another world, she would be held as a feminist icon. But not in this world—not yet.[43]

In 1996, Stuart Taylor, Jr., a legal affairs writer, wrote about the Paula Jones case for the *American Lawyer*'s November 1996 issue. In a breakthrough of sorts for the Clinton critics, the article lent credence to Jones' allegations among some journalists who had been doubters.

One of those struck by Taylor's piece was Evan Thomas, a top editor at *Newsweek*. "With his Andover-Harvard background and WASP pedigree, Thomas was sensitive to Taylor's charge of class bias—a sensitivity that may well have been passed down from his grandfather, Socialist Norman Thomas," a journalist at *Newsweek* wrote.

> Moreover, he felt especially vulnerable on this one: As a regular on the talk show Inside Washington, he had once derided Jones as "some sleazy woman with big hair coming out of the trailer parks," a sneering description for which he had caught some grief. What was more, Taylor was a regular in Thomas's Sunday football games, and he had been lobbying Thomas to give the article a close look.[44]

The Supreme Court was planning to hear Clinton's lawyers argue that presidents should be immune from civil litigation while in office. If Clinton lost, the Jones case would proceed.[45]

The Clinton defenders stepped up their critiques of Jones, as they would do with Lewinsky. Clinton allies condemned the Jones allegations as "tabloid trash."[46]

By 1998, media analyst Howard Kurtz wrote:

> Hillary had long served as a back channel for advisers trying to change her husband's mind about some decision, and now she shifted into what one aide called her "battle mode." Ann Lewis, who was close to Hillary, held a strategy session in the Old Executive Office Building and the first lady decided it was time to publicly emerge as the president's chief defender. The next morning, she declared on the *Today* show that Starr was a "politically motivated prosecutor," part of a "vast right-wing conspiracy" of "malicious" and "evil-minded" people. She also took a whack at the "feeding frenzy" in the media, much of which, in her view, had become part of the conspiracy against the White House. The first lady would not answer questions about Clinton's relationship with Lewinsky, but she understood the value of shifting the spotlight to the political opposition, a tactic that had served her well during the endless Whitewater saga [a lengthy legal investigation that eventually fizzled into alleged Clinton financial abuse in an Arkansas real-estate deal]. [Independent counsel Kenneth] Starr dismissed her charges as "nonsense," but the Clintonites were thrilled with the way she had cast the debate.[47]

"For all the journalistic excess," Kurtz added, "the public reaction, at least initially [before President Clinton admitted he had lied under oath about the affair with Lewinsky], was more restrained."

> Fifty-seven percent of those questioned in a *Washington Post* poll said they believed that Clinton had had a sexual relationship with Lewinsky; like the journalists, they had dismissed his denials as lies. But fifty-nine percent said they wanted him to remain in office, even if he had been having sex in the White House with the young intern. A majority

> favored impeachment only if it turned out that Clinton had lied under oath about the affair. The issue for most people was trust, not sex. … Despite the round-the-clock-media assault, the president's lofty approval rating, seemingly impervious during the campaign finance fiasco, was holding steady.[48]

During his final year in office, after the impeachment crisis, Clinton resorted to abject apologizing and painful public expressions of remorse and admissions of personal failings, far more than any president had ever done. He told a gay rights group in New York:

> It has occurred to me really that every one of us has this little scale inside, you know. On one side there's the light forces, and the other side there's the dark forces in our psyche and our makeup and the way we look at the world. And every day we wake up and the scale is a little bit tilted one way or the other. And life is a big struggle to try to keep things in proper balance. You don't want to have so much light that you're just a fool for whatever comes along. But if the scale tips dark even a little bit, things turn badly for people and those with whom they come in contact.[49]

Clinton's embarrassment had turned into very public introspection as his caustic approach to his adversaries faded.

In 2018, prodded by the feminist "MeToo movement," which focused on supporting women who said they were sexually assaulted, the news media revisited Lewinsky's case with more sympathy than before. Journalist Amanda Hess wrote.

> She has emerged from years of media torture as an unexpected darling of the press. The same cannot be said for Jones, Willey or Broaddrick. In the 90s they were dismissed as "members" deployed in service of what Hillary Clinton called the "vast right wing conspiracy," and with few exceptions, their stories have remained relegated to the margins of respectable conversation. They have been featured not in glossy fashion magazines but in self-published memoirs and political smear campaigns. They have been used as right-wing pawns and left-wing punching bags.[50]

George W. Bush

Emulating his father's use of Lee Atwater and Roger Ailes, George W. Bush had others do the dirty work of politics for him. Among them was adviser Karl Rove, who resorted to arranging attacks when he felt it was necessary to rough up opponents during Bush's successful 2000 presidential campaign and his victorious 2004 re-election bid.

For their part, those opponents were also tough on Bush, mocking his lack of experience with national and international issues, his privileged upbringing, and the perception that he had used his father's connections to advance himself in business and politics over the years.

Bush and his operatives successfully stopped Sen. John McCain, R-Ariz., from winning the Republican nomination over Bush in 2000 through a series of attacks against McCain in the primaries. Bush went on to win the Electoral College in the general election when the Supreme Court in a 5–4 decision awarded Florida to Bush, giving him the electoral majority. Al Gore, his Democratic opponent, won about 500,000 more popular votes nationally than Bush. This outraged many Democrats who believed Bush was not a legitimate president.

There was bitterness all around when Bush took the oath of office in January 2001. The terrorist attacks of September 11 of that year caused the country to rally around him as he began a "global war on terror." Then he ordered invasions of Afghanistan and Iraq to destroy terrorist networks and rid the world of the Iraqi regime of Saddam Hussein, who, while he was a threat to his neighbors, had nothing to do with the 9/11 attacks.

But 9/11 and Bush's strong response transformed American politics and made national security the nation's paramount issue. And this focus on "keeping us safe" became Bush's mantra and his most devastating ammunition against John Kerry, the Democratic nominee in 2004 who was portrayed as weak and an inveterate vacillator.

"It has evolved into one of the most relentlessly negative political campaigns in memory, as attacks on a candidate's character, patriotism, and fitness for office, which once seemed out of bounds, have become routine," wrote reporter Janet Hooks in the *Los Angeles Times*. "More ads than ever focused on discrediting an opponent rather than promoting a candidate, and independent political analysts warned the presidential campaign was breaking new ground in a candidate's willingness to bend the truth."[51]

After it became clear that Kerry would be the Democratic nominee, Bush and his campaign began their all-out attack. "The Bush team labeled Kerry not only as too liberal for the presidency but as someone who did not have the character and integrity required of the job," political scientist Swint wrote. "Bush called him a flip-flopper. ... Of course, Senator Kerry did hand the Bush team some of the best material it could have hoped for to drive home its point."[52] Among his gaffes was seeming to flip-flop in explaining why he didn't support an $87 billion spending bill for the war in Iraq and therefore didn't back the troops.

He explained, lamely, "I actually did vote for the $87 billion before I voted against it."[53]

From then on, the campaign descended into nasty name-calling and harsh charges of ineptitude and lack of ethics.

Another factor intensifying the negativity was the role of independent political organizations known as 527s, named after the section of the Internal Revenue Code specifying their legal status. The code allowed people to organize groups to collect money, often from the super-rich, and spend it on independent political advertising in campaigns. The ads run by these groups were mostly negative, according to an academic study in 2004.[54]

The 527 group that stirred things up the most was Swift Boat Veterans for Truth, run by Floyd Brown, who had done so much damage to Dukakis with the Willie Horton issue during the 1988 campaign of George H.W. Bush. Also participating in the attacks were several Vietnam veterans who had served during the Vietnam war aboard "swift boats" that had patrolled the Mekong Delta. Kerry had done the same job, and the group proceeded to savage him, saying he falsely made himself out to be a hero. What they most objected to were Kerry's anti-war comments after he returned home from the war and his description of what he called atrocities committed by U.S. soldiers. The swift boat veterans said these charges were fabricated, and they called Kerry a traitor.[55]

Kerry at first thought the swift boat allegations would not hurt his campaign, but polls indicated that they damaged him seriously. By the time he responded with aggressive denials, the damage was done, and he couldn't recover. Even accusations that Bush was a "deserter" during the Vietnam war—a false charge that distorted Bush's legitimate service in the National Guard—failed to help Kerry.

As Swint observed:

> Certainly, one of the distinguishing characteristics that made campaign 2004 one of the most negative in modern times was the personal nature of many of the statements and criticisms. Modern campaigns are full of such name calling and personal attacks, but they usually do not come from the actual campaign organizations, from official party sources, or from the candidates themselves [as they did in 2004].[56]

Notes

1 Merle Miller, *Plain Speaking: An Oral Biography of Harry S. Truman*. New York: Berkley Books, 1974, 198.

2 Clare Booth Luce, quoted in Albin Krebs, "Bess Truman is Dead at 97, Was President's 'Full Partner,'" *The New York Times*, October 19, 1982. Archived

at https://www.nytimes.com/1982/10/19/obituaries/bess-truman-is-dead-at-97-was-president-s-full-partner.html.
3 Miller, 198.
4 Quoted in Miller, 280.
5 Emmett H. Buell and Lee Sigelman, *Attack Politics: Negativity in Presidential Campaigns Since 1960*. Lawrence, KS: University Press of Kansas, 2009, 7.
6 ibid.
7 Quoted in Miller, 274.
8 Miller, 279.
9 Harry Truman, "News Conference at Key West," March 30, 1950." Transcript available at https://historymatters.gmu.edu/d/8078.
10 Randall J. Stephens, "Tracing the Origins of Today's Ultraconservatives," *Washington Post*, January 2, 2022, B3.
11 Quoted in John Kelly, "Remembering the Time a President Threatened to Punch a Washington Post Critic," *Washington Post*, February 25, 2017, https://www.washingtonpost.com/local/remembering-the-time-a-president-threatened-to-punch-a-washington-post-critic/2017/02/25/d2053ffc-f9e6-11e6-be05-1a3817ac21a5_story.html.
See also Allan Smith, "Harry Truman Once Wrote a Newspaper Columnist a Scathing Letter for Being Critical of His Daughter," *Business Insider*, February 8, 2017, www.businessinsider.com/harry-truman-letter-daughter-trump-2017-2?amp.
12 Quoted in Kelly.
13 Quoted in "Goldwater's 1964 Acceptance Speech," *Washington Post*, May 1998. https://www.washingtonpost.com/wp-srv/politics/daily/may98/goldwaterspeech.htm.
14 This description is based primarily on Drew Babb, "LBJ's 1964 Attack Ad 'Daisy' Leaves a Legacy for Modern Campaigns," *Washington Post*, September 5, 2014. https://www.washingtonpost.com/opinions/lbjs-1964-attack-ad-daisy-leaves-a-legacy-for-modern-campaigns/2014/09/05/d00e66b0-33b4-11e4-9e92-0899b306bbea_story.html.
15 Edwin Diamond and Stephen Bates, *The Spot: The Rise of Political Advertising on Television*. Cambridge, MA: The MIT Press, 1984, 146–7.
16 Swint, 35.
17 Quoted in "Daisy: The Complete History of an Infamous and Iconic Ad—Part One," www.conelrad.com/daisy/index.php.
18 ibid. See also Robert Dallek, *Flawed Giant: Lyndon Johnson and His Times, 1961–1973*. New York: Oxford University Press, 1998, 174.
19 Swint, 36.
20 Robert Mann, "How the 'Daisy' Ad Changed Everything About Political Advertising," smithsonianmag.com, April 13, 2016, www.smithsonianmag.com/history/how-daisy-ad-changed-everything-about-political-advertising-180958731/.
21 Randall J. Stephens, "Tracing the Origins of Today's Ultraconservatives," *Washington Post*, January 2, 2022, B3.
22 ibid.
23 Angie Maxwell, "What We Get Wrong about the Southern Strategy," *Washington Post*, July 26, 2019, https:www.washingtonpost.com/outlook/2019/07/26/what-we-get-wrong-about-southern-strategy.
24 Quoted in Tim Groeling, *When Politicians Attack! Party Cohesion in the Media*. New York: Cambridge University Press 2010, 7.
25 H.W. Brands, "You're Remembering Reagan Wrong," *Time*, May 16, 2015, https://time.com/3858793/ronald-reagan-history/?amp=true.

26 See Chapters 9 and 10.
27 E.J. Dionne, Jr., *Why Americans Hate Politics*. New York: Touchstone, 1991, 304.
28 ibid., 316.
29 Peter Goldman, Tom Mathews, and the *Newsweek* special election team, *The Quest for the Presidency 1988*. New York: Simon & Schuster/Touchstone, 1989, 305–6.
30 ibid.
31 ibid., 307.
32 ibid., 307–8.
33 ibid., 308.
34 Jean Edward Smith, *Bush*. New York: Simon & Schuster, 2016, 48.
35 ibid., 53.
36 ibid., 48–53.
37 Dionne, 363.
38 Joe Conason and Gene Lyons, *The Hunting of the President: The Ten-Year Campaign to Destroy Bill and Hillary Clinton*. New York: Thomas Dunne Books, 2000, xiii.
39 ibid., xiv.
40 Peter Wehner, "Why Trump Supporters Can't Admit Who He Really Is," *The Atlantic*, September 4, 2020, www.theatlantic.com/ideas/archive/2020/09/predicate-fear/616009/. Original underline. Also see Amanda Hess, "Paula Jones, Reconsidered," November 20, 2018, nytimes.com/2018/11/20/arts/television/Paula-jones-monica-lewinsky-billclinton.html.
41 Amanda Hess, "Paula Jones, Reconsidered," November 20, 2018, nytimes.com/2018/11/20/arts/television/Paula-jones-monica-lewinsky-billclinton.html.
42 ibid.
43 ibid.
44 Michael Isikoff, *Uncovering Clinton: A Reporter's Story*. New York: Crown Publishers, 1999, 104.
45 ibid., 105.
46 ibid., 106.
47 Howard Kurtz, *Spin Cycle: Inside the Clinton Propaganda Machine*. New York: The Free Press, 1989, 198.
48 ibid., 300.
49 Quoted in John F. Harris, *The Survivor: Bill Clinton in the White House*. New York: Random House, 2006, 398.
50 Hess.
51 Janet Hook, "Campaigns Accentuate the Negative," *Los Angeles Times*, Octpber 17, 2004, A1.
52 Swint, 4.
53 Quoted in Jodi Wilgoren, "The 2004 Campaign: Political Memo; Kerry's Words, and Bush's Use of Them, Offer Valuable Lesson in '04 Campaigning," *The New York Times*, May 8, 2004. https://www.nytimes.com/2004/05/08/us/2004-campaign-political-memo-kerry-s-words-bush-s-use-them-offer-valuable-lesson.html.
54 Hook, A1.
55 Swint, 7.
56 Swint, 9.

3

RICHARD NIXON AND THE RISE OF TOXICITY

Richard Nixon earned the nickname "Tricky Dick" early in his career. And throughout his political life, Nixon and his henchmen made American politics more toxic, polarized and deceptive, especially during his 1968 and 1972 presidential campaigns and during the Watergate scandal.

"No figure in American history has a more tarnished image than Richard M. Nixon," wrote political scientist Kerwin Swint.

> After all, how do you come by a nickname like Tricky Dick? In his case it was a well-earned trophy. Through the years of Machiavellian-type political shenanigans, both in political campaigns and in public office, Nixon operated as though his life were at stake. Losing was just not an option.[1]

Nixon "had demons inside him that he had not learned to control," such as deep resentment toward liberals who scorned him as an unscrupulous Neanderthal and a sense that he was persecuted because of his humble beginnings, says David Gergen, a former aide to Nixon and three other presidents.[2]

In his book *Nixonland*, historian Rick Perlstein wrote that Nixon rose to power in large part

> by stoking and exploiting anger and resentment rooted in the anger and resentments at the center of his character. For what was his injunction to join his Silent Majority if not also an invitation to see one's neighbors as aliens, and to believe that what was alien would destroy us? I

DOI: 10.4324/9781003149095-5

> have even suggested that the demons that consumed him, the demons that led to Watergate, were part of a sincere desire to combat what he believed was truly *evil*—a battle with which many of the public in some sense identified, who embraced Nixon despite the anxieties and dreads that drove him, but because of them.[3]

What Richard Nixon left behind, Perlstein added, were

> the very terms of our national self-image: a nation that there are two kinds of Americans. On the one side, that "Silent Majority." The "non-shouters." The middle-class, middle American, suburban, exurban, and rural coalition who call themselves now, "values voters,'" "people of faith," "patriots," or even, simply, "Republicans"—and who feel themselves condescended to by snobby opinion-making elites, and who rage about un-Americans, anti-Christians, amoralists, *aliens*. On the other side are the "liberals," the "cosmopolitans," the "intellectuals," the "professionals"—"Democrats." Who say they see shouting in opposition to injustice as a higher form of patriotism. Or say "live and let live." ... Both populations—to speak in ideal types—are equally, essentially, tragically American. And both have learned to consider the other not quite American at all. The argument over Richard Nixon, pro and con, gave us the language for this war.[4]

Nixon, insecure about his humble origins and seeking to make a name for himself and climb the ladder of success, had a long history of slash-and-burn politics by the time he took over the White House in January 1969. A prime example was his 1950 Senate campaign in California against U.S. Rep. Helen Gahagan Douglas, a Democratic liberal and former actress. Nixon called her, memorably, "the Pink Lady" and "pink right down to her underwear" because she was, he said, a communist or "Red" sympathizer. He mocked her for socializing with "Hollywood left-wing intellectuals at pinko cocktail parties" and for being a sympathizer with communists in the movie industry.[5]

Nixon and other critics never proved that Douglas, a three-term Democratic congresswoman from Los Angeles, was a communist. Actually, she was a mainstream liberal, backing Franklin D. Roosevelt's New Deal social programs and she was pro-civil rights but not a left-wing extremist as Nixon charged. Still, he smeared her as a left-wing extremist.[6] Among his dirty tricks against Douglas, Nixon supporters phoned up to 500,000 California voters and asked if they were aware "that Helen Douglas is a communist."[7]

Douglas went negative, too, dubbing Nixon "peewee" and calling him "Tricky Dick," a nickname that stuck with him for many years. But she lacked Nixon's instinct for the jugular. He followed the counsel of campaign adviser Murray Chotiner about politics and life: "Nice guys and sissies don't win elections."[8]

Nixon won with 59 percent of the vote, and he became a practitioner of attack politics for the rest of his career.

Nixon had a talent for understanding the nation's mood. His highly negative campaign against Douglas came during a period of heightened fear of communism, propelled by the gains of the Soviet Union and China in their battle with the United States for control of other countries. When communist North Korea invaded South Korea in June 1950, fear of communism reached a feverish level. Nixon had already catapulted to national attention as a member of the House Committee on UnAmerican Activities during the late 1940s when he helped to investigate Alger Hiss, a former State Department employee accused and convicted of spying for the Soviet Union. Nixon also allied himself with Sen. Joe McCarthy, R-Wis., and his smear tactics as McCarthy hunted for communists in the government.[9]

"The 1950 campaign [pitting Nixon against Douglas] was significant in that some historians believe it helped set the tone for increasingly negative and personal politics in America," Swint wrote. "In addition, it elevated a very practiced champion of political character assassination to national prominence. It also encouraged the anti-communist 'witch hunt' hearings of Senator Joseph McCarthy in the 1950s."[10]

Overall, negativity was on the rise in America, propelled by fear-mongering, distrust of government, and resistance to change, factors that have ebbed and flowed in the nation for many years. At times it seemed as if the United States was coming loose from its moorings, and many were abandoning fundamental American values such as tolerance and equality. Nixon capitalized on all of this and accelerated the trends.

Nixon's 1968 and 1972 campaigns adopted a harshly negative strategy for dividing the American public. They used wedge issues such as opposition to abortion, support for prayer in public schools, and most of all support for "law and order," fighting crime, and opposition to civil rights to turn working-class whites, especially those in the South, against the Democrats. This proved to be dramatically effective.

Nixon told a town hall meeting in Atlanta on October 3, 1968, the month before the election, "We have reaped not a solution of poverty but we've reaped the riots that have torn 300 cities apart, resulted in 200 dead and 7,000 injured throughout this country." He pledged to restore "law and order" and condemned "those who would destroy America, who would burn it."[11]

"It came to be known as Nixon's Southern strategy: a campaign that used fear of crime and lawlessness to tap into white Southern voters' opposition to racial integration and equality without using overtly racist language," journalist Russ Bynum wrote in 2020.

> It was a strategy that Republicans honed gradually over decades—ultimately achieving dominance across the South and a political realignment that changed the electoral map for presidential candidates, the makeup of Congress and the tenor of the American debate about race.[12]

Political scientist Angie Maxwell wrote of the Nixon strategy,

> The "silent majority" of white Southerners that the candidate needed to attract understood that Nixon's call for the restoration of "law and order," for example, was a dog whistle, signaling his support for an end to protests, marches and boycotts, while his "war on drugs" played on racialized fear about crime. Nixon also adopted a stance of "benign neglect" on civil-rights enforcement, a message that his advocates, such as Democrat-turned-Republican Sen. Strom Thurmond, bluntly conveyed to Southern whites on his behalf. As Thurmond put it, "If Nixon becomes president, he has promised that he won't enforce either the Civil Rights or the Voting Rights Acts. Stick with him."[13]

After he took office as president in January 1969, Nixon stooped to new lows in his slash-and-burn approach in order to guarantee his re-election. And he spawned a cadre of hard-line operatives to carry out his toxic wishes.

The Watergate scandal, which started with the burglary of the Democratic National Committee headquarters at the Watergate office and residential complex in Washington, was part of it, but only the tip of the iceberg.

Washington Post reporters Carl Bernstein and Bob Woodward showed the depth of the caustic politics generated by Nixon in their book *All the President's Men*. A secret source within the government, whom they nicknamed "Deep Throat" after the title of a porn film, described the methods in clandestine meetings with Woodward, sometimes in a deserted Washington garage. "On evenings such as these, Deep Throat had talked about how politics had infiltrated every corner of government—a strong-arm takeover of the agencies by the Nixon White House," Bernstein and Woodward wrote.

> Junior White House aides were giving orders on the highest levels of the bureaucracy. He had once called it the "switchblade mentality"—and had referred to the willingness of the president's men to fight dirty and

> for keeps, regardless of what effect the slashing might have on the government and the nation.[14]

G. Gordon Liddy was a Nixon acolyte who specialized in machismo and negative politics. Dan Zak wrote in the *Washington Post*:

> In the early 1970s, Liddy, as an operative aligned with Richard Nixon, dreamed of a million-dollar plan code-named "Gemstone" that outlined, among other efforts, the assassination of a newspaper columnist [Jack Anderson] and the entrapment of Democratic officials in a blackmail scheme, using prostitutes, a hidden photographer and a houseboat. That plan was pared down to a simple burglary and bugging of the Democratic Party's headquarters at the Watergate complex. Under Liddy's leadership, the plan was botched and traced to the White House.

It was the first event in the Watergate scandal that led to the resignation of President Nixon.[15]

Liddy, who died in 2021 at age 90 after serving prison terms for conspiracy, burglary, and illegal wiretapping, parlayed his macho conservative image into book sales and a talk-radio show. He "lives on in any number of characters afflicting our politics with their theatrical machismo or numb-skulled shenanigans," Zak said.

> There's a little Liddy in [then] New York Gov. Andrew M. Cuomo and his hatchet men, who aren't subtle about conducting loyalty tests or smearing opponents. Trump-World teemed with little Liddys trying to outdo one another with displays of bravado, running off cliffs like Wile E Coyotes, rigging political bombs that detonated in their faces.
>
> Roger Stone, Paul Manafort, Michael Cohen, Rudolph Giuliani. Absent-minded masterminds, all of them, tripping on their own cloaks, daggering their own shanks. Fixers who needed fixing.[16]

"As president, Nixon ordered illegal wiretaps on newsmen who criticized his administration," historian Mark Feldstein wrote,

> and instructed FBI director J. Edgar Hoover to compile a dossier on "homosexuals known and suspected in the Washington press corps." Nixon's Justice Department filed antitrust charges against television networks that criticized him and went to court in an unprecedented attempt to legalize government censorship. Nixon's aides even put together a list of "enemies," including journalists, to be secretly targeted for government retaliation.[17]

Nixon came to hate newspaper columnist Jack Anderson, who wrote many negative stories about him. Nixon told aides "we've got to do something with this son of a bitch"[18] and his operatives moved aggressively. The CIA illegally wiretapped Anderson and put him under surveillance. Nixon wanted his staff to allege that Anderson was gay, but few took the allegation seriously.[19]

In March 1972, Nixon ranted again about Anderson during a meeting with White House special counsel Charles Colson. Colson then contacted Nixon operative E. Howard Hunt and, according to Hunt's sworn testimony before the Senate, Colson said the White House had to "stop Anderson at all costs." Liddy was enlisted to help with an assassination plot. It was never clear whether Nixon was directly aware of the conspiracy, but he had created a toxic environment where such things were contemplated. Eventually, Colson, Hunt, Liddy, and their cohorts concluded that the killing of Anderson was too risky, and they abandoned the idea.[20]

Instead, they turned to bugging the Democratic Party's headquarters in Washington's Watergate office building. The discovery of this plot and the subsequent White House cover-up led to the Watergate scandal and Nixon's resignation. (And Colson, Hunt, and Liddy went to jail for Watergate-related crimes.)[21]

During his 1972 re-election campaign, Nixon and his acolytes played dirty in a number of other ways, such as by undermining possible Democratic opponents such as Ed Muskie, a U.S. senator and former governor of Maine who was initially considered the strongest Democrat. "This was accomplished through espionage, wiretapping, blackmail, forged documents, financial payoffs, burglary, cover-ups, and perjury, all sanctioned by the highest authorities in the land—the president, his senior staff, and the attorney general's office," Swint observed.

> As a campaign strategy, it was incredibly effective—that is, until everyone involved went to jail or resigned from office. What Watergate came to symbolize was an organized conspiracy from the highest office in the world to subvert the democratic process and evade any form of accountability.[22]

Deep Throat told the *Washington Post*, "Fifty people worked for the White House and CRP to play games and spy and sabotage and gather intelligence. Some of it is beyond belief, kicking at the opposition in every imaginable way."[23]Among the tactics he said were used against the opposition: "bugging, following people, false press leaks, fake letters, canceling campaign rallies, investigating campaign workers' private lives, planting spies, stealing documents, planting provocateurs in political demonstrations."[24]

Deep Throat confirmed that "The White House had been willing to subvert ... the whole election process" and "had actually gone ahead and tried to do it."[25]

Nixon's campaign, known as the Committee to Reelect the President, dubbed CREEP by journalists and Democrats, hired operatives to harass and disrupt the campaigns of Democratic candidates using dirty tricks and bizarre stunts. The operatives described their techniques as "ratfucking," and the effort was directed by lawyer Donald Segretti who later served six months in prison for Watergate scandal-related offenses.[26]

Segretti and Ken Clawson, a White House communications official, wrote a letter to William Loeb, the publisher of the influential *Manchester Union Leader*, a conservative newspaper in New Hampshire, claiming that a Muskie aide had joked improperly at a Florida campaign meeting about French Canadians living in New Hampshire. "We don't have blacks, but we have Canucks" (a name referring to French Canadians and considered derogatory by some), the aide supposedly said, according to the letter, and Muskie's laughing response was said to be, "Come to New England and see." Two weeks before the crucial New Hampshire presidential primary, the newspaper published a front-page editorial entitled, "Senator Muskie Insults French-Canadians."

The next day, the *Union Leader* published a *Newsweek* article about Muskie's wife entitled "Big Daddy's Jane" and reported that Mrs. Muskie drank too much, was a chainsmoker, and used offensive language on the campaign plane.

Muskie was outraged. The next morning, he stood on a flatbed truck in a driving snowstorm outside the newspaper's headquarters and attacked Loeb as a "gutless coward." He appeared to get emotional with rage and it seemed to reporters that he was weeping. The incident was widely covered in the news media, and it made Muskie appear to be out of control, a far cry from the steady, cool, and reasonable image he was trying to convey.[27]

"There was no dispute among Muskie backers, his opponents and the press that the incident had a disastrous effect on his campaign," wrote journalists Carl Bernstein and Bob Woodward.

> It shattered the calm, cool, reasoned image that was basic to Muskie's voter appeal, and focused last-minute attention of New Hampshire voters on the alleged slur against the French-Canadians who would be a formidable minority of voters in the Democratic primary.[28]

The Nixon team played other dirty tricks on Muskie but the "Canuck letter" gambit did the most harm. Muskie ended up winning the New Hampshire primary with only 47 percent of the vote, which was far below expectations since he was from the neighboring state of Maine. He never recovered his equilibrium and lost the Democratic nomination to Sen. George McGovern of South Dakota, a weaker national candidate who would lose overwhelmingly to Nixon that fall. All this fit with Nixon's overall plan to maneuver the Democrats into nominating the most vulnerable candidate possible.

Nixon added another fixture to the presidential repertoire: attacking the news media. Previous presidents had quarreled with the press, but Nixon made hostility to the media a central element of his administration. He had his vice president, Spiro Agnew, launch a series of vehement attacks on the media, intensifying the hard feelings between the White House and the Fourth Estate.

Agnew, serving as a hatchet man for his boss, set off a furor when he blasted national television news broadcasters on November 13, 1969. Speaking to the Midwest Regional Republican Committee in Des Moines, Iowa, Agnew said the leaders of ABC, CBS, and NBC were liberals who would never give Nixon and other conservatives fair coverage. These networks were led by a "tiny and closed fraternity of privileged men" who had "a profound influence over public opinion," Agnew declared.[29] Agnew added: "The president of the United States has a right to communicate directly with the people who elected him" without having his words "characterized through the prejudices of hostile critics." In a speech written by Nixon aide Pat Buchanan, Agnew said more government regulation of the media might be justified. When President Nixon read a draft of Buchanan's speech for Agnew, he said approvingly, "This'll tear the scab off those bastards."[30]

A week later, Agnew told an audience in Montgomery, Alabama that newspapers were also on the wrong path of bias against conservatism. In 1970, Agnew went further and condemned liberal journalists as "nattering nabobs of negativism."[31]

TV executives immediately condemned Agnew. NBC President Julian Goodman called his speech "an appeal to prejudice" and implied that Agnew was being anti-Semitic for criticizing the small group of "privileged men" who controlled the networks. Goodman and CBS President Frank Stanton said Agnew was trying to undermine freedom of the press.[32]

Agnew eventually resigned the vice presidency in disgrace in a bribery scandal stemming from his previous career in politics. After Agnew quit, Nixon and his advisers continued the attacks. Nixon said important news organizations, including the television networks, the *Washington Post*, and the *New York Times*, were biased against him and he treated them with hostility.

Reporter Robert B. Semple, Jr. wrote in the *New York Times* as allegations of corruption among Nixon operatives were gaining some traction in the media:

The essence of the Administration's recent counterattack to the charges that some of President Nixon's assistants created or at least condoned a network of political espionage and disruption has been to denounce the charges and the newspapers that print them without explicitly discussing or denying [the charges]. Behind this strategy lie two assumptions that tell much about the Administration's perceptions of the voters and the newspapers that serve them. Judging by recent interviews with Mr. Nixon's aides, these assumptions seem to be widely shared in his inner circle.

The first is that … [a]t the moment, the White House feels, the alleged conspiracy is perceived by most of the public as a distant and even amateurish intrigue far removed from the Oval Office, and thus a denial or even discussion of the charges by the White House would give those charges undeserved visibility and currency.

The second assumption is that the public—softened up by three years of speeches from Vice President Agnew—has less than total confidence that what it reads and hears—particularly in the so-called Eastern or "Establishment" media—is true and undistorted, by political prejudice. Hence the recent Administration attacks on The Washington Post, which has been giving the corruption allegations front-page treatment. …

Repeated requests to senior White House aides to set forth the full story, as they see it, have gone unanswered. This leaves the field to Mr. [Ron] Ziegler [the White House press secretary], who appears increasingly uncomfortable with questions about Mr. Chapin and Mr. Segretti [Nixon aides who were being accused of improper political activities]. …

"Do you know why we're not uptight about the press and the espionage business?" one White House aide—not Mr. Ziegler—asked rhetorically the other day. "Because we believe that the public believes that the Eastern press really is what Agnew said it was—elitist, anti-Nixon, and ultimately pro-[George] McGovern [the Democratic presidential nominee in 1972].

The irony is that Mr. Agnew himself has adopted a low profile and is saying little about the press. But his allies in the White House freely admit that the seeds of suspicion he sowed in times past are bearing fruit today."[33]

Notes

1 Kerwin Swint, *Mudslingers: The Twenty-Five Dirtiest Political Campaigns of All Time*. New York: Union Square Press, 2008, 163.
2 David Gergen Interview, *CBS News Sunday Morning*, May 8, 2022, CBSN.WS/3w9kMT5.
3 Rick Perlstein, *Nixonland: The Rise of a President and the Fracturing of America*. New York: Scribner, 2008, 748.
4 "What Richard Nixon Left Behind": Perlstein, 748.

5 Swint, 165.
6 "Douglas, Helen Gahagan," Biography, US House of Representatives: History, https://history.house.gov/People/Detail/12399.
7 Swint, 171.
8 ibid., 166.
9 See Chapter 8.
10 Swint, 172.
11 Bynum, "At RNC, GOP Echoes Racial Code of Nixon's 1968 Campaign," Associated Press, August 27, 2020, https://apnews.com/article/virus-outbreak-election-2020-race
12 ibid.
13 Angie Maxwell, "What We Get Wrong about the Southern Strategy," *Washington Post*, July 26, 2019, https://washingtonpost.com/outlook/2019/07/26/what-we-get-wrong-about-southern-strategy.
14 Carl Bernstein and Bob Woodward, *All the President's Men*. New York: Simon & Schuster/Touchstone, 1974, 130.
15 Dan Zak, "The Legacy of a Political Super-Klutz," *Washington Post*, April 1, 2021, C1.
16 Zak, C1.
17 Mark Feldstein, "The Nixon White House Plotted to Assassinate a Journalist 50 Years Ago," *Washington Post*, March 25, 2022, washingtonpost.com/history/2022/03/25/nixon.jack.anderson.assassination.
18 Quoted in Feldstein.
19 Feldstein.
20 ibid.
21 ibid.
22 Swint, 132.
23 Bernstein and Woodward, 135.
24 ibid.
25 ibid.
26 Carl Bernstein and Bob Woodward, *All the President's Men*. New York: Simon & Schuster/Touchstone, 1974, 126.
27 Swint, 135–6.
28 Carl Bernstein and Bob Woodward, *All the President's Men*. New York: Simon & Schuster/Touchstone, 1974, 127.
29 Thomas Alan Schwartz, "Nattering Nabobs of News Criticism: 50 Years Ago Today, Spiro Agnew Laid Out Blueprint for Attacking the Press," *Nieman Lab*, November 13, 2019, https://www.neimanlab.org/2019/11/nattering-nabobs-of-news.
30 Theo Lippman, Jr., "Attacks on Press Recall Agnew's Ire," *Baltimore Sun*, July 9, 2006, https://www.baltimoresun.com/news/bs-xpm-2006-07-09-060707.
31 ibid.
32 Thomas Alan Schwartz, "Nattering Nabobs of News Criticism: 50 Years Ago Today, Spiro Agnew Laid Out Blueprint for Attacking the Press," *Nieman Lab*, Nov. 13, 2019, https://www.neimanlab.org/2019/11/nattering-nabobs-of-news.
33 Quoted in Bernstein and Woodward, 169.

4

PRESIDENTS WHO STAYED MOSTLY ABOVE THE FRAY

Several presidents resisted playing negative politics. They showed that staying above the fray won't automatically cost a candidate the White House.

Abraham Lincoln

Abraham Lincoln is generally regarded today with deep respect, even reverence, as one of the best presidents. But he was widely derided during his time in office. "His ancestry was routinely impugned, his lack of formal learning ridiculed, his appearance maligned, and his morality assailed," author Mark Bowden has written.

> We take for granted, of course, the scornful outpouring from the Confederate states; no action Lincoln took short of capitulation would ever have quieted his Southern critics. But the vituperation wasn't limited to enemies of the Union. The North was ever at his heels. No matter what Lincoln did, it was never enough for one political faction, and too much for another. Yes, his sure-footed leadership during his country's most-difficult days was accompanied by a fair amount of praise, but also by a steady stream of abuse—in editorials, speeches, journals, and private letters—from those *on his own side*, those dedicated to the very causes he so ably championed.[1]

New York lawyer George Templeton Strong wrote that Lincoln was "a barbarian, Scythian, yahoo, or gorilla."[2] New York abolitionist Henry

DOI: 10.4324/9781003149095-6

Ward Beecher derided Lincoln as "an unshapely man" who was unsophisticated and unrefined. George McClellan, who had commanded the Union armies under Lincoln and then ran against him unsuccessfully for president, called his former boss a coward, "an idiot," and "the original gorilla." Lincoln was attacked frequently as timid and vacillating, a failure. Among other epithets used against him were "tyrant," "despot," "fiend," "butcher," "monster," "liar," and "ignoramus."

Lincoln did take action against critics of his war policies if he believed they were undermining the war effort, closing down newspapers and allowing editors and other critics to be arrested. But he generally didn't get into personal exchanges with those who mocked him even though, as his wife said, the negative barrages caused him "great pain." After learning of another round of savage attacks against him, he would wave his hand wearily and say, "Let us speak no more of these things."[3]

Lincoln was brilliant at using humor to deflate his opponents and diminish their attacks, a worthwhile technique that seems to be a lost art today. His wit was all the more impressive because his era was so full of anger as the nation descended into civil war. When called two-faced in a debate, for example, he replied with a self-deprecating question underscoring his homely appearance: "If I had another face, do you think I'd wear this one?"[4]

In his re-election campaign of 1864, Lincoln was the target of particularly vicious attacks. As the year began, the North's prospects in the Civil War looked bleak, and casualties were horrendous. Protests had broken out against the military draft imposed by Lincoln and in some cases rioting erupted. In July 1863 anti-draft protests turned violent in New York City, with arson, looting, and the lynching of Black people. Lincoln was widely considered too unpopular to win a second term. Newspaperman Horace Greeley wrote, "Mr. Lincoln is already beaten. He cannot be elected. And we must have another ticket to save us from utter overthrow."[5]

Lincoln was again ridiculed as a liar, a tyrant, an ignoramus, scoundrel, thief, incompetent, and a butcher who sent too many Union soldiers to their deaths.[6]

"Abraham Lincoln's opponents whispered that he, too, was the son of a slave woman, a rumor floated in conjunction with another one asserting that his administration meant to foster miscegenation as well as emancipation," wrote scholars Emmett H. Buell, Jr. and Lee Sigelman. "*Harper's Weekly* listed a score of epithets hurled against him in 1864, including 'Despot,' 'Buffoon,' and 'Monster.'"[7] Republicans countered by disputing the loyalty of former General McClellan, the Democratic nominee in 1864 who had been fired by Lincoln for failing to aggressively pursue the Confederate army.

Political scientist Kerwin Swint wrote,

> The fall campaign was ugly. It seemed that the Democrats thought up every lie they could think of to tell about President Lincoln, and the Republicans tried to think of as many ways to call General McClellan a miserable failure as they could.[8]

But Lincoln endured far worse treatment than McClellan and he mostly refused to respond to the insults and overall derision. He told aides that he believed most Americans knew him well enough not to believe the lies and slanders against him.

What saved Lincoln were major Union victories on the battlefield just before the election. Among them were Union General William Sherman's capture of Atlanta and much of Georgia; General Ulysses S. Grant's success in defeating the rebels at Petersburg, Virginia; and Admiral David Farragut's capture of Mobile Bay.

Lincoln won the election with 55 percent of the popular vote and took 212 electoral votes to McClellan's 21.

Franklin D. Roosevelt

Franklin D. Roosevelt got a taste of caustic politics when he ran on the unsuccessful Democratic ticket for vice president in 1920. Republican presidential candidate Warren G. Harding accused FDR of making "the most shocking assertion that ever emanated from a responsible member of the government of the United States." Harding was referring to a comment Roosevelt had made that as assistant secretary of the Navy he had written the constitution for Haiti. Harding indicated that Roosevelt was too prideful and his remarks smacked of imperialism and colonialism. The Harding campaign reasoned that many Irish-Americans, a growing bloc of voters, would resent FDR's remark because they believed British imperialism was preventing Ireland from attaining independence and they didn't want the United States in Haiti to imitate the Brits. Roosevelt argued blandly that he was misquoted, and this seemed to put the matter behind him.[9] Such restraint in dealing with adversaries became a hallmark of his leadership.

Throughout his 12 years as president from 1933 to 1945, Roosevelt was idolized by many Americans who believed he was a bold decision maker, was finding ways to help them in their time of need during the Depression, and was leading the world's democracies to win World War II. But FDR also endured rough treatment by his critics. They condemned him as a traitor to his class, a dangerous left-winger, a would-be American Caesar, and a socialist who was ruining American democracy and capitalism. First Lady Eleanor Roosevelt also was mocked as a socialist and a behind-the-scenes manipulator.

This also was the era of Gov. and Sen. Huey Long, the firebrand from Louisiana, and the Rev. Charles Coughlin, famous for his ferocious radio broadcasts. They were practitioners of the politics of grievance and forerunners of the political and cultural dividers of today. They often targeted Roosevelt, with Long attacking from the left and Coughlin from the right. But Roosevelt didn't respond as harshly, preferring to mostly ignore them in his public remarks.[10] FDR also responded mildly to Republican presidential candidate Thomas E. Dewey's arguments that he was a pawn of "communist-leaning" trade union organizers.[11]

But in his relatively civil way, FDR sometimes could not resist responding to what he called the "deliberate falsifications and misrepresentations"[12] of elected Republicans and other critics. He was particularly offended by the pro-business Liberty League, composed of rich corporate leaders, for their attacks on programs that helped millions survive the Depression, such as the Social Security assistance program for the elderly. Roosevelt hit back forcefully after the league condemned FDR's New Deal for being based on "ravenous madness" and "the dragon teeth of class warfare," and when the league argued the Social Security amounted to taking money and property from one class and shifting it to another "without due process of law."[13]

Roosevelt and fellow Democrats retorted sharply but not savagely, arguing that the critique was overwrought and based on greed and fear of losing power. He said big business should not always have its way and argued that he was trying to meet the needs of the overwhelming majority of Americans.[14]

FDR refused to step into the gutter despite all the provocations. He believed, correctly, that his ideas and his empathy were so popular that they would carry the day as part of a positive, optimistic message. He didn't want to get dragged into a toxic battle with his critics, and realized that his sunny disposition and his optimism were compelling to voters. Indeed, these traits were the pillars of his political success.

The first of his "fireside chats"—his immensely popular radio talks delivered live to the American people throughout his presidency—was a case in point. This speech, which he gave on March 12, 1933, shortly after his inauguration, was designed to ease worries about the bank closures that were alarming millions of Americans who wondered if their savings would be lost. Roosevelt said he would avoid the mistakes of the past and would use federal power to reopen the banks and prevent losses to everyday people but he didn't directly blame his predecessor Republican predecessor Herbert Hoover by name. Instead, he talked about his own leadership and his ideas for easing the depression and saving the banks. It was a positive message that avoided negativity.

FDR won four times, in 1932, 1936, 1940, and 1944. He benefited because during his era, including World War II, a "vital center" formed in

American politics to unify the country behind a moderate form of liberalism embodied by Roosevelt's New Deal that emphasized big government helping those in need and the United States as a major force for good and stability in international relations.

Roosevelt's response to critics tended to use more humor and a gentler touch than what we see today, much as Lincoln had done. And even though his remarks could be sharp-edged, he avoided getting personal.

When he ran successfully for a third term in 1940, his speech writers Robert E. Sherwood and Samuel Rosenman provided FDR with language that mocked his isolationist and reactionary Republican critics. His speech writers believed he needed a way to respond to the increasingly sharp attacks of Rep. Joseph Martin of Massachusetts, advertising executive Bruce Barton, and Rep. Hamilton Fish of New York. FDR mocked them as if they were members of a reactionary, elitist law firm isolated from the real world —"Martin, Barton and Fish." His crowd loved the taunts, and the gentle mockery got plenty of news coverage.[15]

Historian H.W. Brands pointed out that FDR didn't need toxic politics or personal attacks to win. In fact, such tactics would have hurt him by undermining his image as a man of the people who blamed bad policy not bad people for the country's distress. "[T]he rulers of the exchange of mankind's goods have failed, through their own stubbornness and their own incompetence, have admitted their failure, and abdicated," Roosevelt said in his first inaugural address on March 4, 1933. "Practices of the unscrupulous money changers stand indicted in the court of public opinion, rejected by the hearts and minds of men."[16]

"True they have tried, but their efforts have been cast in the pattern of an outworn tradition," he added. "They know only the rules of a generation of self-seekers. They have no vision, and when there is no vision the people perish."[17]

Roosevelt explained that he had deeper reasons for his restraint in battling with adversaries. "The man of ruthless force had his place in developing a pioneer country," he said in a 1932 speech. But he added that "the lone wolf, the unethical competitor, the reckless promoter" no longer should be part of politics or government because they were likely to pull the nation "back to a state of anarchy."[18]

"Roosevelt seemed to relish the attacks of Republicans, maintaining that he and his New Deal protected the average American against the predations of the rich and powerful," historian William E. Leuchtenburg has written, referring specifically to his 1936 re-election campaign.[19] Mentioning "business and financial monopoly, speculation, reckless banking," Roosevelt declared: "Never before have these forces been so united against one candidate as they stand today. They are unanimous in their hate for me—and I welcome their hatred."[20] He was, in effect, arguing that these anti-Roosevelt forces hated him because he was working for the downtrodden and the desperate, and he saw their negativity toward him as a badge of honor. He didn't need to attack them as savagely as they attacked him. Their opposition alone was enough to bond most voters to him because he persuaded them that their enemies were his enemies.

As his presidency progressed and his health deteriorated, he was tempted to go on the attack as his patience with critics eroded, but he resisted and continued to prefer a lighter touch to skewer his adversaries. On one telling occasion, he turned an attack on his supposed elitism and waste of taxpayer money to a pointed defense of his beloved Sottish terrier Fala. His critics had promoted a rumor that the president had accidentally left Fala behind while visiting the Aleutian Islands and they claimed he sent a Navy destroyer to pick up the dog and bring him to the White House, at a cost to taxpayers of up to $20 million. On September 23, 1944, FDR turned the tables on his adversaries during a campaign dinner with the International Brotherhood of Teamsters union. Roosevelt said he and his family had endured "malicious falsehoods" before, but now he needed to "object to libelous statements about my dog." Roosevelt said the GOP was showing cruelty by using Fala as an excuse to attack the president because their other lines of attack weren't working. Roosevelt went on to win his fourth presidential election a few weeks later.[21]

Dwight Eisenhower

National politics entered a period of relative civility during Dwight Eisenhower's eight years in office from 1953 to 1961. Eisenhower, elected as a Republican after a very successful career as a nonpartisan Army officer, was a towering figure in the United States when he sought the presidency in 1952. He had led U.S. and allied forces in the Normandy invasion that pushed the Nazis out of most of Europe and ultimately ended World War II.

Ike had nothing to prove about his leadership or ability to get things done. He also understood that the country wanted a return to normalcy after so many years of depression and war, and he charted a moderately conservative course that most Americans overwhelmingly supported. His opponents had little chance to defeat him, and Congress mostly went along with his modest agenda that focused on supporting business and strengthening the economy.

President Eisenhower felt no need to savage his opponents and instead emphasized his positive qualities such as trustworthiness, likability, leadership ability, military achievements, and understanding of international affairs. His opponents rarely attacked him personally, seeing no likely advantages to be gained from it. Except for the harsh, belligerent, and phony communist-hunting efforts of Sen. Joseph McCarthy, R-Wis.—which Eisenhower mostly ignored until McCarthy's vitriol ran its course—this was an era, however brief, of relative civility and decorum.[22]

John F. Kennedy

John F. Kennedy, although he was different from Ike in many ways, such as his youth and more liberal approach to domestic concerns, was also a moderate on most issues like his predecessor and was not by instinct a vicious politician. He was a senator from Massachusetts when he won the Democratic presidential nomination in 1960 and, even though the election against then-Vice President Richard Nixon was close, it was not particularly nasty.

Both nominees were establishment politicians from the political mainstream. Where Kennedy got his edge was by emphasizing his charisma and personal traits such as his good looks, his vigor, eloquence, and his pledge to "get American moving again" with a more active and creative White House after the quiet Eisenhower years.

There was a strong consensus on foreign affairs based on the idea that the United States needed to defend freedom around the world and stand up to international communism led by the Soviet Union and China. Neither Kennedy nor Nixon seriously challenged each other's motives or patriotism, which is common among political rivals today. This didn't last very long after Kennedy's assassination in November 1963, which created much cynicism in the United States and deepened the belief that toxicity was spreading in the country.

Gerald Ford and Jimmy Carter

Republican Gerald Ford and Democrat Jimmy Carter were decent men and middle-of-the-road presidents who endured serious crises and setbacks that they seemed powerless to control.

Ford was Richard Nixon's vice president who became president in 1974 after Nixon resigned in disgrace amid the Watergate scandal. He tried to bring a moral compass back to the White House but was overwhelmed by the problems the country was facing, including a weak economy and a messy final withdrawal from the Vietnam war. Ford was not inclined to go negative and never found a way to respond effectively to his critics or effectively defend his administration. He lost in 1976.

Carter, who had been the Democratic governor of Georgia, promised an honest, efficient, and uplifting presidency after the moral failings of Nixon's administration and the economic and international setbacks of the Ford years. Instead, after defeating Ford in 1976, Carter presided over high unemployment, soaring inflation, a mortifying hostage crisis in Iran, serious shortages of oil, and a sense that he was blaming others for his own shortcomings and failures.

Carter was under intense criticism when he ran for re-election in 1980, even from fellow Democrats. He was challenged for the Democratic presidential nomination by Sen. Edward Kennedy, D-Mass., in a bitter campaign that Carter managed to win. But he lost the general election to Ronald Reagan after he came across as hapless and too pessimistic. He ended his presidency as an unpopular figure with little credibility as a politician or a leader.

Barack Obama

Barack Obama could be a tough critic but he was not known as a particularly negative politician and certainly was not vitriolic. "He campaigned as the great unifier and I think that worked," said Frank Donatelli, former White House political director for President Ronald Reagan.[23]

Michelle Obama, his wife, was known for her slogan, "When they go low, we go high." And to a large extent this is how they ran his campaigns and the presidency during his two terms from 2009 to 2017.

One of his biggest tests came during the Democratic primaries of 2008 when he was attacked by rival Hillary Clinton and her allies as inexperienced, immature, and too left-wing. He resisted the Clinton campaign's provocations. Obama responded mildly and won the nomination as an apostle of hope and reconciliation.[24] Many voters were impressed that he kept his promise to practice "a different kind of politics," more upbeat and unifying than the nastiness and pugnacity of his rivals. Voters considered this positivity one of Obama's outstanding character traits and he would have paid a huge price, and possibly lost the nomination, if he had changed his approach.

Obama was attacked by Republicans in the general election as an extreme liberal and weak on a number of issues including preserving national security and stopping illegal immigration. Critics including then-real estate developer Donald Trump claimed, without evidence, that Obama wasn't born in the United States and was therefore disqualified by the Constitution from being president. As this conspiracy theory took hold among some conservatives, Obama had his aides release his birth certificate proving he was born in the State of Hawaii, as he always said. Trump and like-minded conspiratorialists dropped the allegations.

It was another victory for Obama against the forces of toxic politics. In his subdued response, Obama stayed true to his pledge to lift politics into a more positive place and refused to be drawn into the mud.

As he prepared to leave office after two terms, Obama was troubled by the rise in negativity and the distrust of institutions spawned by caustic politics. He put some of the blame on social media such as Twitter which have been widely criticized for failing to curtail misinformation on their networks and for encouraging polarization because their business models reward the harshest and angriest voices, not accuracy or reason.[25]

Obama said Americans must deal with "so much active misinformation" that is "packaged very well" and has the same look as information on mainstream TV news shows. "If everything seems to be the same and no distinctions are made, then we won't know what to protect," Obama said. "We won't know what to fight for. And we can lose so much of what we've gained in terms of the kind of democratic freedoms and market-based economies and prosperity that we've come to take for granted."[26]

"If we are not serious about facts and what's true and what's not, if we can't discriminate between serious arguments and propaganda, then we have problems," the outgoing president told a news conference.[27]

Obama also said rather mildly in November 2016 that "crazy conspiracy theorizing" on Facebook and other social media platforms had created a "dust cloud of nonsense."[28]

In sum, despite harsh attacks against him, which troubled him and made him question the future of accurate, fair dissemination of news and information, Obama mostly resisted hand-to-hand combat with his opponents.

Notes

1 Mark Bowden, "'Idiot,' 'Yahoo,' 'Original Gorilla,': How Lincoln Was Dissed in His Day," *The Atlantic*, June 2013, https://www.theatlantic.com/magazine/archive/2013/06/abraham-lincoln-is-an-idiot/309304/.
2 The criticisms cited in this paragraph are from Bowden.
3 ibid.
4 Quoted in Harold Holzer, "If I Had Another Face, Do You Think I'd Wear This One?" *American Heritage*, Volume 34, Issue 2, February/March 1983, https://www.americanheritage.com/if-i-had-another-face-do-you-think-id-wear-one.
5 Quoted in Kerwin Swint, *Mudslinging: The Twenty-Five Dirtiest Political Campaigns of All Time*. New York: Union Square Press, 2008, 193.
6 Paul Boller, *Presidential Campaigns*. New York: Oxford University Press, 2004, 116.
7 Emmett H. Buell Jr. and Lee Sigelman, *Attack Politics: Negativity in Presidential Campaigns since 1960*. Lawrence, KS: University Press of Kansas, 2009, 5–6.
8 Swint, 199.
9 This account is based primarily on Buell and Sigelman, 6–7.
10 Sen. Long and Fr. Coughlin are both covered in greater detail in later chapters of this book.
11 E.J. Dionne, Jr., *Why Americans Hate Politics*. New York: Touchstone, 1991, 117.
12 Buell and Sigelman, 7.

13 Kim Phillips-Fein, *Invisible Hands: The Businessman's Crusades Against the New Deal.* New York: W.W. Norton, 2009, 11–12.
14 Phillips-Fein, 20.
15 The *New Republic* Staff, "Martin, Barton and Fish: Wynken, Blinken, and Nod; Rangel, Conyers, and Frank," *New Republic*, October 29, 2008, https://newrepublic.com/article/45562/martin-barton-and-fish-wynken-blynken-and-nod-rangel-conyers-and-frank.
16 Quoted in Christian Clarke Casarez, "FDR: Traitor to His Class?" https://lifeandletters.la.utexas.edu/2009/09/fdr-traitor-to-his-class/, September 4, 2009.
17 Clarke Casarez.
18 Quoted in Bill Donahue, "The Rise—and Cost—of He-Man Politics," *Washington Post Magazine*, June 26, 2022, 19.
19 William E. Leuchtenburg, "Franklin D. Roosevelt: Campaigns and Elections," https://millercenter.org/fdroosevelt/campaigns-and-elections, downloaded February 12, 2022.
20 Quoted in Leuchtenburg.
21 This account is drawn from "This Day in History: FDR Defends His Dog in a Speech." Last updated September 21, 2020, https://www.history.com/this-day-in-history/fdr-defends-his-dog.
22 Note to reader: McCarthy did plant the seeds of conspiracy theories and used the kind of political defamation that we often see today but it was Eisenhower and his moderation that political leaders emulated during Ike's era. For a discussion of McCarthy, see Chapter 8.
23 Author's interview with Frank Donatelli, April 6, 2021.
24 Ariel Sabar, "Obama Struggles to Stay above Fray," *Christian Science Monitor*, March 11, 2008, www.csmonitor.com/USA/Politics/2008/0311/p01s01-uspo.html.
25 Olivia Solon, "Barack Obama on Fake News: 'We Have Problems' If We Can't Tell the Difference,'" https://www.theguardian.com/media/2016/nov/17/barack-obama-fake-news-facebook-social-media.
26 Quoted in Solon.
27 ibid.
28 ibid.

5

DONALD TRUMP, THE MOST NEGATIVE PRESIDENT OF ALL

Donald Trump based his presidency to an extraordinary degree on hostility toward his critics, especially the Washington establishment, opposition Democrats, and the mainstream media. He created a cult of personality built upon allegiance to him and his brand of destructive politics. He was the ultimate contrarian and created the most negative U.S. presidency in history. And he continued to spread malice following his defeat in the 2020 election and two impeachments. Trump was trying to keep himself popular with angry white working-class voters and Republican die-hards as he prepared for another presidential run in 2024 which he announced in early 2023. By emphasizing the lie that he had really won the 2020 election and that the Democrats stole victory from him, Trump waged war on truth itself.

"Donald Trump did not—and does not—recognize any distinction between himself and the office of the presidency: He is it, and it is him," columnist Jamelle Bouie wrote in the *New York Times* in 2023.

> This view is as close a fundamental rejection of American constitutionalism as you can imagine—and it helps explain much of the former president's behavior in and out of office. It is why he raged against the "deep state," why he strained against every limit on his authority, why he rejected the idea that he could lose the 2020 presidential election and why he decided he could simply take classified documents to his home in Florida. ... [T]he Republican Party has come to shape itself around his person, it has also adopted his worldview, which is to say, the worldview and ideology of the boss.[1]

DOI: 10.4324/9781003149095-7

This means that the man at the top has full control and exercises extraordinary authority.

"Trump's most significant legacy is that he blew past so many guardrails," said Frank Donatelli, former White House political director for President Ronald Reagan.[2] In an interview for this book, Donatelli explained that Trump intensified support among his core supporters with personal, toxic, and often groundless attacks and charges that stirred up fear and resentment. And Trump left behind a political system that was "much more vitriolic and much more personal" than it had been.

Trump based his political rise and his presidency on a strategy of "stroke your friends and terrify your enemies," Donatelli said. "He was effective in terms of dominating the news and controlling the Republican Party."[3]

"If there is one thing that is becoming increasingly clear about Donald Trump's 2024 bid for the presidency, it is that this campaign is going to be a far darker endeavor than even the two that came before it," *Washington Post* columnist Karen Tumulty wrote.[4] Trump urged voters to think of him as their "retribution" against the establishment and other institutions and the people they hated or feared, an open invitation to play the politics of vengeance and hostility. Tumulty was among the Trump critics arguing that he had "the potential to create a permission structure for violence."[5]

Some said this is what Trump was doing during the winter of 2023 when he said if a Manhattan grand jury indicted him for paying hush money to a porn star, it could lead to "death and destruction." Trump called District Attorney Alvin Bragg, the prosecutor in the case, a "degenerate psychopath."[6] The grand jury did return an indictment of Trump and he pleaded not guilty. There was no death and destruction immediately following the indictment although many Trump supporters were angered and some took to the streets to protest.

Trump, a master salesman, showman, and self-promoter since his years as a real-estate developer and TV reality-show host, believed that attention gave him power. He cultivated his base—mostly white working-class people, conservative Christians, and others who felt maligned, left behind, and demeaned by the larger society and who identified with Trump's philosophy based on resentment, fear, and grievance. Among his techniques were the use of harsh attacks to bully opponents, threatening them with derision and relentless attacks and in some cases lawsuits to pressure them to back off, making unsubstantiated charges, and insulting his adversaries to gain media attention and to discourage opponents from criticizing him in the future. He seemed to believe that his followers, feeling threatened, not only expected him to lash out but wanted him to do so ever more aggressively. He persuaded core supporters that he was the only major political figure who listened and responded to them, and who sought to protect and promote them against perceived enemies such as liberals, socialists, immigrants, minorities, and the mainstream media.

Trump had spent many years shaping his attack strategy as a public figure. From his heyday as a billionaire real-estate developer to his career as a politician, Trump understood that stirring up anger was a key part of his appeal to many Americans—and he did his best to incite fury at the status quo. During his winning 2016 campaign, Trump told journalists Bob Woodward and Robert Costa, "I bring rage out. I do bring rage out. I always have. I don't know if that's an asset or a liability, but whatever it is, I do."[7]

Author David Cay Johnston wrote that Trump "developed a close relationship with one of the most vicious and heartless men who ever lived in America, a mentor who also believed revenge was the best policy and who became a kind of second father: the notorious Roy Cohn."[8]

Johnston added:

> In 1970—two years after getting his college degree from Penn—Donald Trump was still living in Queens. He was an outer-borough guy, part of the group derided as "bridge and tunnel people" by the stylish Manhattanites. Trump wanted to join and eventually lead that fashionable tribe.
>
> Trump has boasted often that he was on the hunt "almost every night" for "beautiful young women," but he was also trying to make other significant connections. One of the first and most important connections was with … Roy Cohn. [Cohn had been the chief lawyer for Senator Joseph McCarthy, whose communist witch hunts made national headlines but who lost most of his credibility when he finally overreached by going after the United States Army.]
>
> By Trump's account, Cohn became a business mentor and nearly a second father to him. Their steadily deepening relationship would link Trump to mob-owned construction companies at a time when other builders were begging the FBI to crack down on the Mafia. It also ensnared Trump in a jewelry tax scam and in a lawsuit that blew up in his face. In Cohn, Trump had someone who could be "vicious" on his behalf and who, he said, looking back in 2005, "would brutalize for you".[9]

In one of his own books, Trump wrote, "I don't kid myself about Roy. He was no Boy Scout. He once told me he'd spent more than two-thirds of his adult life under indictment on one charge or another."[10]

Writer Jonathan Rauch said of Trump,

> With skills he had honed for decades by manipulating journalists, deploying what he called "truthful hyperbole," and starring on reality TV [with his show, *The Apprentice*], he was easily the most artful practitioner of disinformation since the 1930s. Anyone who did doubt his mastery ought to have been convinced when, after four years of softening up the public with one lie after another, Trump executed his coup de grace, an astonishingly comprehensive, brazen, and effective campaign to convince the public that he had won the 2020 presidential election, or at least that the outcome was in doubt.[11]

In particular, Trump learned from Cohn the importance of counterattack—hitting back much harder when adversaries came after him. Trump emphasized this philosophy of life many times during his rise to the White House and his presidency.

Trump also adopted several other Cohn techniques. He emphasized the importance of having inside connections to gain an advantage and making unsubstantiated charges to intimidate his foes. He was adept at using the courts to get his way, often out-maneuvering his opponents through costly litigation and legal challenges that made him an elusive target.[12]

Among the other destructive politicians and operatives whose techniques Trump borrowed were Sen. Joe McCarthy, R-Wis., the notorious smear merchant and communist hunter; former House Speaker Newt Gingrich, R-Ga., who became a Trump backer and TV commentator; Roger Ailes, founder of pro-Trump Fox News, and radio commentator and political bomb-thrower Rush Limbaugh who privately advised Trump. Limbaugh and Trump "helped build the foundations of a philosophy for their followers that was rooted in a sense of victimization, exclusion, and systemic unfairness," according to the *Washington Post*.[13] "In many ways, the GOP had been Donald Trump's for decades," argued journalist Jeremy W. Peters of the *New York Times*.[14] The base of the party, filled with anger and grievance, had been there for the taking but Trump didn't seize it until he ran for president in 2016.

During his successful presidential campaign in 2016, his negativity was stunning. Trump pledged to "drain the swamp" of Washington insiders who, he said, didn't represent the people. After accepting the GOP presidential nomination, Trump told a rally in West Palm Beach, Florida on October 13, 2016:

> Our great civilization, here in America and across the civilized world has come upon a moment of reckoning. We've seen it in the United Kingdom, where they voted to liberate themselves from global government and global trade deals, and global immigration deals that have destroyed their sovereignty and have destroyed many of those nations. But, the

> central base of world political power is right here in America, and it is our corrupt political establishment that is the greatest power behind the efforts at radical globalization and the disenfranchisement of working people. Their financial resources are virtually unlimited, their political resources are unlimited, their media resources are unmatched, and most importantly, the depths of their immorality is [*sic*] absolutely unlimited.[15]

He regularly made outrageous and offensive statements during the 2016 presidential campaign such as when he attacked Texas Sen. Ted Cruz's father for supposed links to the assassination of President John F. Kennedy in 1963. When Trump made the charge, Cruz was running against the real-estate developer for the Republican nomination. Trump apparently got the information about the elder Cruz—which appeared to be fabricated—from the sensationalist tabloid the *National Enquirer.* Social scientist Stevan E. Hobfoll wrote, "Raising the specter of such a wild conspiracy is the pinnacle of inflammatory politics. It is irresponsible, reprehensible, and speaks of either fundamentally flawed judgment or fundamentally flawed ethics by Trump."[16] He dismissed Senator Cruz as "Lyin' Ted." Trump also mocked Ted Cruz's wife as unattractive.

He used destructive tactics against other rivals—noting at one point that "Jeb Bush [the former governor of Florida, son of President George H.W. Bush and brother of President George W. Bush] is an embarrassment to his family." He also made fun of Jeb Bush as "low energy" and a "lightweight." He called Sen. Marco Rubio of Florida "little Marco." He found fault in the looks of businesswoman Carly Fiorina, another GOP opponent in the presidential primaries. He ridiculed the physical disability of a *New York Times* reporter.[17]

He accused former Secretary of State Hillary Clinton, who eventually lost to him in 2016 as the Democratic presidential nominee, of corruption, nicknamed her "crooked Hillary," and encouraged crowds at Trump rallies to chant, "Lock her up." He said House Speaker Nancy Pelosi, D-Calif., was "crazy." He demeaned Rep. Adam Schiff, D-Calif., chairman of the House Intelligence Committee, as "shifty Schiff," "pencil neck," and "watermelon head."

Earlier, he had said Sen. John McCain, R-Ariz., was not a hero because he was shot down during a combat mission and captured by the enemy during the Vietnam war. The real story was that McCain handled himself with courage and fortitude during his time as a prisoner of war, and he was indeed a hero.

Trump's negativity fueled the rise of hyper-partisanship in American political life. It also propelled the decline of truth-telling in politics, and injected more racism, sexism, xenophobia, cruelty, and other social pathogens into the political system and American culture.

After he won in 2016, he intensified toxic politics during his presidency.

"Trump set a standard unmatched in politics for his use of Twitter to assault, belittle and degrade opponents," *Washington Post* columnist Dan Balz wrote. "He reveled in sending out personal attacks."[18]

He made the fundamental mistake of thinking that the techniques that worked for him as a real-estate developer would work for him as president—bulldozing and humiliating opponents, distorting the truth to make himself look as good as possible, reducing everything to financial measurements such as by defining his presidential success in terms of how the stock market was doing. Everything seemed to be about him and his "brand." He relentlessly portrayed himself as an outsider and a winner who savaged his critics to get his way and dominated everyone, with little or no thought about encouraging the compromise and conciliation which facilitate governing.

He surrounded himself with sycophants, such as White House advisers Steve Bannon, Steve Miller, and Kellyanne Conway and cabinet members including Secretary of State Mike Pompeo. If advisers didn't toe his line, he forced them out of government, as he did with Attorney General Jeff Sessions and Defense Secretary James Mattis.

Through 2020, Trump posted more than 56,000 times on Twitter after he started using the social medium in 2009. His tweets were often diatribes against his critics and others, with many misspellings and frequent use of capital letters for emphasis. Twitter became the engine that propelled his endless grievances, contempt, and rage. "He tweeted so often on some mornings in office that it was hard to believe he was doing much else," Sarah Lyall wrote in the *New York Times*.

> Then there were the tweets themselves. … The one where he predicted that if he were to fight Joe Biden, Mr. Biden would "go down fast and hard, crying all the way." The one where he called Meryl Streep "one of the most overrated actresses in Hollywood." The one where he accused former President Barack Obama of wiretapping him. The one where he boasted that his "Nuclear Button" was "much bigger & more powerful" than that of Kim Jong-un, the North Korean leader.[19]

Trump was banned temporarily from Twitter on January 8, 2021, for spreading lies. His last tweet before the ban was another exercise in negativity and spite. "To all of those who have asked," he wrote, "I will not be going to the Inauguration January 20."[20]

His presidency became one emergency after another, ranging from a national immigration "crisis" that didn't exist at that time to government shutdowns caused largely by his own intransigence. These defining moments often were manufactured by Trump, apparently to keep himself at the center of national attention. Even the impeachment crises of 2019–2021 fit this description. The first impeachment charges were based on allegations of abuse of power stemming from Trump's allegedly pressuring the government of Ukraine to investigate and prosecute soon-to-be Democratic presidential nominee Joe Biden for alleged wrongdoing in that country. This wrongdoing was never proven. His second impeachment was over the separate issue of inciting the insurrection at the Capitol on January 6, 2021. In each case, the Democrat-controlled House of Representatives impeached Trump, but the Senate, narrowly divided between Democrats and Republicans, acquitted him.

His mishandling of the coronavirus pandemic was disastrous and showed how his negativity was detrimental to public health and safety. It was a case study in failed presidential leadership. Not only did Trump acknowledge the coronavirus problem too late and cast aspersions on those who recognized its seriousness, he managed the federal response in a ham-handed way, worsening the crisis and allowing the pandemic to intensify.

He initially dismissed the deadly coronavirus that ravaged much of the globe and huge swaths of the United States. The disease was first detected in China during late December 2019, and the Beijing government officially notified the Trump administration of the outbreak in early January 2020. In mid-January, the first confirmed case was diagnosed in the United States. On January 22, 2020, when asked by a CNBC reporter if he was worried about a pandemic, Trump replied, "No, not at all. And we have it totally under control. It's one person coming in from China, and we have it under control. It's—going to be just fine."[21]

On February 28, he said, "One day, it's like a miracle, it will disappear."[22]

As a result of Trump's dismissal of the threat, for several squandered weeks in January and February 2020, he did relatively little to contain the outbreak, aside from blocking travel into the United States from China for thousands of non-Americans. This critical lapse in judgment came despite warnings from medical professionals and disease-control specialists in and out of the U.S. government. Trump's delayed response cost lives and enabled the virus to spread at warp speed. It was a failure of presidential crisis management on a historic scale.

After being caught flat-footed, Trump attempted to rally the federal government behind various strong measures to contain the virus. But these measures didn't succeed, and the pandemic grew worse. An indicator of the negative reaction to his leadership was the performance of the stock market. On February 24, the Dow Industrials declined more than 1,000 points and within a few weeks, the market had lost all of the gains it had made during the Trump presidency, which had been his main selling point for re-election. Unemployment soared, and many businesses were in deep trouble.

In an exhaustive study of the Trump administration's response to the coronavirus during the first 70 days of the crisis, the *Washington Post* reported:

> The country has adopted an array of wartime measures never employed collectively in U.S. history—banning incoming travel from two continents, bringing commerce to a near-halt, enlisting industry to make emergency medical gear, and confining 230 million Americans to their homes in a desperate bid to survive an attack by an unseen adversary.
>
> Despite these and other extreme steps, the United States will likely go down as the country that was supposedly best prepared to fight a pandemic but ended up catastrophically overmatched by the novel coronavirus, sustaining heavier casualties than any other nation.[23]

Among the lapses: the government's failure to develop a diagnostic test to detect the virus quickly; failure to immediately impose massive quarantines to contain the virus's spread; failure to quickly provide emergency supplies such as ventilators and protective material such as surgical masks; failure to make the overall case for strong measures from the outset; and Trump's scoffing at the use of masks to limit the pandemic's spread, which was recommended by the government's health-care professionals and many non-government experts.

Trump violated the standards that our most effective presidents have used in handling crises. After studying presidential leadership under crisis conditions for my book about this topic, I identified five standards that the most effective presidents have used in crisis management: taking action; adapting to changing circumstances; balancing principle with what works; persevering; and having an instinct for achieving success.[24] Trump largely ignored these lessons of history and continued his pattern of doing things his way, seeing only the short term rather than taking the long view.

Trump remained conflicted to the end of his presidency and refused to accept responsibility. He belatedly recognized the need for strong measures to fight the virus, including limits on Americans' social contacts and shutting down businesses and activities deemed non-"essential." But even then, he regularly shifted from dire warnings about the virus to sunny predictions that all would be well, reducing the perceived urgency of the anti-coronavirus campaign. At the same time, he had difficulty showing empathy with the virus's thousands of victims and their families. He largely abandoned the role of consoler-in-chief that other presidents had adopted, such as Ronald Reagan after the explosion of the space shuttle

Challenger in 1986 and Barack Obama after various incidents of gun violence during his administration.

On April 4, 1,344 new deaths were reported in the United States from the coronavirus, according to a survey by Johns Hopkins University, pushing the total over 8,500. On April 7, the total number of deaths exceeded 13,000, and disease experts said the worst was yet to come. As of April 8, 14,599 had died. On April 9, the number increased to 16,458. On April 12, Easter Sunday—which Trump had set informally (and prematurely) as the target date for reopening the economy and ending the most serious anti-coronavirus measures—the death toll exceeded 20,000 and was still rising.[25] It increased to more than 346,000 by the end of 2020, and exceeded 400,000 by the day Trump left office, on January 20, 2021.[26]

"When facing a mortal enemy, above all, we need our commander in chief to unite the nation in collective purpose and shared sacrifice," wrote Susan E. Rice, former national security adviser to President Obama and chosen by President Biden as a senior domestic policy adviser at the White House.

> To defeat the common adversary, we must set aside our differences. President Trump prefers to attack governors, reporters and anyone he deems insufficiently "appreciative" of his anemic efforts. Rather than order the whole nation to stay at home, appoint a senior federal supply czar, fully invoke the Defense Production Act to recruit medical personnel and procure and distribute ventilators and masks to where they are needed most, Mr. Trump has created a Hobbesian jungle where it's every man for himself. States are forced to compete for desperately needed supplies at jacked-up prices. ... By pitting states against one another, Mr. Trump pours salt in our political divisions and cripples our ability to defeat the virus.[27]

Trump and his team were unable to stop the deep economic downturn caused by the near-shutdown of the country to prevent the spread of the virus. At the end of March 2020, 6.6 million Americans filed for unemployment benefits in a single week, a record, according to the *Washington Post*.

On April 3, the *Post* reported:

> The past two weeks have wiped out all the economy's job gains since President Trump's November 2016 election, a sign of how rapid, deep and painful the economic shutdown has been for American families struggling to pay rent and buy prescriptions, food and health insurance.

"The coronavirus recession is shaping up to be the biggest blow to the U.S. economy since the Great Depression, and fears are rising that it will take years to reverse the damage."[28]

Political analyst Jonathan Alter wrote,

> Of course, we now can see that Trump's incompetence runs much deeper and ran much longer than one month of snafus on testing (which he lied about almost daily). "The Lost Month" was actually "The Lost Months." In fact, we lost three full years—years when the Trump administration let its contempt for science and "deep state" civil servants cripple the ability of the federal government to respond to a crisis. Trump didn't fill 700 vacancies at the CDC (Centers for Disease Control), didn't replenish stockpiles of medical supplies (while lying about Obama's response to pandemics), and didn't stop (then-National Security Adviser) John Bolton from closing the pandemic preparedness office at the National Security Council (later lying that he knew nothing of it).[29]

Realizing his re-election was in jeopardy, Trump resorted to his familiar playbook of falsifying what actually happened, refusing to admit mistakes, declining to take responsibility for errors, and trying to divert attention from the crisis at hand by ginning up other issues. He consistently blamed others for his own shortcomings, such as by insisting that China failed in late 2019 to fully report the extent of the virus even though his own advisers were warning him privately about the dangers of the pandemic.

Trump used near-daily media briefings, sometimes lasting two hours, to take credit for what he called an excellent government response to the virus, attempting to rewrite history. At these briefings, he insisted on dominating the proceedings and keeping the real experts, such as Dr. Anthony Fauci, director of the National Institute of Allergy and Infectious Diseases, in secondary roles.[30]

Trump, watching the economy deteriorate rapidly and head toward recession, regularly praised himself for a $2 trillion assistance package passed by Congress to make things right. One major problem was that the Trump administration was having trouble sending the money to those for whom it was intended, because of managerial weakness and three years of hollowing out the government.

In the runup to the November 2020 election, Trump was fully on the attack across many fronts. The main focus was his relentless deriding of the political system that got him to the White House in the first place. He argued repeatedly that the system was "rigged" against him and refused to commit to a peaceful transfer of power if he lost. Speaking at a rally in Minden, Nevada in mid-September, less than two months before the balloting, as his re-election bid moved toward its unsuccessful conclusion, Trump intensified his hostility. He angrily condemned a Democratic ad focusing on allegations that he made disparaging remarks about dead American soldiers. "'Now I can be really vicious,' he said as the crowd roared its support."[31]

The *Washington Post* reported,

> The president, who has long relished his role as a divider who amassed power by creating a climate of fear, went on to describe his opponent, Joe Biden, as "shot" and a puppet of the radical left, before accusing Democrats of trying to "lock law-abiding Americans in their homes" during the pandemic as they fight God, guns and oil. "At no time before has there been a clearer choice between two parties or two visions, two philosophies, two agendas for the future," Trump said. "There's never been anything like this."[32]

Continuing his negative strategy, Trump called protesters against police brutality "thugs," rioters and looters, and he pledged to restore "law and order." This echoed authoritarians and dividers in the past such as Father Coughlin, George Wallace, and Richard Nixon.

Trump also sought to undermine confidence in mail-in ballots. He argued that the Democrats were using mail-ins to "rig this election" and said, perhaps jokingly, that he should be able to "negotiate" for 12 years in the White House even though the Constitution limited him to eight. "We're going to win four more years in the White House and then after that we'll negotiate, right? Because ... based on the way we were treated we're probably entitled to another four after that."

Trump's performance at his first debate with Democratic presidential nominee Biden September 29 underscored his slash-and-burn approach. Describing Trump's attack-filled appearance as "theatrical, scorched-earth nihilism," liberal columnist E.J. Dionne, Jr. wrote,

> The smoldering debris left behind by a political arsonist created one of the low moments of American electoral history and left all but the most fanatical Trump supporters more dispirited than ever about the state of our public life. ... It was not a debate in any meaningful sense. Trump was utterly unconstrained in his interruptions, his obnoxious comments, his snide asides, his attacks on Joe Biden's family, his relentless bullying and ultimately his lack of humanity.[33]

During the general-election campaign, Trump accused Biden of being mentally and physically unable to perform the duties of president, and derided Biden as "sleepy creepy Joe" and "slow Joe."

Trump even mocked his foe for using cosmetic surgery to improve his appearance, although it appeared that Trump himself had used cosmetic enhancements, such as surgery to cover up a bald spot, makeup for his face and double chin, and coloring for his hair. As CNN reported,

> Trump has been throwing every haymaker he can think of, suggesting that Biden is drugged up, that he's senile, that his administration will be dispatching poor people to terrorize the suburbs, that he is "against God," that he's a puppet for a Marxist cabal that will destroy America, and so on.[34]

To his credit, Biden refused to take the bait and lower himself to Trump's level. Dionne added: "Moment after moment, the only words that seemed appropriate were those of the celebrated rebuke that destroyed Sen. Joe McCarthy's political power: 'Have you no sense of decency, sir?'"[35]

In the end, Trump lost to Biden by 7 million popular votes—Biden received more than 81 million to Trump's 74 million—and lost in the Electoral College with Biden receiving 306 electoral votes to Trump's 232.

During the months following his re-election loss, Trump kept up his fusillade of attacks in an effort to continue appealing to his angry, grievance-filled base and remain a force in national politics. He told conservative donors at Mar-a-Lago, his private club in Florida, that Republicans "have to get tougher, they have to get meaner, they have to get better people" in leadership positions. In a classic negative strike, Trump attacked Senate Republican Leader Mitch McConnell of Kentucky, for being "a stiff" and a "stone cold loser" because he accepted the results of the 2020 election that Trump lost. Trump kept repeating his false narrative about massive voter fraud.[36]

Trump extended his negativity in a particularly destructive way—through legal proceedings. Trump allies alleged vast amounts of voter fraud and corruption, but these charges were proven false by the courts, state election officials, the media, and his own Attorney General William Barr. Nevertheless, Trump surrogates persisted and his millions of die-hard followers believed him.

For a few days in the winter of 2020, Trump considered imposing martial law and having the U.S. military "re-run" the election in key swing states that Trump lost.[37]

Trump had helped to persuade one-third of all Americans and two-thirds of Republicans that there had been widespread election fraud, according to a *Washington Post*/ABC News poll in January 2021, just before Biden's inauguration. He never provided the evidence to prove his assertions. "What's unique about Donald Trump is that he took advantage of this widespread distrust of government and media to say everyone is lying to you except for me," historian Kathryn Olmsted told the *Washington* Post.

> We have never had a president so devoted to spreading disinformation and trying to overturn an election. The people who stormed the Capitol are absolutely convinced that the election was stolen. They're not being opportunistic; they really believe this. And all of the social science shows that if someone really believes a conspiracy theory, it is just about impossible to change their minds.[38]

Even Senate Republican Leader Mitch McConnell admitted that Trump inflamed his supporters with "wild falsehoods" that made him "practically and morally responsible" for the January 6 uprising at the Capitol. The rioting was "a foreseeable consequence" of "false statements, conspiracy theories and reckless hyperbole" and a "manufactured atmosphere of looming catastrophe" concocted by Trump, McConnell said.[39]

As media scholar Kathleen Hall Jamieson noted,

> What Trump did was take tactics of deception and played to confirmation biases that were already circulating in our culture, and embodied them in somebody who is president of the United States. He didn't change what was available, but he changed its accessibility. That crazed content has always been there. But it becomes dangerous when it is legitimized and when it has the power of the state behind it.[40]

As Clare Malone wrote on the web site fivethirtyeight,

> Convey a powerful enough image or idea (and make it vague enough) and people will project onto it what they will. This is the heart of any a savvy PR strategy—just ask Beyonce. The great lesson politicians of all stripes have taken from the Trump era is that you can have all the policy ideas in the world but they don't matter if you can't convey a resonant enough message to a broad enough swath of people. Of course Mexico wasn't going to pay for the border wall [as Trump promised during his 2016 campaign], but what a triumphant idea to grasp onto. What a succinct articulation of a set of cultural, racial, economic and political values![41]

"Above all … the Biden illegitimacy myth" functioned "as a prop for Trump's own fragile ego," journalist Anne Applebaum wrote presciently during November 2020, after Trump had lost his bid for re-election. She continued:

> Unable to cope with the loss of the presidency, unable to accept that he was beaten, Trump will now shield himself from the reality of defeat by pretending it didn't happen. His personal need to live in a perpetual fantasyland, a world where he is always winning, is so overpowering that he will do anything to maintain it. In his narcissistic drive to create this alternative reality, he will deepen divisions, spread paranoia, and render his supporters even more fearful of their fellow citizens and distrustful of their institutions. This is a president who never had America's interests at heart. Do not expect loss to change him.[42]

These predictions turned out to be true.

One of the most disgraceful and dangerous episodes of toxic politics was the uprising that occurred on January 6, 2021, a few weeks before Trump was scheduled to leave office. This was the constitutionally prescribed date when Congress was scheduled to certify the state-by-state election results that spelled defeat for Trump. During a rally in Washington a few hours before the start of this count, Trump urged his supporters to march on the nearby Capitol and fight to overturn the results and ensure his victory. He urged them to "show strength" in order to "take back our country." He had been stirring up these same supporters ever since the election by arguing, falsely, that the system was "rigged" against him. Thousands of his supporters ended up conducting what amounted to an insurrection that day by invading the Capitol. They hoped to overturn the election that Trump lost to Biden by stopping official certification of the results at a joint session of Congress.

What happened was a national embarrassment. Trump supporters descended on the Capitol and hundreds pushed past the Capitol Police, who were woefully understaffed. They had made extremely weak preparations for the attempted takeover even though such a move had been a clear option for the angry protesters for weeks. Rioters broke into the Senate chamber and into legislators' offices, including the office of House Speaker Nancy Pelosi, D-Calif. The scenes of mayhem were captured on video and disseminated widely by news organizations and social media. Five persons died including a Capitol policeman who had fought with the rioters. Many people, including scores of law enforcement officers, were injured. Relatively few arrests were made that day—causing outrage among members of Congress—but many were arrested and charged with crimes in the months that followed. Some of the offenders were so proud of what they had done and felt so much above the law that they promoted their exploits on social media, including videos they posted themselves. This facilitated their prosecutions across the country.[43]

Many saw the rioting as an inevitable and dangerous consequence of Trump's war on the truth, his negativity toward Joe Biden and the

Democrats, his authoritarianism, narcissism, and desire to disrupt the status quo in Washington. *Washington Post* media columnist Margaret Sullivan described it as such:

> It should be no surprise. After all, one of the hallmarks of the Trump administration—along with a penchant for cruelty and an endless font of self-dealing—was the lying. From Day One's "alternative facts" about the size of the 2017 inaugural crowd [which Trump and his advisers said falsely was the largest ever for a presidential swearing-in], Trumpian falsehoods became nothing short of routine. They were generously ladled out by a president, his spokespeople and his administration—and then repeated and amplified by his many helpers in the MAGA ["Make America Great Again," Trump's campaign slogan] mediasphere, led by those at Fox News. There were tens of thousands of these falsehoods.[44]

Trump's encouragement of civil disorder at the Capitol led to many condemnations of his actions and his impeachment in mid-January, a week after the mayhem and the week before he was scheduled to leave office with the January 20 inauguration of Joe Biden. He was specifically found by most House members guilty of inciting an insurrection. It came on a 232 to 197 vote on January 13, 2021, with ten Republicans joining Democrats in the majority. Trump thus became the only president to be impeached twice. As noted earlier in this book, he had been impeached once before, in 2019, when the Democrat-controlled House found him guilty of abuse of power and obstruction of Congress after he tried to undermine Biden's presidential campaign by encouraging the Ukrainian president to find dirt on Biden and his son Hunter. The Senate acquitted him in both 2019 and 2021, lacking the two-thirds majority for conviction, although 57 senators including seven Republicans voted that he was guilty of high crimes and misdemeanors in the Capitol riot, just short of the two-thirds needed.

Conservative strategist Peter Wehner wrote,

> We've had plenty of presidents who have failed us, in ways large and small. But this moment is different because Donald Trump is different, and because Donald Trump is president. His relentless assault on truth and the institutions of democracy—his provocations and abuse of power, his psychological instability and his emotional volatility, his delusions and his incompetence—are unlike anything we've seen before. He needs to be stopped. And his supporters can't say, as they did in 2016, that they just didn't know. Now we know. It's not too late—it's never too late—to do the right thing.[45]

"America under Trump became less free, less equal, more divided, more alone, deeper in debt, swampier, dirtier, meaner, sicker, and deader," author George Packer wrote in *The Atlantic* in December 2020.

> It also became more delusional. No number from Trump's years in power will be more lastingly destructive than his 25,000 false or misleading statements. Super-spread by social media and cable news, they contaminated the minds of tens of millions of people. Trump's lies will linger for years, poisoning the atmosphere like radioactive dust.[46]

Packer said,

> So the stab-in-the-back narrative was buried in the minds of millions of Americans, where it burns away, as imperishable as a carbon isotope, consuming whatever is left of their trust in democratic institutions and values. This narrative will widen the gap between Trump believers and their compatriots who might live in the same town, but a different universe. And that was Trump's purpose—to keep us locked in a mental prison where reality was unknowable so that he could go on wielding power, whether in or out of office, including the power to destroy.[47]

"What's happening can only be called a venomous panic attack," wrote *New York Times* columnist David Brooks.

> Since the election, large swaths of the Trumpian right have decided America is facing a crisis like never before and they are the small army of warriors fighting with Alamo-level desperation to ensure the survival of the country as they conceive it. ... The level of Republican pessimism is off the charts.[48]

Brooks pointed out that when a pollster asked in late January 2021 if politics was more about "enacting good public policy" or "ensuring the survival of the country as we know it," 51 percent of Trump-supporting Republicans said survival and only 19 percent said enacting good policy. Another poll in February 2021 found that two-thirds of Trump voters agreed with the statement, "Our lives are threatened by terrorists, criminals and illegal immigrants, and our priority should be to protect ourselves."

Polling indicated that a high level of "catastrophism, nearly despair, had fed into an amped-up warrior mentality" in which Trump supporters became more ruthless in fighting against the forces they perceived as a threat, such as immigrants and Democrats, Brooks noted.

Trump stoked the fires. He even pledged in March 2023 that if he was elected in 2024, he would take vengeance against his adversaries and those who disparaged his supporters. "In 2016, I declared, 'I am your voice,'" Trump told the Conservative Political Action Conference. "Today I add: I am your warrior. I am your justice. And for those who have been wronged and betrayed: I am your retribution."[49]

Some even talked ominously about preparing for civil war. It was another example of how deeply the toxicity had permeated American society.[50]

Trump turned more vituperative and angrier than ever in 2023. A Manhattan grand jury indicted him in March 2023 for allegedly paying hush money to porn star Stormy Daniels in 2016 in order to keep her quiet about having sex with him. Trump had been worried that her allegations would damage his 2016 campaign for president, which he eventually won. The grand jury agreed with Manhattan District Attorney Alvin Bragg that there was sufficient evidence of Trump's guilt, including the charge that he broke campaign-finance laws. Calling it a "witch hunt," Trump denied wrongdoing in the case, which was still working its way through the judicial system as this book went to press. Trump was the first former or current president to face criminal charges.[51] Trump also attacked New York Supreme Court Justice Juan Merchan, who was presiding over the case, as biased against him.[52]

In June 2023, Trump savaged special counsel Jack Smith for persuading a federal grand jury to indict him on 37 charges involving Trump's mishandling of classified government documents after he left office. They included secret files that described the nuclear capabilities of the United States and a foreign government, a foreign country's support for terrorist activities, and a potential U.S. attack on a foreign country. The charges included obstruction of justice, hiding and refusing to return sensitive documents to the U.S. government, making false statements, and endangering national security.[53]

This case and other court proceedings—including a Georgia case accusing him of trying to stop the legitimate victory of Joe Biden in that state, a federal case charging Trump with election obstruction, and a New York case alleging financial wrongdoing in his business operations—had not been resolved when this book went to press. But Trump's claims of being persecuted had already further undermined public faith in governing institutions including the presidency, law enforcement, the Justice Department, the judiciary, and the media.

Notes

1 Jamelle Bouie, "Trump Believes the Presidency Is His," *New York Times*, June 25, 2023, SR3.
2 Author's interview with Frank Donatelli, April 6, 2021.
3 Author's interview with Frank Donatelli, January 25, 2022.
4 Karen Tumulty, "Donald Trump Is Promising the Apocalypse," *Washington Post*, March 29, 2023, A27. https://www.washingtonpost.com/opinions/2023/03/28/trump-2024-battle-apocalypse-rhetoric/.
5 ibid.
6 Quoted in Tumulty.
7 Excerpt from *Rage* quoted in Elizabeth Stuart and Jamie Gangel, "New Woodward Book to Cover Last Days of Trump Presidency," *CNN Politics*. Published July 1, 2021. https://www.cnn.com/2021/07/04/politics/bob-woodward-robert-costa-donald-trump-new-book/index.html.
8 David Cay Johnston, *The Making of Donald Trump*. Brooklyn, NY: Melville House, 2016, 32–4.
9 ibid., 33–4.
10 Donald Trump and Tony Schwartz, *Trump: The Art of the Deal*. New York: Ballantine, 2015, 99, quoted in Johnson, 34.
11 Quoted in Robert G. Kaiser, "Can reality prevail once again in an age of information warfare," *Washington Post*, July 25, 2021, B1.
12 Johnston, 32.
13 Carlos Lozada, "How Trump's Political Style Smothered the GOP's Substance," *Washington Post*, February 6, 2022, B1.
14 ibid.
15 Video of Presidential Candidate Donald Trump Rally in West Palm Beach, Florida, October 13, 2016, C-SPAN, downloaded December 18, 2023.
16 Steven E. Hobfoll, *Tribalism: The Evolutionary Origins of Fear Politics*. Cham, Switzerland: Palgrave Macmillan, 2018, 51.
17 ibid., 113–14.
18 Dan Balz, "Garland, Tanden and the Double Standards of GOP Lawmakers," *Washington Post*, February 24, 2021, A4.
19 Sarah Lyall, "Twitter Without Trump: A Nation Calmly Scrolls," *New York Times*, April 18, 2021, 1.
20 Quoted in Lyall, 1.
21 Quoted in PolitiFact and Jon Greenberg, "'We Have It Totally under Control.' A Timeline of President Donald Trump's Response to the Coronavirus Pandemic," Poynter Institute. https://www.poynter.org/fact-checking/2020/we-have-it-totally-under-control-a-timeline-of-president-donald-trumps-response-to-the-coronavirus-pandemic./.
22 Dana Milbank, "Trump Blew It—Not the WHO, Fauci or the Jews," *Washington Post*, April 7, 2020, A23.
23 Yasmeen Abutaleb, Josh Dawsey, Ellen Nakashima, and Greg Miller, "70 Days of Denial, Delays and Dysfunction," *Washington Post*, April 5, 2020, A1.
24 Kenneth T. Walsh, "Introduction," *Presidential Leadership in Crisis: Defining Moments of the Modern Presidents from Roosevelt to Trump*. New York: Routledge, 2020.
25 Madeline Holcombe, "US Coronavirus Fight Enters Crucial Weeks after Reaching a Grim Milestone," cnn.com April 5, 2020. Also see chart, *Washington Post*, April 13, 2020, A1.
26 ibid.

27 Susan E. Rice, "Trump Is the Wartime President We Have (Not the One We Need)," *New York Times*, April 7, 2020, nytimes.com/2020/04/07/opinion/trump-coronavirus-us.html?action=click&module=Opinion&pgtype=Homepage.
28 Heather Long and Abha Bhattarai, "As Economy Craters, 6.6 Million More Jobless," *Washington Post*, April 3, 2020, A1.
29 Jonathan Alter, "Trump's Lost Months Are Killing Us. Here's How to Make Them Politically Fatal for Him," April 4, 2020, yahoo.com/news/trump-lost-months-killing-us-011244950.html.
30 David Greenberg, "Spin Won't Save Trump," *Politico* Magazine, April 5, 2020, politico.com/news/magazine/2020/04/05/spin-wont-save-trump-165091.
31 Quoted in Maeve Reston, CNN "Trump Relishes His Role as a Divider as He Vows to Be 'Vicious,'" CNN report, September 13, 2020.
32 Quoted in Reston.
33 .Dionne, Jr. "Trump Leaves Nothing But Nihilism in His Wake," *Washington Post*, October 1, 2020, 23.
34 Juliana Silva and Bill McGowan, "Trump's Amateurish Mistake ahead of Debates," CNN. Cnn.com/2020/09/24/opinions/trumps-amateurish-mistake-ahead-of-debatesi-bden-silva-mcgowan/index.html.
35 Dionne.
36 Shane Goldmacher, Maggie Hagerman, and Jonathan Martin, "G.O.P. and Trump Enter an Inescapable Tango at a Retreat in Florida," *New York Times*, April 11, 2021, 23.
37 Amy Gardner, Tom Hamburger, and Michelle Ye Hee Lee, "Defeats Pile Up in Trump's Bid to Undo Loss," *Washington Post*, November 21, 2020, A1.
38 Quoted in Jose A. Del Real, "The Trump Presidency Was Marked by Battles over Truth Itself. Those Aren't Over," *Washington Post*, January 18, 2021. https://www.washingtonpost.com/politics/the-trump-presidency-was-marked-by-battles-over-truth-itself-those-arent-over/2021/01/18/3bee0050-5750-11eb-a931-5b162d0d033d_story.html.
39 Quoted in George F. Will, "Now Begins McConnell's Project to Shrink Trump's Influence," *Washington Post*, February 15, 2021, A17.
40 ibid.
41 Clare Malone, How Trump Changed America," fivethirtyeight.com, November 7, 2020, https://fivethirtyeight.com/features/how-trump-changed-america/.
42 Anne Applebaum, "Trump Won't Accept Defeat. Ever," *The Atlantic*, November 7, 2020, www.theatlantic.com/ideas/archive/2020/11/trumps-forever-campaign-is-just-getting-started/617021/.
43 Stephen Collinson, "Trump's Legacy of Mistrust Sends Congress into Total War," cnn.com, January 29, 2021, cnn.com/2021/01/29/politics/donald-trump-republicans-joe-biden-coronavirus-index.html?utm_content=2021-01-29.
44 Margaret Sullivan, "Culture of Lying Made Conviction Impossible," *Washington Post*, February 15, 2021, C1.
45 Peter Wehner, "Why Trump Supporters Can't Admit Who He Really Is," *The Atlantic*, September 4, 2020, www.theatlantic.com.ideas/archive/2020/09/prpredicate-fear/616009/.
46 George Packer, "A Political Obituary for Donald Trump," *The Atlantic*, January/February 2021, December 9, 2020, www.theatlantic.com/magazine/archive/2021/01/the-legacy-of-donald-trump/617255/.
47 ibid.

48 David Brooks, "The G.O.P. Is Getting Even Worse," *New York Times*, April 22, 2021, nytimes.com/2021/04/22/opinion/trump-gop-html?action=click&module=Opinion&pgtype=Homepage.
49 Quoted in Aaron Blake, "Trump's Dark 'I Am Your Retribution' Pledge—and How GOP Enabled It," *Washington Post*, March 6, 2023, downloaded March 9, 2023.
50 Brooks.
51 "Trump Indicted in New York: Donald Trump Is Indicted in New York." *New York Times*. Last Updated April 4, 2023. https://www.nytimes.com/live/2023/03/30/nyregion/trump-indictment-news.
52 Shayna Jacobs, Dylan Wells, David Nakamura, and Jacqueline Alemany, "Trump Pleads Not Guilty to 34 Counts," *Washington Post*, April 5, 2023, A1.
53 Devlin Barrett, "Trump Difference: All in What He's Not Charged With," *Washington Post*, June 12, 2023, A1. Also see *New York Times* Editorial Board, "The Justice Department Had No Choice," *New York Times* Sunday Review, June 11, 2023, SR 11.

6

JOE BIDEN ATTEMPTS TO RESTORE CIVILITY

Joe Biden faced a wave of attacks from his political adversaries not only against him personally but against American democracy as he prepared to take office on January 20, 2021. It was one of the most polarizing and caustic moments in U.S. history, and it included outgoing President Donald Trump inciting his supporters to take over the U.S. Capitol in an effort to overturn Trump's loss and reverse Biden's victory. As described in Chapter 5, the rioters failed but the violence set a very negative note on which to start the Biden era. Trump's fierce negativity had contaminated the political atmosphere.

In defeating Trump, Biden generally refused to get into the mud with his opponent and he mostly avoided directly responding to Trump's insults and snide remarks. Maintaining decorum, Biden remained true to his record of more than four decades of civility and service in Washington, including eight years as vice president for Barack Obama and 36 years as a U.S. senator from Delaware.

Biden did sink into the pit occasionally. He called Trump a "clown" during a televised debate and strongly criticized Trump for being incompetent, lacking compassion for others, and dividing the country. But he could have gone negative in a much more sustained way. Mostly he was calm and steady during the 2020 campaign, stayed above the fray, and resisted the depths of negativity to which Trump sank. Biden largely ignored Trump's taunts such as calling Biden "sleepy Joe," and deriding Biden for being too old and decrepit to be president even though Biden at 78 was only four years older than Trump and seemed to be in much better physical shape.

DOI: 10.4324/9781003149095-8

Biden struggled to overcome a tendency to commit gaffes and unforced errors, which had plagued his two previous unsuccessful presidential campaigns. He pushed compelling messages—that Donald Trump didn't have the right temperament to be president because he was too divisive and filled with resentments, and that Trump's policies were further dividing the country and weren't helping most Americans.

Attorney General William Barr gave Biden an unexpected lift in December 2020, about a month before Biden's inauguration in January. Barr undercut Trump, his boss, by saying there was no need for special counsels to investigate Hunter Biden, Joe Biden's son, for any possible illegalities (as Trump wanted), or to investigate election fraud. Barr said the Justice Department had found irregularities in the balloting, but nothing that was extensive enough to overturn Biden's victory. A few days later, Barr announced he was quitting as attorney general.

Yet Trump persisted in claiming election fraud even though Biden won the election with 81 million popular votes to Trump's 74 million, a margin of 7 million votes, and he captured the electoral majority 306–232. Trump still searched for ways to overturn the election. He failed to do so, but few fellow Republicans were willing to chastise him for being a sore loser and trying to delegitimize his successor. This suggested to many Democrats that the GOP had little interest in cooperating with Biden. They were correct, but Biden took many months before he acknowledged that the GOP leaders wanted to paralyze his administration to make it easier to defeat him in 2024.

Biden had good reason to go after Trump. The outgoing president, deeply upset at losing, left a mountain of problems behind, in some cases making them worse in order to make Biden's job as difficult as possible. As the *Washington Post* pointed out a month before Biden's inauguration, the list of crises that Biden faced included "a massive cyber intrusion, a still-raging global pandemic, a slowing economic recovery and a lingering reckoning over the nation's racial tensions."[1]

The *Post* argued:

> President Trump is not making his [Biden's] job any easier and, in several ways, appears to be actively making it harder—going to extraordinary lengths to disrupt and undermine the traditional transition from one administration to another despite the nation's many crises. ... In his final weeks in office, Trump is making a series of moves aimed at cementing his legacy and handicapping Biden's presidency—from abruptly pulling troops from war zones to cracking down on Iran to encouraging the Justice Department to investigate his political enemies. The result is a situation without precedent in American history: One president ending his term amid crisis is seeking to delegitimize a

> successor and floating the prospect of mounting a four-year campaign to return to power.[2]

New York Times columnist Frank Bruni wrote,

> Is normalcy obsolete? In the many weeks since it became clear that he lost the election, Donald Trump has successfully marketed an outrageous alternate reality, so that 70 percent of registered Republicans, according to a Quinnipiac poll this month, believe that Biden's victory was illegitimate. Trump has taken his refusal to concede to historic, previously unthinkable lengths. And an overwhelming majority of Republican members of Congress have played along, actively or passively, many of them knowing better, all of them traitors to democracy and profiles in cowardice.
>
> To this crew Biden is supposed to extend an olive branch?[3]

Still, Biden persevered in attempting to restore civility and a spirit of compromise. This was his nature.

In a speech on December 14, 2020, Biden said, "We need to work together to give each other a chance to lower the temperature. We may come from different places, hold different beliefs, but we share in common a love for this country."[4]

During a group interview with columnists on December 23, less than a month before his inauguration, Biden said,

> I respectfully suggest that I beat the hell out of everybody else. I won the nomination, got everybody to come around and won by over seven million votes. So I think I know what I'm doing and I've been pretty damn good at being able to deal with the punchers. I know how to block a straight left and do a right hook. I understand it. ... I haven't changed how I approach politics since I got involved. And part of it is establishing with your opponents that if they want to play, I'm ready to fight. But one of the things that happens is when you get into one of those kinds of blood matches ... nothing gets done.[5]

He argued that in the end the Republicans would use common sense and work with him.

Biden was staking his presidency on his belief that the country, including many Republicans, wanted to move away from the Trumpian approach of demonizing and attacking. During a meeting with supporters during his transition to power, Biden said, "I may eat these words, but I predict to you: As Donald Trump's shadow fades away, you're going to see an awful lot change."[6]

As explained in Chapter 1, there had been bitter divisions in past presidential elections. For example, the 1876 contest between Republican Rutherford B. Hayes of Ohio and Democrat Samuel J. Tilden of New York had been one of the most hotly disputed in U.S. history. The electoral votes of Louisiana, South Carolina, and Florida were fiercely contested. In January 1877, Congress set up an electoral commission to decide the outcome—made up of eight Republicans and seven Democrats. The commission gave Hayes a final electoral vote of 185 to 184, awarding him the presidency amid intense acrimony.

Trump, however, created an even worse situation by building up a false impression among many of his followers—a large proportion of the country—that Biden had really lost. His constant repetition of baseless allegations of fraud and corruption poisoned much of the electorate against Biden. Trump was playing the politics of revenge and fear and using attacks on the democratic system as fundamentally unfair to him in order to delegitimize Biden's presidency.

On January 8, 2021, Biden welcomed Trump's announcement that he would not attend his successor's inauguration, which every president had done since 1869 when Andrew Johnson boycotted Ulysses S. Grant's swearing-in. Biden said, "It's a good thing him not showing up. ... He's exceeded even my worst notions about him. ... He is one of the most incompetent presidents in the history of the United States of America."[7]

But Biden's bitterness quickly receded, at least publicly. In his inaugural address on January 20, the new president pledged to work immediately with his adversaries to solve the "cascading crises" that he faced, including the coronavirus pandemic, an economic downturn, serious unemployment, racial tension, climate change, and deep polarization. "Let's start afresh, all of us," he declared. "Let's begin to listen to one another again." Biden added: "Politics doesn't have to be a raging fire destroying everything in its path ... Every disagreement doesn't have to be a total war."[8]

During the first 100 days after his inauguration—the traditional time frame for assessing new presidents since Franklin D. Roosevelt took office in 1933 with a burst of activity—Biden did attempt to restore some measure of civility to the government, politics, and a badly fractured American society. His presidency became a test of whether the political pendulum could swing back to a more uplifting form of politics and whether governing could again be based on finding common ground instead of dividing people and emphasizing attacks and personal destruction.

Biden used FDR as his role model in many ways, especially in expressing optimism that the United States could solve its problems and displaying an eagerness to take action. Biden was inspired by Roosevelt's dynamism and activism illustrated by FDR's moving 13 major programs into law within 90 days.[9] The problem for Biden was that FDR had overwhelming Democratic control of Congress and most legislators were eager to follow his lead. Under Biden, the House and Senate were closely divided with minimal Democratic majorities in each chamber.

Biden and his aides delved into the history of FDR's presidency, notably his fabled and extremely active first 100 days. Among the books on their reading list were *FDR* by Jean Edward Smith and *The Defining Moment* by Jonathan Alter.[10] Biden also consulted with historian Jon Meacham, who assisted in writing Biden's inaugural address.

Biden signed more than 40 executive orders, proclamations, and memoranda reversing many of Trump's policies on issues including immigration, climate change, racial justice, and transgender rights. He accelerated the administering of vaccines to combat the coronavirus pandemic, which was the highest priority of most Americans for his administration, according to polls.[11]

At the same time, he pushed for congressional passage of a $1.9 trillion economic/pandemic relief package and signaled that, while he would listen to Republican alternatives to key provisions, he would not allow substantial delay in enacting the package. This angered GOP legislators who said Biden's pushing of his far-reaching bill without Republican support showed he wasn't really interested in compromise or working with the GOP. Democrats responded that the Republicans had a track record, under President Obama, of pledging good-faith efforts at compromise on key legislation only to have the measures delayed with little or no compromise from the Republicans in the end. Biden argued that the nation's needs were urgent, and he would move ahead aggressively with or without the GOP. But he refrained from Trump-style attacks, ridicule, and insults.

Biden's tactics worked for a while, as both the House and Senate approved his bill, but there was no unity between the major parties. The vote was almost totally partisan, with nearly all Democrats and no Republicans supporting Biden's relief package. On March 11, 2021, Biden signed the measure into law and gave a prime-time address to the nation. He avoided recriminations and emphasized that he wanted the country to move on, unite, and return to "normalcy" both in ending the pandemic through widespread vaccination and in stopping the vicious polarization that marked the Trump era.

But Biden's agenda stalled, especially his efforts to pass a massive program of social spending which he called "Build Back Better." Republicans remained adamantly opposed and they blocked passage. His proposed reforms in voting rights were also stymied.

In early April 2022, Biden won Senate confirmation of his nomination of Judge Ketanji Brown Jackson to the Supreme Court, the first

African American woman to serve on the high court. But her hearing was acrimonious, with Republican senators accusing her, unfairly, of being soft on child molesters and generally weak on crime in her lower-court rulings. She was confirmed on a 53–47 vote, with all Democrats, two independents who leaned Democrat, and only three Republicans supporting her.

The paucity of GOP support despite her excellent credentials showed how far the culture of polarization had spread. The unhinged anti-Jackson reactions of various GOP hard-liners was another indication of the depth of the political contamination. Rep. Marjorie Taylor Greene, R-Ga., said the pro-Jackson votes from Republican Sens. Susan Collins, Lisa Murkowski, and Mitt Romney proved that they were "pro-pedophile," a ridiculous allegation that had no merit. The anti-Jackson screeds of GOP Sens. Tom Cotton, Ted Cruz, and Josh Hawley were in the same category.

Biden improved the presidency's relationship with the news media, in part because Biden showed respect for the Fourth Estate and stopped calling journalists "the enemy of the people," as Trump had done.

At the annual White House Correspondents' Association dinner on April 30, 2022, an event designed to honor the media and which Donald Trump boycotted while he was president, Biden was conciliatory and laudatory. "The free press is not the enemy of the people," Biden said. "Far from it. At your best, you're guardians of the truth."

The closest to criticism that Biden came was when he urged journalists to avoid sensationalism and irresponsible reporting. "The First Amendment grants a free press extraordinary protection," Biden declared. "But with it comes, as many of you know, a very heavy obligation to seek the truth as best you can, not to inflame or entertain but to illuminate and educate." Biden added: "There's incredible pressure on you all to deliver heat instead of shed light … American democracy is not a reality show."

As president, he adopted some unpopular policies, and he sank into a stalemate with Congress for many months. For a while at mid-term, his approval ratings sank below 40 percent, a very mediocre number, and he seemed unable to persuade the country that he was capable of reducing inflation, cutting crime, controlling the flow of undocumented migrants over the U.S. southern border, or uniting America. Biden slipped up sometimes as a conciliator. In January 2022 he was asked whether inflation might be a political liability in the mid-term elections that year. The query came from Fox News reporter Peter Doocy, who often asked Biden and his staff pointed questions. Biden tried to ignore Doocy and then, as reporters were ushered out of the room, Biden said in front of an open microphone, "What a stupid son of a bitch." He quickly phoned Doocy and apologized, saying "It's nothing personal, pal," but it was too late to keep the incident from causing a media frenzy for a day. Yet it was a testament to Biden's newfound discipline in avoiding embarrassing off-the-cuff remarks that such incidents had become unusual.

The question remained whether he could achieve his goals in the hyper-polarized atmosphere. At mid-point of his term, Biden's agenda continued to stall.

One of his disadvantages was the perception among many legislators and voters that at 81 he was too old to serve another term as president. He was already the oldest president in U.S. history. All this depressed his approval ratings with the public and weakened him politically. And there seemed to be little Biden could or was willing to do to mitigate appearances that he was suffering from cognitive and physical decline. His all too frequent stumbles—such as falling while climbing the steps of Air Force One, taking a header when he tripped in front of a podium at the Air Force Academy, and falling off a bicycle—were embarrassments, done in full view of the TV cameras and spread widely on the networks and social media.

Biden had difficulty reading texts of long speeches, and if he veered from prepared remarks he often found himself on tangents that made little sense to his listeners. He seemed to shuffle his feet and walk stiffly with an old man's gait more often than ever. Democratic strategists told reporters (including me) privately that they were alarmed that Biden wasn't taking the age issue seriously enough, wasn't pacing himself well enough, and wasn't limiting his exposure to situations where his advanced age would be highlighted.

Biden's presidency got a boost in the mid-term election of 2022 when the Democrats defied expectations and held onto control of the Senate, even though it was by a small margin, and minimized their losses in the House of Representatives, although the Republicans did take control by a narrow margin. Biden and his allies argued that the Democrats did better than expected largely because the GOP nominated too many extremist conservative candidates who were unelectable but who had been endorsed by Donald Trump because he thought they would be loyal to him.

Biden benefited by rising to the occasion during Russia's invasion of Ukraine and rallying many nations against Russia, imposing sanctions on Russia, and providing much-needed arms to the Ukrainians. This briefly muted some of the criticism that Biden was too old to serve effectively.

Biden managed to engineer a deal with majority Republicans in the House to increase the debt ceiling and approve a new budget. After winning approval of both the House and the Democrat-controlled Senate at the 11th hour before the United States government was scheduled to default on its financial obligations, Biden argued that the deal proved bipartisan deal-making was still possible despite the hyper-partisan atmosphere.

"Passing this budget agreement was critical," Biden said. "The stakes could not have been higher. No one got everything they wanted, but the American people got what they needed. We averted an economic crisis and an economic collapse."

"When I ran for president," Biden added,

> I was told the days of bipartisanship were over, that Democrat and Republicans could no longer work together. But I refused to believe that, because America can never give in to that way of thinking. The only way American democracy can function is through compromise and consensus, and that's what I've worked to do as president.[12]

Biden spoke too soon. Hard-line conservatives in the House quickly rebelled because of the agreement and led the way in ousting Speaker Kevin McCarthy, D-Calif., for working too closely and compromising with Biden and the Democrats. This raised the prospect of long-term dysfunction on Capitol Hill.

On an ominous note for Biden, House Republicans led by new Speaker Mike Johnson of Louisiana started an impeachment investigation against him, arguing vaguely that he had failed as an effective leader and was hurting the country in a number of ways. Supporters of impeachment, such as firebrand conservative Rep. Lauren Boebert, R-Colo., condemned Biden's "dereliction of duty" and "abuse of power" that led to chaos and a flood of unwelcome migrants, allegedly violent and destitute, into the United States at the U.S. border with Mexico.[13] Other Republicans said Biden and his family were corrupt. It was clear that Biden had a long way to go to restore comity and find common ground with his adversaries.

Notes

1 Toluse Olorunnipa, Josh Dawsey, and Anne Gearan, "Trump Will Exit Amid Crises, Efforts to Disrupt Successor," *Washington Post*, December 22, 2020, A6.
2 ibid.
3 Frank Bruni, "Biden's Withering Olive Branch," *New York Times*, December 23, 2020, downloaded from nytimes.com.Bruni, December 23, 2020.
4 Quoted in Bruni.
5 Jonathan Capehart, "Biden Insists He's Ready for a 'Punch in the Mouth' from Republicans," *Washington Post*, December 24, 2020, retrieved from washingtonpost.com, December 26, 2020.
6 Bruni.
7 Eric Bradner, "Biden Says Trump Skipping Inauguration is 'a Good Thing,'" January 8, 2021, https://www.cnn.com/2021/01/08/politics/biden-trump-inauguration/index.html.
8 Author's coverage of Biden's inaugural address.
9 Jeff Greenfield, "The Trials Ahead," *Washington Post*, January 24, 2021, B1.

10 Peter Baker, "Copying Roosevelt, Biden Wanted a Fast Start. Now Comes the Hard Part," *New York Times*, January 30, 2021, A1.
11 ibid.
12 John Wagner and Cleve R. Wootson Jr., "Biden Readies His Pen on Debt," *Washington Post*, June 3, 2023, A1.
13 Maegan Vazquez and Marianna Sotomayor, "House Votes to Send Articles of Impeachment against Biden to Committees," *Washington Post*, June 23, 2023, A4.

7

FIRST LADIES' BENIGN INFLUENCE, WITH EXCEPTIONS

America's first ladies have rarely been a divisive or caustic force in the White House or the nation. Nearly all of them have devoted themselves to benign projects that emphasized the positive side of American life, and they tended to focus on being as supportive of and comforting to their husbands as possible.

Among the first ladies who played this traditional role were:

- Bess Truman and Mamie Eisenhower, who focused on taking care of their husbands as traditional wives;
- Jacqueline Kennedy, who specialized in restoring the historic décor of the White House and being a devoted mother to the first couple's young children, and enjoyed being a fashion icon;
- Lady Bird Johnson, who promoted highway beautification;
- Pat Nixon, another traditional wife who did not crave public attention;
- Betty Ford, who advocated for breast cancer detection and treatment after suffering herself from breast cancer, and also was a vocal supporter of programs to foster mental health;
- Rosalyn Carter, a private adviser to her husband;
- Nancy Reagan, who devoted herself to creating a happy home life for her husband and protecting him from advisers whom she believed were not serving him well and who also developed a popular campaign urging children and teenagers to "just say no" to drugs;
- Barbara Bush, a devoted wife who also emphasized the need to improve reading skill among young people;

DOI: 10.4324/9781003149095-9

- Laura Bush, a former librarian who advocated for reading as did her mother-in-law Barbara;
- Michelle Obama, who preached the importance of good nutrition and exercise and urged fellow Democrats to reject harshly negative politics practiced by her husband's critics with the slogan, "When they go low, we go high";
- Melania Trump, who, in promoting a message she called "Be Best," focused on improving children's health and well-being.

Three exceptions stand out: Edith Wilson, a first lady who exercised power as acting president when her husband was very sick and became a target for critics of the Wilson administration; Eleanor Roosevelt, a forceful advocate of women and minorities, including support for the expansion of civil rights and voting rights and ending discrimination against African Americans, both before and after her husband's 12 years in office, and who became a lightning rod for Franklin's opponents; and Hillary Rodham Clinton, who advanced the power of the first lady to new levels but dialed back her influence after she ran into headwinds of opposition.

Edith Wilson

Edith Bolling Galt met Woodrow Wilson when he was president in 1915. She was a 43-year-old widow at the time, and he was a 59-year-old widower still devastated by the death of his wife Ellen in 1914. They married less than a year after they met following an intense courtship. As first lady, Edith "dazzled the American people with her gracious manner and fashionable couture," according to one media account. She also took a keen interest in the policies President Wilson was promoting and he carefully kept her informed. "Privately, Edith worked arduously at the president's side," PBS has reported. "She was apprised of state matters and, after the outbreak of the First World War, even decoded secret transmissions. All the while, Edith was attendant to her husband's increasingly burdened health."[1]

After the president suffered a debilitating stroke in 1919, Edith worked behind the scenes to help him perform his duties. He stopped appearing at public events, and Mrs. Wilson regularly informed other officials of what Woodrow had "decided" on various issues, even though it is likely that she was making those decisions herself, based on what she thought her husband wanted.[2]

"Edith imposed a self-described 'stewardship' of the Presidency," PBS noted.

> Seeking to protect her husband's health at all costs, she allied with his loyal physician to shield the president from all outside visitors. She

> served as the only conduit to the president. White House usher Ike Hoover recalled, "If there were some papers requiring his attention, they would be read to him—but only those that Mrs. Wilson thought should be read to him. Likewise, word of any decision the president had made would be passed back through the same channels.[3]

Some historians say she actually ran the government from 1919 until her husband left office in a much-diminished condition in March 1921 (after eight years as president). "There is no question in my mind that there are times she could not or would not consult him," Edith Wilson biographer Rebecca Boggs Roberts told NPR in an interview discussing her book *Untold Power: The Fascinating Rise and Complex Legacy of First Lady Edith Wilson*. Sen. Albert B. Fall, R-N.Mex., called her "the presidentress who had fulfilled the dream of suffragettes by changing her title from First Lady to Acting First Man."[4]

Edith Wilson was sensitive to such accusations that she was "usurping her husband's power," Roberts says, so she wielded her vast authority secretly. In the process, she took on a negative role, descending into deception and spreading falsehoods about the condition of her husband. "His left side was paralyzed," Roberts adds. "She lied to the public, to the press, to the Congress, to the Cabinet, to the vice president, and to the president himself," assuring everyone his health was improving. "He never knew how sick he was, and all controversial and upsetting news was kept from him."

She might have been the most powerful first lady in history and accepted her husband's decidedly negative view of various issues and people, including his caustic assessment of the Republicans in the Senate who blocked his pet project, the League of Nations. The league was designed to rein in authoritarian, aggressive nations and protect small countries. The organization was never approved in the United States. After World War II, a more powerful version of it was created by the United States and other countries as the United Nations. Woodrow and Edith Wilson never forgave opponents in Congress for blocking the league.[5]

Eleanor Roosevelt

Eleanor Roosevelt, the wife of Franklin D. Roosevelt, publicly supported the expansion of civil rights and government help for those in need, especially for African Americans, which was a controversial position at the time. This caused her husband to insist that she stop her vigorous advocacy for African Americans because it was angering white voters and members of Congress, particularly from the South. FDR believed Eleanor's activism on this issue would cost him support for other programs on his agenda, and she reluctantly agreed to soften her public comments. She was a strong supporter of FDR's New Deal that used government to help the poor and the middle class during the Depression, and she remained a powerful public advocate for these programs even after his death and after her 12 years as first lady.

Because of her immersion in controversial causes, Eleanor Roosevelt became a divisive figure. She was popular among many Americans because she effectively championed the underdogs in American society. On the other hand, FDR's opponents blasted Eleanor for endorsing excessive government power and she became a symbol for government overreach and siding with African Americans.[6]

Historian Blanche Wiesen Cook said in a 2013 interview:

> Eleanor Roosevelt was reviled by the Dixiecrats [conservative southern Democrats], by the conservatives, by members of Congress and by the press because she stood for justice and she stood for civil rights at a time when, even during World War II, the military is segregated, blood plasma is segregated, it's segregated black and white. Everywhere she goes, she is demanding racial justice.[7]

But Franklin immensely valued her willingness to be his "eyes and ears." He was limited in his activities because his legs had been paralyzed from polio as a young man, and FDR sent Eleanor on many "fact-finding" missions to find out how his policies were working and what Americans wanted and needed from the government. She visited soup kitchens, coal mines, farms, cities, military bases, and many other places and reported back to her husband after the trips. He came to value her reports, and Eleanor enjoyed doing them because they made her a vital part of the administration, enabled her to make a difference in setting policy, and kept her husband in contact with the country.[8] Partly because she was so successful as his personal reporter, President Roosevelt had an unparalleled grasp of the conditions and attitudes in the country, and he became one of America's most iconic and empathetic leaders.

FDR wanted her to collect information from everyday people in as many walks of life as possible on how their lives were going, what problems they had, what they wanted from their president and their government, and how his policies were affecting them.

During the first summer of her husband's presidency, she visited Appalachia and found the conditions appalling. She wore a hard hat and miner's overalls and descended into a deep mine shaft to learn about mining operations and the difficult conditions experienced by workers. She noticed the ragged clothes on the wash lines and talked to people in their backyards and shanties. At Scott's Run near Morgantown, West Virginia,

Eleanor found a boy in a shack hugging his pet rabbit. His sister had just told him it was the only thing left to eat.[9]

After Eleanor reported her findings to Franklin, he immediately created a program to resettle as many Appalachian residents as possible in areas with better economies.

"The following year," historian Doris Kearns Goodwin says,

> Franklin had sent Eleanor to Puerto Rico to investigate reports that a great portion of the fancy embroidered linens that were coming to the United States from Puerto Rico were being made under terrible conditions. To the fury of the rich American colony in San Juan, Eleanor took reporters and photographers through muddy alleys and swamps to hundreds of foul-smelling hovels with no plumbing and no electricity, where women sat in the midst of filth embroidering cloth for minimal wages. Publicizing these findings, Eleanor called for American women to stop purchasing Puerto Rico's embroidered goods.[10]

Eleanor told a radio interviewer,

> I realized that if I remained in the White House all the time I would lose touch with the rest of the world … I might have had a less crowded life, but I would begin to think that my life in Washington was representative of the rest of the country and that is a dangerous point of view.[11]

And she became famous because of her travels. When she visited migrant-labor camps in California's San Joaquin Valley, she saw some shacks built of boards, tarpaper, and tin cans pounded flat as she was being driven through the area by car. She ordered the driver to stop, got out, and walked across a field toward some migrant workers. One of them wrinkled his face as he strained to see who was coming and he recognized the first lady immediately. "Oh, Mrs. Roosevelt, you've come to see us," he said matter-of-factly, so familiar was he with her trips to similar places.[12]

Eleanor learned during her travels that African Americans were increasingly impatient, and many were angry, over the pervasive racial discrimination, segregation, and oppression. Gradually during the thirties, she became one of the strongest civil-rights advocates in the country and befriended many in the civil-rights movement, including educator Mary McCLeod Bethune and activist Walter White.

In 1939, she resigned from the Daughters of the American Revolution when they prohibited American opera singer Marian Anderson from performing at Washington's Constitution Hall because she was Black. Eleanor persuaded her husband and Interior Secretary Harold Ickes to let Anderson sing at the Lincoln Memorial instead.

Historian Goodwin writes,

> More than anyone else in the White House, Eleanor was responsible, through her relentless pressure of War Department officials, for the issuance of the two directives that forbade the designation of recreational areas by race and made government-owned and -operated buses available to every soldier, regardless of race. (In 1948, President Harry S. Truman would issue Executive Order 9981, lifting the final barrier for full equality when he ended segregation in the armed forces.)[13]

She eventually had many outside allies in her campaign to improve social conditions and promote equality, such as civil rights and labor leaders, but inside the White House she was also influential even if many times her views did not prevail because Franklin felt she was pushing too hard and trying to move too fast.

Eleanor also learned much from the letters she received from everyday people, and she publicly encouraged them to write her. In August 1933, she made this request in an article she penned for Woman's Home Companion under the headline "I Want You to Write to Me." Mrs. Roosevelt said,

> Whatever happens to us in our lives, we find questions constantly recurring that we would gladly discuss with some friend. Yet it is hard to find just the friend we should like to talk to. Often it is easier to write to someone whom we do not expect ever to see.[14]

This caused a flood of mail, a pattern that continued for years. Mrs. Roosevelt received 300,000 pieces of mail in 1933, 90,000 in 1937, and 150,000 in 1940. She clearly had persuaded millions of Americans, through the many interviews and speeches she gave, the radio shows on which she appeared, and the trips she made, that she cared about them and wanted to know the details of their problems so she could help either by telling her husband, referring their cases to appropriate agencies of the federal government, or through her own intervention. Citizens' letters addressed many aspects of life at the time, reflecting the widespread desperation and anxiety caused by the Depression among unemployed workers, farmers who were losing their land through foreclosure, people who needed medical care, and others in dire straits. "I think I have been asked to do something about everything in the world except change the weather!" Mrs. Roosevelt wrote in 1940.[15]

As World War II advanced, Franklin didn't have as much time for Eleanor and her domestic intelligence reports, which hurt her feelings, but she kept at it. She called Franklin's attention to the need for a larger food allowance for unemployed mothers, more focus on preventing illiteracy, the need for better housing, more pensions for the elderly, and more attention to guaranteeing civil liberties.[16] She spread the word through speeches, press conferences, media interviews, and her popular syndicated newspaper column.

Harry Hopkins, a key FDR aide and friend who was in charge of a vast work-relief program, was a strong ally of Eleanor's in advocating more government help for those in need. Hopkins and Mrs. Roosevelt shared a deep conviction that the unemployed were worthy and decent people who had no jobs through no fault of their own and were fully deserving of government assistance.

They told Franklin how desperate people were, and how much they needed help, serving as the most committed and sensitive opinion analysts possible. "Both Harry Hopkins and Mrs. Roosevelt were driven during the depression by a sense of urgency," said Works Progress Administration (WPA) Administrator Elizabeth Wickenden.

> They never forgot there were these millions of people who had absolutely nothing, who had once held a steady job and had a sense of self-respect. From their wide travels across the country they kept in their minds a vivid picture of the lives of these people, and that image drove them to push the government to create as many jobs for as many people as it possibly could.[17]

Amid a rash of racial disturbances across the country in 1943, including ugly incidents between white and Black welders in Mobile, Alabama and a vicious race riot in Detroit, Michigan, Eleanor's sense of urgency increased.

She sent Franklin a stream of memos warning about the horrendous living conditions of Black people in many areas and she said rising racial tension was a problem that the president needed to address. She called for a national interracial conference of Black and white leaders, but her husband declined to put his imprimatur on the idea. FDR also refused to make a national statement or speech about race because he felt it would anger Southern members of Congress whose votes he needed for war bills and social programs.[18]

Realizing how much American life was changing during World War II, she successfully advocated government funding for day-care centers and after-school programs for children while their mothers worked, and their fathers were fighting the war. She successfully promoted Frances Perkins to secretary of labor, the first time a woman had held a Cabinet position.

But she paid a price for her activism and her social advocacy. Her conservative critics were very hostile to her and regularly pilloried her as a socialist, a radical, and a harridan. She rarely hit back, feeling that responding would push critics to new lows and make matters worse.

Hillary Clinton

Hillary Clinton was an outlier in many ways among first ladies and, for a while, provided a cutting edge for her husband's administration. She pushed for women's rights both in the United States and around the world, sometimes turning harshly negative toward what she considered patriarchal societies where she said men were holding women back.[19]

This negativity was nothing new for her. During his 1992 presidential bid, Bill Clinton was attacked for smoking marijuana as a young man, for alleged draft dodging, and making improper sexual advances. Partly at the urging of Hillary Clinton, a key adviser, he created a "war room"—actually, a rapid-response team—to immediately respond to rumors and innuendo by counter-attacking as much as possible.

During her early years as first lady, Hillary got involved in divisive policy debates such as pushing for health care reform, a massive piece of legislation. Bill Clinton again created a war room to win passage for this health-care bill, which failed.

The instinct to demean the Clintons' adversaries was a key tactic during Bill's second term as his defenders derided women who accused him of sexual improprieties. The women's reputations were sullied but a number of their accusations later proved true, such as the claim by former White House intern Monica Lewinsky that President Clinton had an inappropriate sexual relationship with her. And as described earlier in this book, Hillary Clinton was a key part of Bill Clinton's public defense and his team's efforts to undermine the credibility of his accusers.

Hillary Clinton said a "vast right-wing conspiracy" had been created to destroy her husband's presidency and defended him for many months during impeachment proceedings for lying under oath and obstructing justice in the Lewinsky sex-and-lies scandal. After Bill Clinton admitted that he had indeed lied about having an improper sexual relationship with Lewinsky, a former White House intern, Hillary backed off from her very public profile until she decided to run for office herself, winning a seat in the U.S. Senate from New York.

After Bill Clinton left the presidency after two terms, Hillary Rodham Clinton served effectively as a Democratic U.S. senator from New York from 2001 to 2009 and was secretary of state under President Obama from 2009 to 2013. As the Democratic nominee for president in 2016, she described supporters of her opponent, Republican nominee Donald Trump, as a "basket of deplorables," which alienated many swing voters who felt supporting Trump was perfectly legitimate and believed Hillary

Clinton did not understand their problems or their lives. She had become a very divisive figure, and this comment seemed to summarize her negative outlook for many voters. She lost to Trump decisively.

Notes

1 Public Broadcasting Service. "Edith Bolling Galt Wilson," *PBS: American Experience*. Accessed August 1, 2023. https://www.pbs.org/wgbh/american-experience/features/wilson-edith-wilson/.
2 Steve Inskeep and Barry Gordemer, transcript of "Biography of First Lady Edith Wilson Examines the Complexities of Women and Power," National Public Radio (NPR). Updated March 11, 2023, https://www.npr.org/2023/03/08/1161859597/biography-of-first-lady-edith-wilson-examines-the-complexities-of-women-and-power.
3 Public Broadcasting Service.
4 Quoted in Shiloh Holley, "Edith Bolling Galt Wilson (1872–1961)," *Encyclopedia Virginia*, Virginia Humanities. Published December 7, 2020. Accessed August 2, 2023. https://encyclopediavirginia.org/entries/wilson-edith-bolling-galt-1872-1961/.
See also William Hazelgrove, *Madam President: The Secret Presidency of Edith Wilson*. New York: Regnery History, 2016.
5 Public Broadcasting Service.
6 Iván Román, "Eleanor Roosevelt's Unprecedented Activism—From Inside the White House,"*History.Com*. Updated March 7, 2023. https://www.history.com/news/eleanor-roosevelt-first-lady-humanitarian-activist.
7 ibid.
8 Doris Kearns Goodwin, *No Ordinary Time: Franklin and Eleanor Roosevelt: The Home Front in World War II*. New York: Simon & Schuster, 1994, 27. Also see Conrad Black, *Franklin Delano Roosevelt: Champion of Freedom*. New York: PublicAffairs, 2003, 128.
9 Goodwin, 29.
10 ibid.
11 ibid.
12 ibid., 38–9.
13 ibid., 627.
14 Quoted in Frances M. Seeber, "'I Want You to Write to Me': The Papers of Anna Eleanor Roosevelt," Summer 1987 issue of *Prologue*, 1, available at Franklin D. Roosevelt Presidential Library and Museum.
15 Seeber, 2.
16 Goodwin, 86.
17 Quoted in Goodwin, 87.
18 Goodwin, 447.
19 Peter Baker and Amy Chozick. "Hillary Clinton's History as First Lady: Powerful, But Not Always Deft," *The New York Times*, December 5, 2014, https://archive.is/20190405162012/https://www.nytimes.com/2014/12/06/us/politics/hillary-clintons-history-as-first-lady-powerful-but-not-always-deft.html.

The riot at the U.S. Capitol on January 6, 2021, was an extension of the negative politics that has existed in America, waxing and waning over the years and surging again now. Thousands of trouble-makers, urged on by former President Donald Trump, marched on the Capitol and hundreds broke in, with the goal of stopping the transfer of power from Trump, who lost the 2020 election to Joe Biden. The effort failed but it showed how the toxic environment is endangering American democracy.

Source: AP Photo/John Minchillo

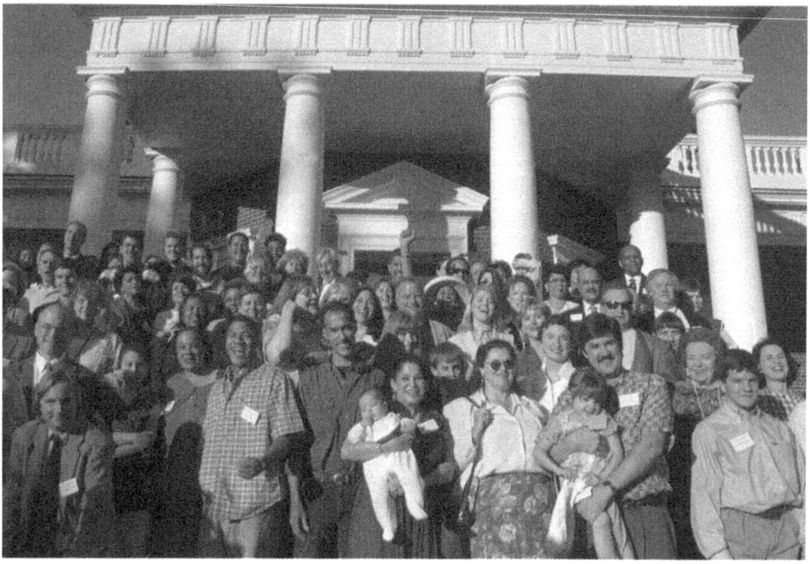

One of the first would-be character assassinations in American politics was journalist James Callender, whose caustic pen found ready targets in various Founding Fathers. However, Callender's most notorious allegation concerned Thomas Jefferson. Frustrated that Jefferson had not granted him a government post, Callender began a smear campaign against the third president, alleging amongst other things that Jefferson had fathered children with one of his enslaved women, Sally Hemings.

Although Callender's claims were met with skepticism in his own time, modern DNA testing has since proved the allegation true. Pictured above is the 1999 "family reunion" between descendants of Jefferson and Hemings at Monticello.

Source: AP Photo/Leslie Close

Andrew Jackson was at the center of negative politics in the mid-1820s and early 1830s. Criticized by some opponents as a would-be monarchist and others as an uncultured upstart, Jackson was the alternative target of vicious attacks and their instigator. Jackson had married his beloved wife Rachel before her divorce from her previous husband was finalized. The couple said they thought the divorce proceeding had been completed. But Rachel Jackson was lambasted by her husband's opponents as a bigamist and an adulteress. The allegations took a drastic toll on her health, and she died shortly before her husband took office, leaving Jackson devastated by the loss and angry at those who had enabled it.

Source: Library of Congress Print and Picture Collection (Photos 3a and 3b)

The character issue has been a staple of presidential politics for many years. One of the most dramatic examples contains the attacks on Grover Cleveland in the 1884 campaign for fathering a child out of wedlock. However, aspersions on his character had little impact at the polls, and Cleveland won the presidency anyway.

Source: Library of Congress Print and Picture Collection

During the Great Depression, Franklin D. Roosevelt was attacked by those on the right as a traitor to his upper-class background for his many programs designed to help the poor and the middle class, while also being accused of not doing enough by those on the left. Nevertheless, he largely refrained from political mudslinging of his own, projecting a sunny, optimistic outlook above the fray.

Source: National Archives and Records Administration

Eleanor Roosevelt was a lightning rod for criticism during the administration of her husband Franklin. Opponents said she was too liberal and was taking too many stands on policy issues, going far beyond the traditional role of first lady.

Source: *Los Angeles Daily News* via UCLA Library Digital Collections

The "Daisy Ad" was probably the most effective negative TV commercial in political history. President Lyndon Johnson used it to decimate Republican challenger Barry Goldwater by portraying him as a warmonger in the 1964 campaign, which Johnson won in a landslide.

Source: Screenshot of *Daisy Ad* via Wikimedia Commons

Wading through the toxic mire of politics sometimes involves risking one's life. Only a few weeks into his presidency in 1981, Ronald Reagan was shot as he returned to his limousine following a speaking engagement. Although his wounds were critical, he was able to survive thanks to the diligent care of the medical staff at GWU Hospital and eventually made a full recovery. Not every politician is as fortunate as Reagan was.

Nearly 50 years prior to Reagan's attack, Louisiana governor Huey P. Long was shot and killed in 1935 by the son-in-law of a political opponent. A magnetic, controversial figure with strong populist appeal, the "Kingfisher" was one of FDR's harshest critics on the left and was preparing to run for president when he became another victim of toxic politics.

Source (Photo 8a): AP Photo/Ron Edmonds
Source (Photo 8b): Harris & Ewing Collection (Library of Congress)

Republican opponents attacked Democrat Bill Clinton's character as a way to undermine him. He gave them ammunition by at first denying that he had an affair with former White House intern Monica Lewinsky but later admitting it. His perjury led to his impeachment by the House of Representatives in 1998. He was acquitted by the Senate in one of the most negative periods in U.S. political history.

Source (Photo 9a): William J. Clinton Presidential Library
Source (Photo 9b): AP Photo/Marty Lederhandler

Although he was untouched by scandal and projected a cool, unflappable persona, Barack Obama was nevertheless attacked repeatedly and viciously by his opponents. One tactic was to claim he was not born in the United States, which critics said made him ineligible for the presidency. It was a false charge and Obama eventually disproved it.

Source (Photo 10a): Executive Office of the President/Lawrence Jackson
Source (Photo 10b): AP Photo/David Zalubowski

Richard Nixon set the standard as one of the most negative presidents in modern history. He and his operatives harassed his rivals both openly and privately, often intentionally provoking retaliatory ire. This "attack dog" approach to his opponents eventually proved to be Nixon's downfall in the aftermath of the Watergate scandal.

Nixon's toxic legacy has tarred nearly all subsequent presidencies. However, Donald Trump is perhaps "Tricky Dick's" most obvious disciple. An intimidator, agitator, and master showman, Trump wields his bravado, quick temper, cult of personality, and eagerness to dominate people as weapons against his allies and adversaries alike.

Source (Photo 11a): National Archives and Records Administration
Source (Photo 11b): The White House

Although Joe Biden has attempted to stay civil amid attacks against him, he remains a target for much criticism among his opponents. Much of the censure around Biden concerns his advancing age. Critics said he had lost cognitive and physical abilities and was no longer fit to be president. Biden, who turned 81 in November 2023, had great difficulty countering these accusations, and his image as an effective leader was badly tarnished.

Source: The White House

Father Charles Coughlin, the famous right-wing "radio priest," gained a vast following during the 1930s and 1940s with his pro-fascist, anti-communist attacks. He was a forerunner of the many media commentators today who make their living by stirring people up and tearing their opponents down. A more recent example of talk radio as a powerful, toxic force in politics is Rush Limbaugh, a caustic conservative broadcaster who hosted a massively influential radio talk show from 1984 until his death in 2021. *The Rush Limbaugh Show* intensified the caustic environment of modern politics, leavened at times by his sense of humor and his desire to entertain his audiences as well as outrage them.

Source (Photo 13a): Library of Congress Print and Picture Collection
Source (Photo 13b): AP Photo/Chris Carlson

Sen. Joe McCarthy, R-Wis., was one of the most famous caustic politicians and political rogues ever as he hatched fake charges and invented conspiracies about communists in government that played on fears of a communist takeover. Eventually, he went too far, and his influence faded, but during the 1950s he was one of the nation's most influential politicians. The name for making unsupported and unfair charges came from him: "McCarthyism."

Source: AP Photo/Herbert K. White

George Wallace, racist populist, was Democratic governor of Alabama and became a national figure with his anti-African American campaigns of hate and vitriol. A merchant of malice during his heyday, he was known for always being on the attack and for exploiting Americans' fears and resentments.

Source: AP Photo

Pat Buchanan (top), a conservative speechwriter and strategist, sought the presidency unsuccessfully by challenging Republican incumbent George H.W. Bush in 1992. He was a bellicose, conservative hard-liner, an antecedent to Donald Trump. Newt Gingrich (below), former speaker of the U.S. House of Representatives, promoted division and stoked anger against Democrats, the establishment, and the mainstream news media. He was another forerunner of Trump.

Source (Photo 16a): AP Photo/Eric Draper
Source (Photo 16b): AP Photo/Ron Edmond

The latest wave of vitriolic rogues, provocateurs, and apostles of discord has included media figures associated for at least part of their careers with Fox News—figures such as Roger Ailes, who ran the network from 1996 to 2016, and influential commentators Tucker Carlson and Sean Hannity. All were masterminds of attack and they developed ardent followings among conservatives. They helped make Fox News a powerful influence in shaping right-wing politics.

Source (Photo 17a): AP Photo/Jim Cooper
Source (Photo 17b): AP Photo

PART II

A Rogues' Gallery of Toxic Influencers

8

INFLUENTIAL CAUSTIC POLITICIANS

Throughout U.S. history, politicians who were provocateurs, demonizers, and merchants of discord have stirred up the toxins in American life. Their tactics varied but they shared some common attributes such as being creative, adept at exploiting grievance and resentment, and effective in coarsening the political culture. The stories of these architects of negativity provide many insights into the reasons caustic politics has become so popular. No analysis of negative politics would be complete without a discussion of these operators. We begin with a look at four national officeholders who intensified the negativity, whose impact has endured, and who in many cases paved the way for today's toxic politicians.

Huey Long: Populist Authoritarian

Huey Long, nicknamed "The Kingfish," started out as a mainstream liberal and backer of Franklin D. Roosevelt, but Long's zeal for action, his desire to accumulate and wield power, and his ambition to rise to the very top got the best of him.

As governor and U.S. senator from Louisiana, he became a demagogue and used explosive politics to get his way, conquer his adversaries, and advance himself. "I used to get things done by saying 'please,'" he once said. "Now I dynamite 'em out of my path."[1] Historian David Kennedy described Long's regime in Louisiana as "the closest thing to a dictatorship that America has ever known."[2]

Despite his relatively short time on the national scene, Long made a lasting impact on American politics by showing how a clever leader can

DOI: 10.4324/9781003149095-11

marshal the power of aggrieved and furious voters who feel ignored and exploited by "elites." President Roosevelt regarded Long as "one of the two most dangerous men in the country."[3] (The other "most dangerous" man cited by FDR was Gen. Douglas McArthur.)

Eighty years later, Donald Trump followed in Long's footsteps as a ferocious advocate of change but from a conservative rather than Long's liberal standpoint.

Long was born on August 30, 1893, one of nine children, in poverty-stricken northern Louisiana. He attended several colleges and worked as a traveling salesman before passing the bar exam and becoming a lawyer in 1915. He represented poor clients and made a name for himself as a crusader against entrenched interests such as Wall Street and big oil companies.[4]

Entering politics, he started as a Democrat but gradually developed his own liberal-populist party based heavily on creating a cult of personality. He sought to redistribute the nation's wealth, severely tax the rich, and massively increase federal spending—far beyond what FDR tried to do. It was a measure of Long's influence and his accurate reading of the public desire for a more activist federal government that over time Roosevelt began moving in Long's left-wing direction in the mid- and late 1930s.

Historian William Ivy Hair wrote that Long created a political identity that had great appeal.

> He was a young warrior of and for the plain people, battling the evil giants of Wall Street and their corporations; too much of America's wealth was concentrated in too few hands, and this unfairness was perpetuated by an educational system so stacked against the poor that (according to his statistics) only fourteen out of every thousand children obtained a college education. The way to begin rectifying these wrongs was to turn out of office the corrupt local flunkies of big business … and elect instead true men of the people [such as Huey Long].[5]

His first bid for governor failed in 1924; he attacked incumbent John M. Parker as a puppet of big business, denounced Standard Oil, and said local political bosses were corrupt and had too much power. He came in third in a Democratic primary although he did well in the poor rural north of the state.[6]

Four years later, he won the governorship at age 35, making him the youngest person ever elected to the job in state history. He had built on his name recognition from 1924 and four years of campaigning as a fierce populist and unrelenting critic of the status quo. And to his credit, he didn't use the harsh racism against African Americans that was part of Southern politics at the time.

As governor, he moved boldly to build huge public works projects such as roads and bridges, putting many people to work, and he expanded social programs. He was impeached in 1929 by the Louisiana House of Representatives for abuse of power but the Louisiana Senate couldn't muster the votes to remove him from office. He stirred up passions pro and con, even to the point where the debate over impeachment in the Louisiana House of Representatives caused a brawl on the House floor. There were media reports that Long himself was involved in altercations with critics at various times.[7]

Long's popularity grew and he was elected to the U.S. Senate in 1930 after another harsh campaign in which he attacked incumbent Joseph E. Ransdell, whom Long had supported in 1924. Long mocked Ransdell, 72, for being too old and nicknamed him "Old Feather Duster."[8]

For a while, Long served as governor and senator at the same time, which was legal in Louisiana but highly unorthodox. He finally arranged for an acolyte to take over the governorship and do his bidding at home while Long was a senator in Washington.

He came to believe Roosevelt was too timid and that FDR would never fully redistribute national wealth as Long wanted. He criticized FDR's creation of Social Security, designed to help the elderly by providing a regular income, calling the program too weak. In 1933 and 1934, Long proposed a radical plan to help the poor and the middle class, including limiting fortunes to a maximum of $100 million, restricting annual income to $1 million, and limiting individual inheritances to $5 million. He proposed guaranteeing every family a household payment of $5,000 as an annual income, and proposed many other federal programs including public works projects, pensions for the elderly, and a 30-hour work week.[9]

Long was also an isolationist on foreign policy, in contrast to Roosevelt's internationalism.[10]

A natural showman, Long used rhetoric that was understandable to everyday people, especially rural voters, many of whom adored him. With a strong dose of humor, he complained about both major parties as he popularized his own party under the slogan, "Every Man a King: Share Our Wealth."

In a famous speech, Long expressed his opinion of the Democratic and Republican parties, describing them as

> just like the old patent medicine drummer that used to come around our country. He'd play a banjo and he'd sell two bottles of medicine. One of those bottles of medicine was called High Popalorum and another one of those bottles of medicine was called Low Popahirum ... Finally somebody around there said is there any difference in these bottles of

> medicines? "Oh," he said, "considerable. They're both good but they're different," he said.
>
> "That High Popalorum is made from the bark off the tree that we take from the top down. And that Low Popahirum is made from the bark that we take from the root up."
>
> And the only difference that I have found between the Democratic leadership and the Republican leadership was that one of 'em was skinning you from the ankle up and the other from the ear down.[11]

As the Louisiana Legislature continued to pass legislation to implement Long's agenda—as a sort of laboratory for his national ideas—tensions rose dramatically in Long's home state. Although everyday people still admired him, opposition grew from the powerful forces he was attacking including former officials and the oil industry.

Adding to his controversial persona, Long used authoritarian methods to enhance his power. He was willing to punish his opponents with no hesitation, such as by dismissing hundreds of government employees in Louisiana when they disagreed with his policies and replacing them with supporters. He blocked authorization and funding for projects and programs supported by politicians and others who opposed his initiatives, and he removed their family members from government jobs as punishment. He was furious at negative coverage in the newspapers, and he founded his own newspaper, the *Louisiana Progress*, to promote him and his ideas and attack his enemies. He helped create an oil company to compete with the industry giants in Louisiana. Even after taking a seat in the U.S. Senate, he oversaw the passage of bills in the Louisiana Legislature.[12]

"The accusation of fascism was nothing new for Long," author Annika Neklason wrote in *The Atlantic*. "He was a controversial figure in American politics, attracting a passionate base of support on one hand for effectively pushing progressive legislation and widely condemned on the other for alleged corruption and abuses of power."[13]

Instead of merely denying these allegations, which included comparisons with Adolph Hitler in Germany and Benito Mussolini in Italy, Long "tended to play them off,"[14] arguing that he was using authoritarian methods to carry out the people's will.

On September 8, 1935, Carl Weiss, the son-in-law of a judge whom Long was trying to remove from office, shot Long at the state Capitol. Weiss was shot and killed by Long's bodyguards, and Long died of his wounds on September 10.[15]

Journalist Annika Neklason articulated the obvious parallels between Huey Long and Donald Trump.

Both men rose to national political prominence in the aftermath of a global financial crisis, with ethnic violence on the rise, automation putting workers' jobs in doubt, and autocratic leaders gaining political power worldwide. Both made waves with sweeping populist rhetoric and policy proposals that challenged their parties' more moderate establishments and promised to make government work for the common people. Both encapsulated their pledge to elevate the nation in a catchy slogan: Trump's "Make America Great Again" and Long's "Every Man a King." And both, once in power, showed little concern for norms and standard legislative procedures when pursuing their goals.[16]

Sen. Joe McCarthy: Communist Hunter

Sen. Joe McCarthy, R-Wis., led "witch hunts" to find and root out alleged communist influence in America, including in the federal government, the U.S. Army, and Hollywood. He eventually lost much of his public support because he was so extreme, but he retained a cult following and McCarthy remained a potent and negative force in American life whose influence has lasted to this day. He pioneered the use of innuendo, insinuation, false charges, and character assassination under the guise of patriotism. Today these techniques are common, partly because McCarthy showed they can be effective in undermining the opposition and at the same time making the originator of the noxious charges famous.

"He plainly had no ethical or ideological compass, and most of his colleagues regarded him as a troublemaker, a loudmouth, and a fellow entirely lacking in senatorial politesse," wrote journalist Louis Menand in the *New Yorker* in July 2020.[17]

But McCarthy, who relished his nickname "Tail Gunner Joe" from his service as a Marine during World War II, became a sensation and a household name during the late 1940s and 1950s. His brand of toxic accusations based on little or no evidence played into the nation's insecurities. Americans' fears were growing over the potential for communist subversion within the United States and overseas, fueling the bombastic legislator's rise to fame. These fears became known as the "Red Scare," and much of it was propelled by McCarthy.

He came from a middle-class family and was a striver from the start. He worked as a chicken farmer at the age of 17 on his father's property near Appleton, Wis., then was hired as a grocery-store clerk and quickly became the store's manager. He had only a grammar-school education and at age 21 enrolled at Little Wolf High School in Manawa, Wis. and completed four years of high school work in nine months, graduating in 1930. He moved on to Marquette University and studied engineering for two years, paying for his studies by selling flypaper door to door and managing two service stations at the same time. He switched to law school and became a licensed attorney in 1935.[18]

McCarthy, then a Democrat, ran for district attorney in 1936 but lost. In 1939, he ran for judge in Wisconsin's Tenth Circuit and won. He was a hard-working candidate and recruited a small army of dedicated volunteers. He also began using negative politics, accusing the 66-year-old incumbent of being too old to do the job. McCarthy also said the incumbent enriched himself during his many years in public office, a powerful allegation during the Depression when so many were in dire economic straits.[19]

In personal terms, he was engaging and glib, and while he professed commitment to his Roman Catholic faith and abstemious values, he became a heavy drinker and enjoyed gambling, especially poker, roulette, and slot machines—habits in which he indulged for the rest of his life.[20]

The start of World War II for the United States with the Japanese attack on Pearl Harbor on December 7, 1941, changed his life, as it transformed so many others. As a judge, he could have taken an exemption from the draft, but he joined the Marine Corps on June 4, 1942, at age 33. He was appointed a first lieutenant after applying immediately for a commission. He served in the Pacific with distinction and participated in several combat missions as a tail gunner with a Marine air squadron.[21]

While stationed at Guadalcanal, he changed his party registration to Republican, more advantageous at the time in his home state. In 1944, still in Guadalcanal, he ran long-distance for the U.S. Senate from Wisconsin, challenging incumbent Republican Alexander Wiley. Wiley won the GOP primary, however. In December 1944, McCarthy resigned his commission in the Marines. He returned to Wisconsin where he was re-elected district judge in April 1945.[22]

In 1946, McCarthy upset Sen. Robert La Follette, Jr., member of a famous political family in Wisconsin, in a Senate Republican primary. He went on to defeat Democrat Howard McMurray in the general election. In the Senate, he quickly became known for his ambition, his belligerence, and his willingness to bully witnesses at hearings. But he didn't immediately find an issue to make him a national figure.

McCarthy's rise started on February 9, 1950, when, as a virtually unknown freshman senator, he made a fiery Lincoln Day speech at the Ohio County Republican Women's Club in Wheeling, West Virginia. McCarthy waved a piece of paper and announced that he had a list of 205 known members of the Communist party who were "working and shaping policy" in the State Department. It was the start of "McCarthyism." Even today, this epithet is used to describe unethical political tactics based on hurling dramatic accusations without proof. Picked up by the

Associated Press, McCarthy's allegations about the State Department drew him immense attention nationally.[23]

Journalist Menand describes the start of the McCarthy witch hunts as follows, reiterating that McCarthy did not have the infamous list:

> He did not have even a single name. ... It didn't matter. He had grabbed the headlines, and that was all he cared about. He would dominate them for the next four and a half years. Wheeling was McCarthy's Trump Tower escalator [when Donald Trump made a splashy arrival at a news conference announcing his 2016 presidential candidacy]. He tossed a match and started a bonfire.[24]

As with Trump, McCarthy was a showman who understood and could exploit the media of his day.

He timed his February 1950 speech perfectly. Communism seemed to be on the march. The Soviet Union had unexpectedly detonated an atomic bomb in August 1949, causing fear in the West.[25] Communist forces won the Chinese civil war that same year, creating the People's Republic of China. North Korea, run by communists, invaded pro-Western South Korea in 1950, and the United States entered the war as an ally of South Korea. Communists were gaining popular support in some European countries and elsewhere around the world. Americans dreaded communist subversion at home, and McCarthy played on their concerns.[26]

"In the hyper-suspicious atmosphere of the Cold War, insinuations of disloyalty were enough to convince many Americans that their government was packed with traitors and spies," wrote the editors of history.com. "McCarthy's accusations were so intimidating that few people dared to speak out against him."[27]

The Republican-controlled House Un-American Activities Committee (HUAC) began to publicize members' charges that communists were infiltrating the U.S. government and various businesses such as the entertainment industry and the media. Responding to public fears, Congress in 1950 approved the McCarran Internal Security Act requiring that all "subversives" in the United States undergo government supervision. President Harry Truman vetoed the act, saying it violated the Bill of Rights, but Congress overrode his veto.

Seeking to counter Republican allegations that he was soft on communism, Democrat Truman began a loyalty program of his own designed to weed out "subversives." He also denied Congress access to many administration security files. "Ironically," wrote journalist Tom Wicker, "these policies lent legitimacy to the idea of foreign subversion. *Must be something to hide*, suggested critics from both parties."[28]

"McCarthy was a bomb thrower—and, in a sense, that is all he was," Menand wrote.

> He would make an outrageous charge, almost always with little or no evidentiary basis, and then he would surf the aftershocks. When these subsided, he threw another bomb. He knew that every time he did it reporters had two options. They could present what he said neutrally, or they could contest its veracity. He cared little which they did, nor did he care that, in his entire career as a Communist-hunter, he never sent a single "subversive" to jail. What mattered was that he was controlling the conversation.[29]

McCarthy also had a way with words—specializing in the language of attack and derision—and this drew media coverage and public attention. Among his memorable phrases: blasting liberals as "prancing mimics of the Moscow party line," attacking "egg-sucking phony liberals," and mocking "dilettante diplomats" who "whined" and "whimpered" before the communists.[30]

McCarthy persisted despite setbacks. The month after his Wheeling speech in 1950, a Senate subcommittee began an investigation and found no proof of subversive activity at the State Department. And even though many legislators considered his scare tactics and smears over the Red Menace overdone, McCarthy kept up the pressure.

He followed up on his initial, sketchy accusations in a number of ways and received enormous publicity. In what one commentator called his distinctive "nasal monotone," he gave a Senate speech on February 20 to packed visitors' galleries. He demonstrated "sheer audacity and his contempt not only for the truth but for the listening senators he must have known could see through his deceptions and distortions," journalist Wicker wrote. "But he knew power-hungry Republican senators—even the respectables of the Senate club—would not expose him because *they didn't want to*."[31]

He dominated hearings on alleged communist subversion and made another media splash. "Even insubstantial charges were never quite disposed of by denials, which themselves called attention to the accusations," Wicker added. "The constant allegations that the Democrats and the Truman administration had been subverted from abroad and infiltrated at home suggested that smoke must be hovering over *some* hidden administration fire."[32]

Re-elected strongly in 1952, McCarthy became chairman of the Senate Committee on Government Operations in 1953. This gave him a bigger platform for his Red-baiting. In a series of hearings, McCarthy acted as an angry inquisitor and made wild accusations that certain people were communists and tarnished the reputations of many. One study found that more than 2,000 government workers lost their jobs because of McCarthy's charges even though he generally provided little evidence.[33]

His newly hired chief of staff of the Permanent Subcommittee on Investigations J.B. Matthews attacked Protestants as the "largest single group supporting the Communist apparatus in the United States today." This drew the wrath of Protestant voters and legislators. President Dwight Eisenhower, a Protestant and a Republican, condemned the attack as "irresponsible" and "alien to America." McCarthy fired Matthews but the incident raised more doubts about the Wisconsin senator's habit of overreaching and his creating an atmosphere of false charges and toxic politics.[34]

McCarthy also expanded his accusations to include gay men and lesbians. He alleged that homosexual governmental employees "could be blackmailed by enemy agents over their sexuality and thereby betray national secrets," according to biography.com.

> In 1953, Eisenhower signed Executive Order 10450, which sanctioned the administrative policy of tracking down gay and lesbian governmental employees and having them fired due to the labeling of "sexual perversion" as an undesirable trait for employment. Scores of employees were thus fired or resigned out of fear of persecution, with various surveillance measures instituted to try and track down citizens' intimate habits.[35]

Starting in 1951, McCarthy claimed without evidence that Defense Secretary and former Gen. George Marshall, throughout his career, had been "always and invariably serving the world policy of the Kremlin" and was part of "a conspiracy on a scale so immense as to dwarf any previous venture in the history of man."[36]

McCarthy's worst misstep came when he tried to expose alleged communist influence in the armed forces during a month of televised Senate hearings in the spring of 1954. He was questioning the patriotism of the military, a respected institution, with no proof, and following up on the allegations he had made against Marshall, an esteemed figure who had also been secretary of state under President Truman. McCarthy accused Marshall of contributing to the United States' "loss" of China to the communists and being guilty of "a conspiracy of infamy."[37]

In hearings that were widely viewed on television, Americans saw McCarthy hector and abuse witnesses and fail to offer evidence for his accusations of subversion. At one point, he attacked the patriotism of a young lawyer who was an acquaintance of the Army's chief counsel Joseph Welch. This caused Welch to ask the senator with just the right tone of outrage and sadness, "Have you no sense of decency, sir? At long last, have you left no sense of decency?"[38]

Behind the scenes, McCarthy was not dealing well with the stress. He endured stomach pain and severe headaches. His drinking problem got worse, as recounted by biographer Tom Wicker:

> What had been a shot of bourbon at work was now a tumbler. Where he had once relied on a surreptitious drink to get through a public speech, he now needed several to get through a morning of normal work. ... When the hearings adjourned at 4:30 p.m. he would gather with his aides for several hours, then eat a hurried dinner before returning to the office to look at more files and plan strategy for the next day. ... McCarthy would often sit up all night, shifting papers and sipping straight vodka until 6:00 a.m.[39]

The Senate voted to censure him on December 2, 1954 with a bipartisan vote of 67–22. His colleagues condemned him for "inexcusable," "reprehensible," "vulgar and insulting" behavior "unbecoming a senator."[40]

The censure showed that McCarthy had lost much of his power among his Senate colleagues. Most of them were fed up with his conduct and no longer feared him. "Even worse, the press paid him little attention; those who knew McCarthy believed that the loss of headlines and an entourage of reporters pained him more than the indifference of his colleagues," Wicker wrote.[41]

President Eisenhower, who disliked the Wisconsin senator's arrogance and his smearing of opponents, said, "It's no longer McCarthyism. It's McCarthywasism."[42]

Despite the rebuke, he went on to serve in the Senate until his death from hepatitis two-and-a-half years later at age 48.

The parallels between McCarthy and Trump are unmistakable. Both had the support of important forces in the mass media of their day. McCarthy had the Hearst newspaper chain and popular columnists Westbrook Pegler and Walter Winchell. Trump had Fox News. Both were dramatists who knew how to attract attention and had no qualms about defaming and insulting those who stood in their way or people they selected as their targets.

And there is a direct personal connection between McCarthy and Trump. Roy Cohn, one of McCarthy's lawyers, later became a key adviser to Trump when he was a businessman. In addition to the use of unsubstantiated statements, Cohn advised Trump to attack anyone who stood in his way and to call attention to himself with dramatic charges. Trump carried these lessons into his successful 2016 campaign for the White House, into his presidency, into his unsuccessful bid for re-election in 2020, and into his bid to re-take the White House in 2024.

The political establishment was adamantly against McCarthy and Trump for much of their careers, but the two insurgents used this opposition to their advantage by making the insiders their targets day in and day out. This tapped into a strain of opinion held by many everyday Americans who believed their government was no longer on their side.

Hated and loved, McCarthy proved the power of negativity and caustic politics, and some of his methods—such as the personal insults and the incendiary but baseless charges that the media couldn't resist covering—remain in use.

Menand observed:

> Right from the start, McCarthy had prominent critics. But almost the entire political establishment was afraid of him. You could fight him, in which case he just made your life harder, or you could ignore him, in which case he rolled right over you. He verbally abused people who disagreed with him. He also had easy access to money, much of it from Texas oilmen, which he used to help unseat politicians who crossed him.[43]

"To his supporters he could say and do no wrong," Menand added, noting that pollster George Gallup in 1954 said, "Even if it were known that McCarthy had killed five innocent children, they would probably still go along with him."

This is remarkably similar to Trump's boast during the 2016 campaign that he could shoot someone on Fifth Avenue in New York and his supporters would still love him. The die-hard backers of both McCarthy and Trump liked the way their hero bullied adversaries, dominated people, said outrageous things, and could be very entertaining.

Another parallel to Trump was McCarthy's temperament. Like Trump, McCarthy was described as

> incapable of sticking to a script. He rambled and he blustered, and if things weren't going his way he left the room. He was notoriously lazy, ignorant, and unprepared, and he had a reputation for following the advice of the last person he talked to. But he trusted his instincts. And he loved chaos. He knew that he had a much higher tolerance for it than most human beings do, and he used it to confuse, to distract, and to disrupt.[44]

"Like Trump, McCarthy burst on the political scene as a self-proclaimed outlier, nominally part of the Republican Party but with a style all his own," wrote historian Beverly Gage for the *Washington Post*. She continued:

> Though nearly everyone in Washington could be considered "anti-communist" in the early 1950s, McCarthy knew how to turn vague affinities into shocking headlines, accusing the Truman administration of harboring secret communists at the highest levels. Even without Twitter, McCarthy dominated the news cycle, introducing one outrageous claim and then switching to another if the first came under challenge. As with Trump, not everything he said was false, but the constant slippage between truth and lies served to destabilize the national conversation and upend political norms.[45]
>
> Millions of Americans loved what they saw, At the peak of his influence, McCarthy boasted a 50 percent approval rating; like Trump, he divided the country with near-perfect precision. Among Republicans, he was even more widely admired, if not quite universally. ... Trump's story of what happened in the 2020 election bears all the hallmarks of McCarthyite myth: conspiring elites, hidden corruption, even the threat of an imminent socialist takeover.[46]

George Wallace: Racist Divider

As the governor of Alabama and a presidential candidate, George Wallace was an important force behind the rise of racist populist attack politics in the United States during the 1960s and 1970s.

He also employed some of the methods adopted later by Trump in his presidential campaigns and presidency, such as making shocking statements that drew intense media coverage, using insults and extreme rhetoric, inflaming his base voters, and holding big rallies to get news coverage and stir up his admirers. Trump and Wallace shared "the demagogue's instinctive ability to tap into the fear and anger that regularly erupts in American politics," wrote Dan T. Carter in the *New York Times*.[47] He continued:

> Both George Wallace and Donald Trump are part of a long national history of scapegoating minorities: from the Irish, Catholics, Asians, Eastern European immigrants and Jews to Muslims and Latino immigrants. During times of insecurity, a sizable minority of Americans has been drawn to forceful figures who confidently promise the destruction of all enemies, real and imagined, allowing Americans to return to a past that never existed. ... [Both Wallace and Trump] learned how to exploit the deepest fears and hatreds of white Americans frightened about the present and despairing of the future.[48]

Wallace was elected Alabama governor in 1962 and rose to national fame by standing outside a building at the University of Alabama on June 11,

1963, to deny admission to Black students and briefly defy federal orders to desegregate. He declared, "Segregation today; segregation tomorrow, segregation forever." The administration of President John F. Kennedy forced him to back down, but he became a hero to opponents of integration and racist elements of society from coast to coast.

He ran for the Democratic presidential nomination in 1964 and fell far short. However, he showed potential strength and did well in a few Democratic primaries outside the South such as in Indiana, Maryland, and Wisconsin.

After the '64 campaign won by Democratic President Lyndon Johnson, Wallace returned to Alabama to shore up his power base. The Alabama Constitution prohibited anyone from serving consecutive terms as governor, so Wallace arranged for his wife Lurleen to run for governor in 1966. She won but George Wallace was calling the shots. He continued to use the governor's office as a power base to raise money and promote his ideas.[49]

In 1968, Wallace ran for president again, this time as the candidate of his own American Independent Party, opposing desegregation and civil rights and attacking liberals as weak and un-American. He was a natural showman with a gift for memorable phrasing, such as when he called Democratic leaders "pointed-head college professors who can't even park a bicycle straight."[50]

Wallace's racist themes and overall negativity found a receptive audience across the country, especially among working-class whites. Many Americans were attracted to his strongman's rhetoric and anti-Washington attacks as the nation endured a tumultuous year with setbacks in the Vietnam war, huge anti-war demonstrations, the assassinations of the Rev. Martin Luther King, Jr. and Democratic presidential candidate Robert Kennedy, riots in more than 100 cities, and pervasive racial tensions.

Journalist Dan T. Carter drew comparisons between Wallace's and Trump's oratory style:

> On paper his speeches were stunningly disconnected, at times incoherent. But videotapes of those 1968 rallies captured a performance. A wild energy seemed to flow back and forth between Mr. Wallace and his audiences as he called out their mutual enemies: bearded hippies, pornographers, sophisticated intellectuals who mocked God, traitorous anti-Vietnam War protesters, welfare bums, cowardly politicians. And the television networks, drawn to covering conflict, gave his rallies plenty of attention since they sometimes turned violent and seemed exciting and entertaining.[51]

Wallace won 10 million votes or 13 percent of the popular vote and 46 electoral votes in 1968, carrying five Southern states and demonstrating that overtly racist appeals had strong appeal throughout the country, not just in the former Confederate states of the South.[52] Republican Richard Nixon won the White House with his own divisive and conservative campaign although he was not as overtly racist as Wallace.

Wallace, returning to his power base in advance of another presidential run in 1972, won the Alabama governorship again in 1970. He ran a racist primary campaign against Gov. Albert Brewer, a moderate Democrat who had succeeded to the governorship from being lieutenant governor when Lurleen Wallace died of uterine cancer in 1968. George Wallace would tell rallies in small towns, "You know, 300,000 nigger[53] voters is mighty hard to overcome."[54] This stimulated turnout among his racist supporters. Wallace successfully linked Brewer to Black voters and Brewer, a genteel centrist from a wealthy white family, failed to come up with a strategy to defend himself. He seemed weak and reluctant to fight. Wallace mocked Brewer as "sissy-britches" and said he wasn't strong enough to stand up for Alabama.[55] On policy, Wallace billed himself as a populist and called for increasing state services, cutting taxes, and terminating the spread of "filthy literature and narcotics."

Political scientist Kevin Swint described Wallace as

> a born campaigner. He appeared at huge outdoor rallies orchestrated by his campaign. Local speakers would warm up the crowd by warning of the dangers posed by "immoral politicians." Then Wallace would burst onto the stage, while a band played "Dixie" in the background. His speeches were pure red meat. He railed against racial integration, school busing, and federal legislators.[56]

This model for campaign rallies was replicated by Trump a half century later—the theatrics, the tirades, the warnings about immoral and nefarious politicians, the red meat. The issues were different, but the negativity was the same.

Wallace won the runoff over Brewer with 51.5 percent of the vote, capturing the state's blue-collar voters who were worried about what Wallace said might be a Black "takeover."[57]

While governor of Alabama, Wallace ran for president again in 1972 as a Democrat proclaiming a goal of safeguarding "states' rights" and of limiting federal power. He had an impact that has persisted ever since.[58] Wallace won Democratic primaries in Florida, Maryland, Michigan, North Carolina, and Tennessee.

In his state and national roles, Wallace made it easier for racists and demagogues to peddle their offensive wares by showing that such a negative strategy could succeed in many places around the country.

During his 1972 run, Wallace was shot by would-be assassin Arthur Bremer while campaigning in Laurel, Maryland. He suffered major injuries to his spinal cord and was paralyzed from the waist down. Suffering from severe pain, he used a wheelchair for the rest of his life. Although he lost the Democratic nomination to Sen. George McGovern, D-S.Dak., in 1972, Wallace remained a voice for division and racism nationally, even though his reach was limited by his poor health. He was elected to third and fourth terms as Alabama governor in 1974 and 1982.

Several years before he died at age 79 in 1998, Wallace changed his views, denounced racism, and apologized to people he had "offended and hurt."[59]

But his impact was to help normalize baleful populism.

Newt Gingrich: Scorched Earth

Newton "Newt" Gingrich rose from back-bencher in the U.S. House of Representatives to speaker of the House through scorched-earth tactics. Many politicians, especially fellow Republicans, adopted his philosophy that politics is a war for power and embraced a strategy of making unrelenting attacks on opponents, including the news media. His impact has been lasting.

From the start of his career as a conservative politician from Georgia, Gingrich did not respect Washington traditions such as decorum and civility. He hated the Washington Establishment. He distrusted the news media. He loved attention. In all these areas, he was a forerunner of Donald Trump.

As speaker of the House of Representatives in the mid-1990s, "[He] was enshrining an attitude—angry, combative, tribal—that would infect politics for decades to come," journalist McKay Coppins wrote in *The Atlantic*. Coppins continued:

> Political scientists who study our era of extreme polarization will tell you that the driving force behind American politics today is not actually partisanship, but negative partisanship—that is, hatred of the other team more than loyalty to one's own. Gingrich's speakership was both a symptom and an accelerator of that phenomenon.[60]

"While he looked as if he might fit naturally in a seminar room, deep down Gingrich had the take-no-prisoners mentality of the toughest partisan figures who had ever served on Capitol Hill," historian Julian E. Zelizer wrote in his biography of Gingrich. "He had practically written the handbook on cutthroat congressional tactics and spinning the media for partisan advantage; indeed, during his speakership, conservatives had literally circulated a memo on how to speak like Newt."[61]

Gingrich set forth his wrecking-ball theories during his successful congressional campaign in 1978 while he was a professor at West Georgia College. "One of the great problems we have in the Republican Party is that we don't encourage you to be nasty," he told a group of college Republicans at a conference in Georgia. "We encourage you to be neat, obedient and loyal, and faithful, and all those Boy Scout words, which would be great around the campfire but are lousy in politics." He declared that politics is a "war for power."[62]

Gingrich was perseverant, even when his prospects for success seemed remote. As described by Zelizer:

> When Ronald Reagan was president from 1981 from 1989, Gingrich had worked diligently as a backbencher to remake the Republican Party's then-staid, country-club, business-oriented brand into something far more hard hitting and confrontational. He committed himself to being a foot soldier in the Reagan Revolution. His goal: shove the national policy agenda to the right and wrest power away from the Democrats who had controlled the House for three decades, ... To almost everyone, it was a pipe dream.[63]

Gingrich saw his own political success as a harbinger. He won his House seat in 1978 after it had been in Democratic hands for decades precisely because he used cutthroat tactics aimed at discrediting his opposition. He advised other Republicans to follow his example.[64]

He attempted to demolish bipartisan coalitions that led Republicans, as the minority in Congress, to compromise with majority Democrats to get things done. Then he waged war on Congress and official Washington for being dysfunctional, and aimed to persuade most Americans to throw the majority Democrats out.

In 1989, Gingrich said in his incendiary way:

> The left-wing Democrats will represent the party of total hedonism, total exhibitionism, total bizarreness, total weirdness, and the total right to cripple innocent people in the name of letting hooligans loose. ... These people [Democrats] are sick. They are so consumed by their own power, by a Mussolini-like ego, that their willingness to run over normal human beings and to destroy honest institutions is unending.[65]

Social scientist Stevan E. Hobfoll called Gingrich "one of the principal architects of the politics of hatred and fear-mongering brought into the modern mainstream."[66]

Eventually, he turned against fellow Republicans as they tried to work with Democrats. He called Sen. Bob Dole of Kansas, a leader of GOP moderates, the "tax collector for the welfare state." He dismissed House Republican Leader Bob Michel of Illinois, a genial, conciliatory pol of the old school, as irrelevant because "he represented a culture which had been defeated consistently."[67] And he branded Democrats with labels such as pro-communist and un-American.

Gingrich was always seeking to dramatize his ideas and his own role as a revolutionary battling with Washington's elites. He took full advantage of C-SPAN, then a new cable television network that carried congressional proceedings live. Gingrich regularly condemned the Democrats in speeches to an empty House chamber, which viewers didn't realize because the cameras were stationary, focused on the legislator speaking at the moment and didn't show all the empty seats.

"The No. 1 fact about the news media is they love fights," he said, with considerable accuracy. "When you give them confrontations, you get attention; when you get attention you can educate."[68]

Over time, Gingrich and his allies in Congress and in the broader political system moved from fights over legislation to weaponizing those legislative battles and using "wedge issues" such as abortion, regulation, and immigration to divide the country in a permanent war on his opponents.

Coppins described Gingrich's political strategy:

> [H]e set out to circumvent the old power structures and build his own. Rather than letting the party bosses in Washington decide which candidates deserved institutional support, he took control of a group called GOPAC and used it to recruit and train an army of mini-Newts to run for office.[69]

He sent out cassette tapes and memos to conservative candidates, counseling them on how to communicate more like Newt, which is to say, more negatively. One memo included recommended words to use in attacking Democrats, including "sick ... pathetic ... lie ... anti-flag ... traitors ... corrupt."[70]

Gingrich led House Republicans to victory in the 1994 mid-term elections by helping to make the balloting a national referendum on Democratic control of Congress. He blamed the Democrats for paralysis in Washington, even though he and his cohorts did all they could to block legislation. He came up with a "Contract With America," a list of conservative proposals he pledged to implement if the GOP won a majority such as budget cuts and anti-crime legislation.

In the end, the Republicans took control of the House in 1994, picking up a remarkable 54 seats, and also taking control of the Senate and various governorships and state legislatures. The new House chose Gingrich as speaker, one of the most powerful positions in government. In addition to pushing for his conservative agenda, Gingrich tried his best to undermine Democratic President Bill Clinton, advocating the impeachment of Clinton for perjury, obstruction, and other offenses linked to his affair with former White House intern Monica Lewinsky. The House did impeach him, but the Senate acquitted Clinton. Many Americans thought Gingrich had gone too far in both the impeachment and in pushing conservative proposals that had shaky support nationally.

The GOP lost seats in the House in November 1998, and many congressional Republicans blamed Gingrich for the setback. Adding to his problems was a congressional ethics investigation that led to a reprimand of Gingrich for financial improprieties, and the disclosure that he had an extramarital affair with a congressional employee. Gingrich resigned as speaker after the 1998 election. He resigned his seat in Congress in January 1999.

But Gingrich's impact outlasted his direct hold on power.

As Trump moved closer to winning the 2016 Republican presidential nomination, he briefly considered Gingrich to be his vice presidential running mate. The two men ended up rejecting the idea—Gingrich told Trump allies they were too much alike for him to draw many voters to the ticket and he concluded that Trump needed a more stabilizing force such Sen. Mike Pence of Indiana, whom Trump chose to be his vice president.

Zelizer highlighted the direct link between Gingrich's influence and the Trump presidency.

> In any case, Gingrich believed he had already made an enormous impact on GOP politics and helped to create the foundation for Trump's ascendancy. Gingrich could feel as though he had won. Trump was thriving in the political world that Gingrich had created. Gingrich would always be Michelangelo to Trump's *David*.
>
> In Gingrich's world, Republicans practiced a ruthless style of partisanship that ignored the conventional norms of Washington and continually tested how far politicians could go in bending government institutions to suit their partisan purposes. Republicans went for the head wound as Trump's adviser Steve Bannon said, when Democrats were having pillow fights. The new GOP goal was not to negotiate or legislate but to do everything necessary to maintain partisan power. If it was politically useful to engage in behavior that could destroy the possibility of governance which rendered bipartisanship impossible and would unfairly decimate their opponents' reputations, then so be it.[71]

In *The Atlantic*, journalist McKay Coppins compared Gingrich and Trump as both embodying

> a combination of self-righteousness and smallness, of pomposity and pettiness, that personifies the decadence of this era ... Few figures in modern history have done more than Gingrich to lay the groundwork for Trump's rise. During his two decades in Congress, he pioneered a style of partisan combat—replete with name-calling, conspiracy theories, and strategic obstructionism—that poisoned America's political culture and plunged Washington into permanent dysfunction. Gingrich's career can perhaps be best understood as a grand exercise in devolution—an effort to strip American politics of the civilizing traits it had developed over time and return it to its most primal essence.[72]

During Trump's term in office, Gingrich became a key adviser to the president, egging him on as he emerged as a wrecking ball aimed at destroying the norms and traditions of civility and cooperation in Washington and in American life. Gingrich also became a regular commentator on the pro-Trump Fox News, known for his incendiary remarks and huge ego.

Gingrich described himself grandly as a "transformational figure" and "the most serious, systematic revolutionary of modern times."[73] These self-descriptions were hyperbolic, typical of Gingrich, but his impact as a toxic politician was powerful and pervasive.

Notes

1 Quoted in David Zinman, "Remembering Huey Long: 'This is the Kingfish Speakin'," *The Courier*, August 28, 2020, archived at https://www.houmatoday.com/story/news/2010/08/26/remembering-huey-long-this-is-the-kingfish-speakin/26932782007/.
2 David M. Kennedy, *Freedom from Fear: The American People in Depression and War, 1929-1945*. Oxford: Oxford University Press, 2001, 236.
3 Quoted in T. Harry Williams, *Huey Long*. New York: Vintage, 1981, 640.
4 William E. Leuchtenburg, "FDR and The Kingfish," *American Heritage*, Fall 1985, https://www.americanheritagecom/fdr-and-kingfish.
5 William Ivy Hair, *The Kingfish and His Realm: The Life and Times of Huey P. Long*. Baron Rouge, LA: Louisiana State University Press, 1996, 88.
6 Alan Brinkley, *Voices of Protest: Huey Long, Father Coughlin, and the Great Depression*. New York: Vintage Books, 1983, 19.
7 Jennifer Latson, "The Strange Career of Assassinated Louisiana Politician Huey Long," *Time*, September 8, 2015, https://time.com/4020709/huey-long-anniversary/.
8 Quoted in Thomas Harnett Kane, *Huey Long's Louisiana Hayride: The American Rehearsal for Dictatorship, 1928–1940*. New York: William Morrow, 1941.
9 Glen Jeansonne, "Challenge to the New Deal: Huey P. Long and the Redistribution of National Wealth," *Louisiana History: The Journal of the Louisiana Historical Association* (Autumn 1980), 21, www.jstor.org/stable/4232034.
10 Williams, 1969, 1981, 623–34.
11 Huey P. Long, "Huey P. Long on the Difference between Democrats and Republicans," delivered September 2, 1935, Oklahoma City Fairgrounds.

Video recording, 0:00 to 1:08, https://www.youtube.com/watch?v=8MKb35NK0F0.
12 Brinkley, ibid. Hair, ibid. Niklason, ibid.
13 Annika Neklason, "When Demagogic Populism Swings Left," *The Atlantic*, March 3, 2019, https://www.theatlantic.com/politics/archive/2019/03/huey-long-was-donald-trumps-left-wing-counterpart/583933/.
14 ibid.
15 Boyce Rensberger, "Clues from the Grave Add Mystery to the Death of Huey Long," *Washington Post*, June 29, 1992, www.washingtonpost.com/archive/politics/1992/06/29/clues-from-the-grave-add-mystery-to-the-death-of-huey-long/cbdd5297-27a1-4534-96bb-6817daf3573/.
16 Neklason.
17 Louis Menand, "Joseph McCarthy and the Force of Political Falsehoods," *New Yorker*, July 27, 2020, www.newyorker.com/magazine/2020/08/03/joseph-mccarthy-and-the-force-of-political-falsehoods.
18 Tom Wicker, *Shooting Star: The Brief Arc of Joe McCarthy*. New York: Harcourt, 2006, 24–5.
19 ibid., 30–4.
20 ibid., 25–6, 36.
21 ibid., 37–9.
22 ibid., 40–4.
23 ibid., 5.
24 Menand.
25 Wicker.
26 history.com editors, "Joseph McCarthy," history.com. Published October 29, 2009, www.history.com/topics/cold-war/joseph-mccarthy.
27 ibid.
28 Wicker, 19.
29 Menand.
30 Wicker, 84.
31 ibid., 65.
32 ibid., 77.
33 history.com editors.
34 Wicker, 121.
35 Biography: Joseph McCarthy, biography.com, August 2, 2019, www.biography.com/political-figure/joseph-mccarthy.
36 Menand.
37 Wicker, 96–8.
38 history.com editors.
39 Wicker, 151–2.
40 history.com editors.
41 Wicker, 183.
42 Quoted in Ted Morgan, *Reds: McCarthyism in Twentieth-Century America*. New York: Random House, 2001, 505.
43 Menand.
44 Menand.
45 Beverly Gage, "McCarthyism Didn't Die with Its Leader's Fall, Says Historian Beverly Gage. Trumpism Won't, Either," *Washington Post*, December 6, 2020, B1.
46 ibid.
47 Dan T. Carter, "What Donald Trump Owes George Wallace," *The New York Times*, January 8, 2016. https://www.nytimes.com/2016/01/10/opinion/campaign-stops/what-donald-trump-owes-george-wallace.html.

48 ibid.
49 Kerwin Swint, *Mudslingers: The Twenty-Five Dirtiest Political Campaigns of All Time*. New York: Union Square Press, 2008, 224.
50 Quoted in Ken Ringle, "The Enduring Symbol of an Era of Hate," *Washington Post*, Tuesday, September 15, 1998, E1. Archived https://www.washington-post.com/wp-srv/politics/daily/sept98/wallace15.htm.
51 Carter.
52 Richard Pearson, "Former Ala. Gov. George C. Wallace Dies," *Washington Post*, September 14, 1998, A1.
53 As in earlier chapters, the author has elected to present such quotes in their uncensored state including profanities and racial slurs in order to fully represent the offensive and inflammatory nature of such statements.
54 Quoted in Swint, 223.
55 Swint, 226.
56 ibid.
57 ibid., 228–30.
58 ibid., 230–1.
59 Pearson.
60 McKay Coppins, "The Man Who Broke Politics," *The Atlantic*, October 17, 2018, www.theatlantic.com/magazine/archive/2018/11/newt-gingrich-says-youre-welcome/570832/.
61 Julian E. Zelizer, *Burning Down the House: Newt Gingrich, the Fall of a Speaker, and the Rise of the New Republican Party*. New York: Penguin Press, 2020, 3.
62 Quoted in Coppins.
63 Zelizer, 4.
64 ibid.
65 The comments by Gingrich in this paragraph were quoted in Stevan E. Hobfoll, *Tribalism: The Evolutionary Origins of Fear Politics*. London: Palgrave Macmillan, 2018, 29–30.
66 Hobfoll, 29.
67 Quoted in Coppins.
68 ibid.
69 Coppins.
70 ibid.
71 Zelizer, 5.
72 Coppins.
73 Quoted in Coppins.

9

THE ROLE OF THE MAINSTREAM NEWS MEDIA

It's not only politicians who are to blame. The news media also are at fault for fostering and promoting toxic culture.

Presidents and other politicians tend to accuse the mainstream news media of being obsessively harsh and destructively negative. This is no longer a partisan critique pushed mostly by Republicans, as it had been for many years. Now most politicians seem to share this critique. President Bill Clinton, a Democrat, said while in office, "The press destroys people. It's how they get their rocks off. It's how they enjoy themselves."[1]

Donald Trump, a Republican, labeled the mainstream media as "fake news." Joe Biden, a Democrat, said the nature of news reporting is to focus on the negative while ignoring the positive side of life.[2]

According to Gallup, only 34 percent of Americans have at least a "fair amount" of trust in news media. This is a sharp decline from 72 percent in 1976, when the media were appreciated for speaking truth to power in the aftermath of the Vietnam war and the Watergate scandal.[3]

I am referring here to the mainstream news media, ranging from the *New York Times* and the *Washington Post* to the broadcast television networks and the cable news operations. I will discuss the opinion commentators and other proselytizers of division later in this book.

As a lifelong journalist and White House correspondent for three decades, I still believe that we in the media should hold our leaders accountable. But in recent years, our natural negativity has devolved into a constant refrain about what is wrong. There is relatively little coverage of the positive side of politics and American life, although the bright side is just as real and valid as the dark side.

DOI: 10.4324/9781003149095-12

I remember learning in journalism school a slogan popular in the news business: "If it bleeds, it leads." This idea was frowned upon by the professors but reflected the prevailing philosophy in much of the news business. It was based on the idea that to increase readership and advertising revenue, the media needed to focus on the negative—such as violence, crime, and conflict.

When it came to politics, exposing lies, falsehoods, and corruption was our goal. This far overshadowed any positive news we might deign to cover.

My view is that the media should always make a commitment to the watchdog role of journalism, protecting the public interest and working to insure that government is honest and effective. But over time the Fourth Estate has unfortunately played more of an attack-dog role, eager to bite and not just bark.

President Biden was on the mark when, miffed at tough questions from the media after his first meeting as president with Russian leader Vladimir Putin in Geneva during 2021, he remarked, "To be a good reporter, you got to be negative, that you got to have a negative view of life, it seems to me." He criticized reporters for "never" asking a positive question. Biden later apologized for the harsh tone of his comment, but not for the substance.[4]

There is no doubt that doing positive stories about government and political leaders has become relatively unusual. A reporter is too often considered a shill by his or her professional colleagues when doing a positive story even when praise is justified. And positive stories are often considered boring by the public and by editors and reporters; this has reduced the media's interest in them.

For my generation—the baby boomers—the focus shifted too often from straight news reporting to investigative and advocacy journalism. Too many of us thought it would lead to power, wealth, and fame. Investigative reporting was further romanticized by the portrayal of journalists in the popular culture such as in the movie *All the President's Men* based on the Watergate scandal. Actors Robert Redford and Dustin Hoffman played Watergate reporters Bob Woodward and Carl Bernstein, giving journalists an aura of glamor. There was also *The China Syndrome* focusing on a reporter played by Jane Fonda as she investigated potentially deadly mishaps at a nuclear plant. Again, the reporter was portrayed as a heroic figure.

Over time, more journalists sought to make an impact, more than anything else, either to right society's wrongs or to make a difference and increase his or her influence on the wider world.

Since the 1960s, the media have "increasingly embraced 'attack journalism,'" writes communications professor Tim Groeling. "[T]here seems to be a consensus within the scholarly literature that negativity dominates modern news coverage."[5]

Groeling reasons that competition, changing standards of performance, and post-Watergate/Vietnam cynicism were some of the reasons for the trend.[6]

But politicians began to take their criticism of the media directly to the public. In 1969, then-Vice President Spiro Agnew, reflecting the views of President Richard Nixon, his boss, called the media "nattering nabobs of negativism," which, although overwrought, was in many ways accurate.[7] In 1993, Bill Clinton, when he was enduring sharp criticism from the media, said "success and lack of discord are not as noteworthy as failure."[8] Former Rep. Newt Gingrich, R-Ga., became House speaker during Clinton's presidency in part because of the popularity among fellow Republicans of his constant attacks on Clinton, Democrats, and the media.[9]

As media critic David Shaw has written, "The news media are biased. We're biased in favor of change, as opposed to the status quo. We're biased in favor of bad news, rather than good news. We're biased in favor of conflict, rather than harmony."[10]

Take media coverage of the coronavirus pandemic in 2020 and 2021. A study co-authored by Dartmouth College economics professor Bruce Sacerdote focused on news coverage by major television networks and other organizations such as the *New York Times*. The study found that about 87 percent of coronavirus coverage in national U.S. media during the pandemic was negative compared with 53 percent in U.S. regional media and 51 percent in international media. The coverage was negative in both liberal-oriented media outlets such as MSNBC and conservative-oriented outlets such as Fox News.[11]

"When Covid cases were rising in the U.S., the news coverage emphasized the increase," reported David Leonhardt of the *New York Times*. He continued:

> When cases were falling, the coverage instead focused on those places where cases were rising. And when vaccine research began showing positive results, the coverage downplayed it, as far as Sacerdote could tell. ... If we're constantly telling a negative story, we are not giving our audience the most accurate portrait of reality ... The researchers say they are not sure what explains their findings, but they do have a leading contender: The U.S. media is giving the audience what it wants .... When the researchers examined which stories were the most read or the most shared on Facebook they tended to be the most negative stories. To put it another way, the stories that people choose to read skew even more negative than the stories that media organizations choose to publish.[12]

Political scientist Kathleen Hall Jamieson has written that when the press covers issues,

> more often than not it focuses on attack and counterattack, including dismissal of the status quo, which raises the anxiety. The status quo doesn't work, neither do any of the alternatives. That invites cynicism as well. But the press that is the carrier of the message is now inviting cynicism about everyone, including itself. You can't survive that way.[13]

As I wrote in my book *Feeding the Beast*,

> To citizens who wonder why the media are so negative, there is a simple answer: lies. Too many have been told over the years to justify much trust in government. Journalists have been conned and attacked too often by any number of officials at the White House, and by several Presidents, on Watergate, the Vietnam war, the Iran-Contra scandal, the Monica Lewinsky affair, and many other issues.[14]

Just as important, the concept of objective reality is under attack. Charlie Warzel, an analyst for the *New York Times*, wrote in 2020, "My biggest takeaway of the last four years is probably realizing the extent to which big chunks of America are living in a different universe of news/facts with basically no shared reality."[15]

In 2023, CNN chairman and CEO Christ Licht was fired following a series of blunders that attempted to reduce CNN's reputation for overt liberal bias. Joe Walsh, a conservative commentator and former U.S. representative from Illinois took to Twitter to express his thoughts regarding Licht's firing:

> CNN is trying to give America something that, sadly, Americans don't seem to want right now ... CNN is trying to give viewers down-the-middle, balanced programming. But in these hyper-partisan times, viewers don't want that. They want advocacy journalism. Viewers don't want to be informed, they want their own views validated. They want, "My side good, the other side bad" every day. So they tune into MSNBC or Fox News or they go to their super partisan websites every day to get that, and we get more and more divided every day. This needs to change, but I don't see it changing any time soon.[16]

Margaret Sullivan, media columnist for the *Washington Post*, has written,

> [A]s scholars have observed, calling out falsehoods forcefully may actually cause people to hold tighter to their beliefs.

> That's the "backfire effect" that academics Brendan Nyhan and Jason Reifler wrote about in their study "When Corrections Fail" about the persistence of political misperceptions: "Direct factual contradictions can actually strengthen ideologically grounded factual beliefs." …
>
> Most people don't have the time or energy to do research projects on the news they are reading, or the claims they are hearing from the White House, or the conspiracy theories that flood their Facebook feeds.
>
> Most people no longer share with their fellow citizens the trust in news organizations—or in political actors—that would give them confidence in a shared basis of reality. And worst of all, the flow of disinformation on social media is both vile and unstoppable. …
>
> As Americans, we're in trouble when it comes to a common ground of reality on which to stand.
>
> And no amount of fact-checking is going to solve that overwhelming problem.[17]

Despite the credibility gap, the media, especially TV, continue to reward the outlandish, the combative, and the obnoxious with attention, undermining public confidence in journalism. "You want to raise your profile as a member of Congress, raise re-election funds, perhaps try to run for higher office? Become more extreme. Say wilder things and the TV bookers will invite you back," media critic Tom Rosenstiel observed.[18]

Social media platforms such as Twitter and Facebook have exacerbated these trends toward playing up conflict and the negative. And the public believes it's harming the country. Sixty-four percent of Americans said social media have a mostly negative effect on "the way things are going in the country today," according to a Pew Research Center poll. Many are troubled by the misinformation, hate, and harassment they see on social media.[19]

A poll by NBC News in May 2021 found that 64 percent of Americans said social media platforms did more to divide the nation than to bring it together. This included 77 percent of Republicans, 65 percent of independents, and 54 percent of Democrats. Only 27 percent of adults believed social media did more to bring the nation together. In March 2019, 57 percent of respondents had said social media platforms did more to divide the nation while only 35 percent said they did more to unite the country.[20]

Yet social media is becoming a habit. Largely because of the entertainment value, Americans are drawn to social media despite their concerns that the platform intensifies national divisions.

Sixty-six percent of adults say they use social media once a day or more, while only 33 percent say they don't use social media that often, according to the NBC News poll. Forty-nine percent of those who use social media every day say social media platforms make their lives better while only 37 percent say they make their lives worse.[21]

The role of editorial cartoonists over the years provides a microcosm of how the news media have fueled and shaped negativity. The cartoonists were forerunners of today's visual-based media that are drawn to and intensify conflict and hostility, albeit often in the cause of social reform and exposing abuses of power.

"Anyone on social media knows the power of memes to drive home an argument and influence others' views," wrote Patrick J. Kiger on history .com.

> But the tactic of using a viral image to persuade people goes back to long before the existence of the Internet or Facebook. One of its earliest practitioners was American founding father Benjamin Franklin who, in 1754, published a cartoon, "Join, or Die," depicting a snake severed into pieces that symbolized the American colonies.[22]

This first political cartoon, drawn by an unknown artist, was printed in the *Pennsylvania Gazette*, a newspaper published by Franklin. It was designed to bring the American colonists together to fight the French and their Native American allies and persuade the British government to back a unified colonial government during the French and Indian War. Later, the cartoon was used to unite the American colonies in the runup to the Revolutionary War against Britain.

"Franklin's cartoon made such a powerful impression on Americans that it took on a life of its own,"[23] Kiger wrote. During the Stamp Act protests of 1765–66, colonists re-embraced Franklin's design as "a symbol of their desire to unify in opposition to unfair taxation."[24]

In 1774, Paul Revere used a new engraving of the design in the masthead of *The Massachusetts Spy*, and several other pro-rebellion colonial papers followed suit.[25] Today, Franklin's severed snake "remains one of the most famous political cartoons ever published."[26]

Another milestone in the development of the political cartoon was a drawing entitled "King Andrew the First," by another unknown artist and published in 1832 using lithography, a reproduction process that was faster and less expensive than engraving. It depicted President Andrew Jackson clad in royal robes and wearing a crown, trampling the Constitution, all designed to suggest that Jackson was abusing his presidential powers. It was a harsh attack and was widely distributed by Jackson's opponents in the 1832 election campaign, but Jackson won anyway. However, the cartoon showed how visual imagery could capture a moment and spread a theme.

Thomas Nast, who came to the United States from Germany with his family as a boy, drew one of the most memorable and influential political cartoons for *Harper's Weekly* during the presidential campaign of 1864. It showed a Confederate soldier standing confidently as he shakes hands with a peg-legged Union veteran while a woman cries over the grave of another Union soldier. Entitled "Compromise with the South," it blasted American politicians such as Democratic presidential nominee George McClellan for casting doubt on the worth of the Civil War and the enormous sacrifices made by Northern troops. Republican incumbent Abraham Lincoln, seeking a second term, distributed copies of Nast's cartoon widely and it was credited with helping Lincoln win.[27]

"Known as the father of political cartoons, no other artist wielded more power in influencing public opinion of the American political scene than Thomas Nast during the 19th Century," wrote Stella Wei in illustrationhistory.org.[28]

He achieved his fame working at the widely circulated *Harper's Weekly* for 25 years starting in 1862. Readers appreciated what one historian called his "artistic talent, keen political perception, devastating satire, inventive genius, and unquenchable conviction."[29]

One of his achievements was to ridicule the corruption of New York City leader William "Boss" Tweed and his Tammany Hall cronies.

Eventually, Nast had a dispute with his bosses at *Harper's Weekly* and left the publication, which deprived him of access to readers and income. One of the reasons for the falling-out was that his superiors wanted him to tone his cartoon down because they judged, accurately, that middle-class Americans in the late 1800s showed a growing preference for a more civil politics than what Nast was providing. Nast didn't want to comply, and he left his job, never to recover his influence.

"Even though Thomas Nast eventually faded out of popularity, the legacy he left behind is impossible to ignore," Wei wrote.

> During his own days, he not only acted as the pictorial advocator but also contributed to the development of political cartooning in America. The power of his imagery is proved in his success … swaying public opinion, most notably in his achievement defeating the Tammany Ring and Boss Tweed. The symbols and imagery he created such as the dollar sign and the Republican elephant have become an unforgettable element of the American culture.[30]

Over time, in part thanks to Nast's influence, political cartoons in newspapers became known for their biting wit and brutal treatment of public figures. As editorial cartoonist Pat Oliphant has pointed out,

"Cartoonists need villains" and the political system has provided many of them. Oliphant also said, "A legitimate political cartoon has to draw blood."[31]

In the 1884 presidential campaign, the *New York World* ran on Page One a cartoon ridiculing a dinner held by rich supporters of Republican nominee James G. Blaine, entitled "The Royal Feast of Belshazzar Blaine and the Money Kings." It depicted a poor family begging for food from the fat cats. The Democrats spread copies of the cartoon in New York State. Blaine lost the state and the election to Democrat Grover Cleveland.

More recently, Herbert L. Block, known as Herblock, published savage caricatures in the *Washington Post* of Richard Nixon, including a famous cartoon showing the future president emerging from a sewer. In using his cartoons to attack Sen. Joseph McCarthy, R-Wis., for his communist witch hunts during the 1950s, Herblock coined the term, "McCarthyism."

Cartoonists who had strong impact included Nast, Oliphant, Jules Feiffer, and Bill Mauldin.

The influence of political cartoons has diminished, paralleling the overall decline in the influence of newspapers and the rise of visual and electronic media including television and the internet. Americans, especially young people, tend to find editorial cartoons old-fashioned and boring, and they prefer interactive media. Editorial cartoons also require more effort to understand the ideas being conveyed, and Americans apparently don't want to devote the time or energy to following cartoons. And the decline of newspapers in the United States has discouraged owners from investing in cartoonists.

But the mainstream news media's overall addiction to negativity has only gotten more intense, as this chapter has described. It's part of the long-term battle between the entertainment function of the media and the educational function. We in the mainstream news media have leaned too far toward entertaining, not educating.

Notes

1 Dick Morris quoting Clinton to TV interviewer Charlie Rose, 1997, as reported in Rune Olso, *Behind the Curtain of Power.* Pittsburgh, PA: Dorrance Publishing, 2021, 91.
For a more comprehensive discussion of Clinton's views on the media, see Dick Morris, *Behind the Oval Office: Winning the Presidency in the Nineties.* New York: Random House, 1997.

2 Margaret Sullivan, "What Biden—and a Lot of Other People—Get Wrong about Journalists," *Washington Post*, June 22, 2021, downloaded June 28, 2021. https://www.washingtonpost.com/lifestyle/media/media-biden-journalists-negative/2021/06/22/b47db2de-d2a9-11eb-9f29-e9e6c9e843c6_story.html.

3 Megan Brenan, "Americans' Trust in Media Remains Near Record Low," Gallup, October 18, 2022. https://news.gallup.com/poll/403166/americans-trust-media-remains-near-record-low/.
4 Quoted in Oliver Darcy, "Biden Apologizes after Losing Temper While Addressing CNN's Kaitlan Collins: 'I Shouldn't Have Been Such a Wise Guy,'" https://amp.cnn.com/cnn/2021/06/16/media/biden-apology-kaitlan-collins/index.html/.
5 Tim Groeling, *When Politicians Attack! Party Cohesion in the Media*. New York: Cambridge University Press, 2010, 50–1.
6 ibid.
7 Quoted in Robert Mitchell "'Nattering Nabobs of Negativism': The Improbable Rise of Spiro T. Agnew," *Washington Post*, August 8, 2018. https://www.washingtonpost.com/news/retropolis/wp/2018/08/08/nattering-nabobs-of-negativism-the-improbable-rise-of-spiro-t-agnew/.
8 Groeling, 51. See Clinton news conference, May 7, 1993.
9 Groeling, 51.
10 Quoted in Groeling, 43. I also make this point in my book, Kenneth T. Walsh, *Feeding the Beast: The White House Versus the Press*. New York: Random House, 1996, 346–50.
11 David Leonhardt, "Bad News Bias," *New York Times*, March 24, 2021, updated April 22, 2021, www.nytimes.com/2021/03/24/briefing/boulder-shooting-george-segal-astrazeneca.html.
12 ibid.
13 Quoted in Walsh, *Feeding the Beast*, 346–7.
14 ibid., 348.
15 Quoted in Margaret Sullivan, "Fact-Checking Trump Is an Increasingly Fruitless Task," *Washington Post*, August 31, 2020, C1.
16 Joe Walsh, @WalshFreedom, June 8, 2023, 10:09 a.m.
17 Sullivan.
CNN media analyst Brian Stelter also discussed the problem of alternative realities in his 2020 book *Hoax: Donald Trump, Fox News, and the Dangerous Distortion of Truth*. New York: Atria/One Signal, 2020.
18 Tom Rosenstiel, "What Can Journalists Do about the 'Unreality Crisis?'" American Press Institute, www.americanpressinstitute.org/publications/articles/what-can-journaists-do-about-the-unreality-crisis/.
19 Brooke Auxier, "64% of Americans Say Social Media Have a Mostly Negative Effect on the Way Things Are Going in the U.S. Today," pewresearch.org/fact-tank/2020/10/15/64-of-americans-say-social-media-have-a-mostly-negative-effect-on-the-way-things-are-going.
20 Mark Murray "Poll: Nearly Two-Thirds of Americans Say Social Media Platforms Are Tearing Us Apart," May 9, 2021, www.nbcnews.com/politics/meet-the-press/poll-nearly-two-third-americans-say-social-media-platforms-are-n1266773.
21 Murray.
22 Patrick J. Kiger, "How Ben Franklin's Viral Political Cartoon United the 13 Colonies," history.com, October 23, 2018, www.history.com/news/ben-franklin-join-or-die-cartoon-french-indian-war.
23 ibid.
24 ibid.
25 ibid.
26 ibid.

27 Dan Gilgoff, "Political Cartoonists Impact Presidential Races," *U.S. News & World Report*, February 28, 2008, www.usnews.com/news/articles/2008/02/28/political-cartoons-impact-presidential-races.
28 Stella Wei, "Thomas Nast: The Rise and Fall of the Father of Political Cartoons," January 7, 2021, www.illustrationhistory.org/essays/thomas-nast-the-rise-and-fall-of-the-father-of-political-cartoons.
29 John Chalmers Vinson, quoted in Wei.
30 Wei.
31 Patrick Oliphant, "Why Political Cartoonists are Losing Their Influence," NiemanReports, Winter 2004, December 15, 2004, https://niemanreports.org/articles/why-political-cartoons-are-losing-their-influence/.

10

PUBLIC COMMENTATORS AND POLEMICISTS

For many years, public commentators and cultural influencers from outside elective office have used the media to advance their agendas and promote themselves with an emphasis on fear, division, and resentment.

They pioneered or perfected various techniques to increase the effectiveness of toxic politics and were widely imitated. They specialized in inflaming people and generating conflict. They saw themselves and their followers as victims, aggrieved and righteous—and someone else was generally at fault. They cherry-picked facts and shaded stories to ensure their followers felt threatened and disgusted by their neighbors and their government, which is when violence tends to happen. A number of these followers, marinating in fear, proceeded to do things they wouldn't ordinarily do, "as we've seen again and again from Rwanda to the former Yugoslavia," according to journalist Amanda Ripley.[1]

As individuals, the most successful have had much in common. They possessed charisma, drive, and ambition. They were extremely competitive, often ruthless, and preoccupied with winning. In many cases, they had big personalities and huge egos and often exhibited a talent for self-promotion, showmanship, and public relations. They also had a special ability to find the flaws of their opponents and target them in the most effective ways. These are traits that would lead to success for any entrepreneur, not just someone in politics.

Republicans and conservatives dominated the group in recent years, showing a special capacity for inciting and inflaming people, but Democrats have played these roles, too. Liberals seem to have as much interest in promoting negativity as conservatives, but they haven't been as good at it.

DOI: 10.4324/9781003149095-13

My theory is that the conservatives, feeling more aggrieved and resentful and worried that their potential to take or hold power is fading for various reasons, are more willing to say outrageous things and demean their adversaries. This makes them more entertaining and able to draw attention to themselves, their candidates, and their causes, which in turn makes them more effective.

This group is dominated by men. But I believe it's only a matter of time before women gain more influence in the world of toxic politics, as they move further into the top ranks of power, politics, and the media. It has already started happening, at least among public officials. House Speaker Nancy Pelosi (D-CA), didn't pull her punches during her many years as leader of the House of Representatives. She tangled frequently with then-President Donald Trump and Republican leaders in the House and Senate, often exchanging harsh words with them.

Former Secretary of State and 2020 Democratic presidential nominee Hillary Clinton was also tough on her opponents. Attacked and baited by Trump in the 2016 campaign, she called him unfit for the presidency and dismissed Trump's hard-core supporters as a "basket of deplorables."

Rep. Marjorie Taylor Greene, R-Ga., showed an ability to make headlines with her conspiracy theories, including her bogus arguments that the 2020 election was stolen from Trump. Elected in 2020 from a safe GOP district, she targeted Rep. Alexandria Ocasio-Cortez, D-N.Y., whom Greene accused of being pro-terrorism and anti-American. Greene at one point verbally confronted Ocasio-Cortez in the halls of a congressional office building and got a lot of media attention for the gambit. Before she was elected, Greene supported the execution of leading Democratic politicians for supposed treason. Her incendiary remarks and her combative behavior drew a censure from the Democratic majority in the House and as punishment she was temporarily denied committee assignments but, in another illustration of the hyper-partisanship in Washington, committee assignments were restored to her when Republicans took over the House in 2023.

Public commentators and toxic influencers have been part of the American political landscape almost since the beginning of the Republic. They include the following rogues' gallery.

James T. Callender: The First Character Assassin in American Politics

James T. Callender was a Scottish immigrant, pamphleteer, newspaper editor, and writer in the early days of the United States. He took on the role of character assassin.

As a supporter of Thomas Jefferson, in 1797 he published an accusation that Alexander Hamilton, a Jefferson rival, had an affair with Maria Reynolds, a married woman, and had used federal money to illegally speculate in government securities. Callender's anti-Federalist attacks during John Adams' administration resulted in his prosecution under the Sedition Act, which made it a crime to make false statements that were critical of the federal government. He was convicted and in May 1800 began serving nine months in jail and paid a $200 fine.[2]

By the time Callender was released from confinement in the spring of 1801, Jefferson had been elected president, and he expected Jefferson to reward him for his loyalty with the job of postmaster in Richmond, Virginia. Jefferson did pardon him along with others who had been prosecuted under the Sedition Act. But Jefferson had soured on his former defender after concluding that Callender was too radical and offensive. Jefferson even wrote that Callender "presents human nature in a hideous form."[3] Jefferson didn't give Callender the postmaster job.

Callender was enraged, and he made it his mission from then on to embarrass Jefferson and damage him politically. One of his allegations that received widespread attention was the salacious charge that Jefferson fathered several children with Sally Hemings, a slave at Monticello, Jefferson's Virginia estate. Evidence has emerged in recent years that Callender was correct although there were only rumors at the time. DNA studies and other evidence have indicated that Jefferson and Hemings did have a prolonged affair and she bore several of his children.

Callender's original allegation was published during 1802, Jefferson's second year in office, in Callender's Virginia newspaper, the *Richmond Recorder.* He also had it reprinted in the *Literary Gazette* of Walpole, New Hampshire.

Callender wrote:

> It is well known that the man, whom it delighteth the people to honor, keeps, and for many years has kept, as his concubine, one of his own slaves. Her name is Sally. The name of her eldest son is Tom. His features are said to bear a striking although sable resemblance to those of the president himself … By this wench Sally, our President has had several children. There is not an individual in the neighbourhood of Charlottesville who does not believe the story. … The African Venus is said to officiate, as housekeeper, at Monticello.[4]

Law Professor Annette Gordon-Reed has noted that Callender's weak character and partisanship undermined his credibility with historians. "He was a despicable individual ruled by venom and racism," Gordon-Reed said.[5] But there is no doubt that he put the Jefferson-Hemings relationship on the public record for the first time.

After their break, Callender did all he could to undermine Jefferson. Fueling his desire to publicize the Sally Hemings story was Callender's hatred for Black people and his opposition to what he considered the repulsive practice of miscegenation.[6]

"James Callender's modus operandi was to take the basic kernel of truth that existed in a given situation and use his white-hot prose style to exaggerate matters to make a better story,"[7] Gordon-Reed wrote. And he was animated by grievance, anger, and resentment. This is the same approach that other attack specialists have used since then.

Callender had a history of controversy that helps to explain his rise as a shaper of opinion. He was born in Scotland and worked during the 1790s as a political philosopher and pamphleteer. His attacks on Great Britain and its leaders including the King of England became extremely strident. He referred to the British government as a "mass of legislative putrefaction."[8] His treatise "The Political Progress of Britain" was banned by the British government in January 1793. Callender, facing sedition charges, sailed to America in May 1793, hoping to express himself freely in the newly formed United States.[9]

He worked as a journalist in Philadelphia and quickly began attacking aspects of U.S. politics and government. One of his targets was the Constitution's provision to elect the U.S. president through the Electoral College which he branded undemocratic—a criticism still made today. He even criticized George Washington, the nation's first president, for having "debauched" and "deceived" the new nation's citizens by calling too much attention to himself and acting like "an idol."

Callender got the reputation of an extremist. He lost his job as a writer for the *Philadelphia Gazette* and proceeded to produce pamphlets, as he had done in Scotland. Thomas Jefferson noticed him and liked the way he praised Jefferson and his Republican party. Callender was in debt and Jefferson helped him get a job on the *Aurora*, a Republican paper, in addition to giving him money outright. Jefferson wanted Callender to continue his attacks on Federalist leaders, who were increasingly Jefferson's bitter adversaries.

The Callender story ended badly. Condemned as a scurrilous hack and unable to make a decent living, Callender descended into bitterness and alcoholism. He drowned in the James River in July 1803 at the age of 44 or 45. He apparently fell into the water while intoxicated.

Journalist John Dickerson summarized Callender's legacy:

> A scoundrel and a drunk, James Callender has long been treated as a historical cur, but the chaos he unleashed in both parties uncovered the truth that the men of virtue who founded the country were not as virtuous as they pretended, either in their private lives or in the way they

> carried out their public debates. Thomas Jefferson, in particular, was willing to endorse, finance, and encourage the basest personal attacks on his rivals while bemoaning the coarse nature of the public press. It was a hypocrisy that swelled until … Callender punctured it. A country moving toward popular sovereignty was destined to have more of these clashes, as the habits of the elites were brought to the public by the press.

The United States has been facing the consequences ever since.

The Rev. Charles Coughlin: The Pro-Fascist Radio Priest

Father Charles Coughlin was a forerunner of the modern radio and television commentators who spout various forms of populism and prejudice. He pioneered many of the same methods used in recent years by Donald Trump.

The son of a seaman and a seamstress, Coughlin was born on October 25, 1891, in the port town of Hamilton, Ontario, Canada. He was educated at St. Michael's College in Toronto and after considering a career in politics, he entered the Roman Catholic priesthood, ordained in Detroit in 1923. He became a small-town pastor in Michigan but realized he had a gift for public speaking and began broadcasting sermons and speeches on radio. His following grew quickly.[10]

Charismatic and seething with anger, Coughlin exhibited impressive skills as a dramatist and public advocate. He was a direct antecedent of the media evangelists of the later 20th century such as the Revs. Jerry Falwell and Pat Robertson. He also created the format of hostility and attack used by many radio talk-show hosts today. He reached the height of his fame and influence from 1926 to 1942. For a while, his radio audience reached an estimated 30 million listeners per week.[11]

In his biography of Fr. Coughlin, sociologist Donald Warren described the radio priest's influence and audience:

> In his ascendancy he commanded an army of the disaffected that numbered within its ranks elderly pensioners, farmers, rural and small-town merchants, and disillusioned urban middle-class men and women of many religious denominations whose allegiance to the "Good Father" was most often expressed by mailing in one- or two-dollar contributions to his radio program, "The Golden Hour of the Shrine of the Little Flower," broadcast from Royal Oak, Michigan.[12]

As with many would-be American demagogues, including Sen. Joe McCarthy and Trump, Coughlin exploited the nation's fears at a time of widespread, unsettling, and, in some cases, alarming change. He railed against communism, capitalism, Wall Street, big banks, "atheistic Marxists," labor unionism, and "international financiers" (a reference to Jewish bankers), and eventually turned against President Franklin D. Roosevelt for being "anti-God" and a tool of the elites. Coughlin admitted he was taking "the road of fascism" but argued that it was better than the alternatives.[13]

As the Depression worsened in 1930, he became more incendiary and resentful. *The New York Times* reported:

> Father Coughlin started giving his listeners the scapegoats that many seemed to want. ... His first targets were the Communists. "Choose today!" he intoned. "It is either Christ or the Red Fog of Communism!"[14]

In other broadcasts, he attacked "every money-changer in Wall Street," "the wolf in sheep's clothing of conservatism ... bent upon preserving the policies of greed," and then-President Herbert Hoover. He condemned "modern capitalism because by its very nature it cannot and will not function for the common good. In fact, it is a detriment to civilization."

Sociologist Donald Warren explained that

> During the Great Depression of the 1930s radical-right conspiracy theories appealed to many average, middle-class citizens. These victims of economic catastrophe needed to blame someone—some group or malevolent cabal—for destroying their chance to achieve the American dream. Millions of bewildered and angry men and women turned to this radio priest for solace and solutions. In his weekly newspaper, Social Justice, and in his radio broadcasts, the priest became the voice of the people against a political elite and against alien minorities whom they thought were intent on betraying the nation.[15]

After supporting Franklin D. Roosevelt in his successful campaign against Republican incumbent Herbert Hoover in 1932, Coughlin condemned FDR for being too liberal. In June 1936, Coughlin announced that he had formed his own Union Party and would promote Rep. William Lemke, a U.S. representative from North Dakota, as its presidential candidate. But FDR won overwhelmingly, defeating both Lemke and Republican nominee Alf Landon.

As the 1930s progressed, Coughlin's right-wing positions, including favorable comments about dictators Adolf Hitler in Germany and Benito Mussolini in Italy, were troubling his superiors in the Catholic Church. He was rebuked for extremism by his archbishop, Edward Mooney of Detroit, and the Vatican.[16]

After the Japanese attack on the United States at Pearl Harbor and America's entry into World War II against Japan and Germany in 1941, Coughlin claimed that the war was caused by a conspiracy involving FDR, the British, and Jews. This finally took his accusations too far for many of his listeners and he began to lose influence. The Catholic hierarchy forced him to stop his radio programs, and the federal government under Roosevelt's Attorney General Francis Biddle accused Coughlin's magazine of giving aid and comfort to the enemy. The Post Office banned it from using the mail, forcing it out of business.[17]

In an interview on his 77th birthday, long after his heyday, Coughlin displayed an odd combination of defiance and acceptance. He said he

> couldn't honestly take back much of what I said and did in the old days when people still listened to me. ... The press ignored it at the time, but the real reason I couldn't take any more of Roosevelt was because he recognized the atheistic, godless government of the communists in Russia.[18]

He added: "I could have bucked the government and won—the people would have supported me. But I didn't have the heart left, for my church had spoken. It was my duty to follow, for disobedience is a great sin."[19]

He died at age 88 in 1979.

The radio priest was a pioneer in attack politics who showed how effective a preacher-showman could be. As sociologist Warren described it:

> Charles Coughlin's emergence as a national media celebrity defined a critical turning point in American public life and popular culture. He was the first public figure to obliterate the distinction between politics, religion, and mass media entertainment. No longer could the skills of the theater be subordinated to the talents of the policymaker. Both increasingly would be merged in the merchandizing of ideas through the electronically projected sound in the ear and image on the screen. The radio priest stood at the dawn of an age in which radio and later television could create media celebrities who could rival in their power those public figures who held office or claimed a political following.[20]

Pat Buchanan: Grievance Merchant and Riding to the Sound of the Guns

Pat Buchanan was another forerunner of Donald Trump.

Throughout his long career in public life, Buchanan shifted from journalist to pundit to polemicist over the course of a half-century. He ran unsuccessfully for the Republican presidential nomination twice and was the failed Reform Party nominee in his third race. But he remained a strong conservative voice and set a path for conservative populism that endures today.

Even though he never was popular enough to win the White House, Buchanan was very influential in gaining attention for many of the same ideas and tactics that carried Trump to the presidency in 2016. Among them were stirring up anger and resentment among working-class whites against immigrants, globalism, and political elites who seemed to disdain the values and needs of the working class.

Buchanan, born on November 2, 1938, came from a middle-class Roman Catholic family of nine children in Washington, D.C. He remained a practicing Catholic as an adult, and he and his wife attended Mass every Sunday into their old age. He was a reporter for the *St. Louis Globe-Democrat*, became an editorial writer there, and after three-and-a-half years began working as an adviser and speech writer to Richard Nixon in 1965. He shared with Nixon an intense combativeness and hatred of the news media, which they considered far too liberal and biased against conservatives.

Buchanan went on to become a White House speech writer for Nixon and was White House communications director for Ronald Reagan. But he had a falling out with George H.W. Bush, Reagan's vice president, because he didn't think Bush was conservative enough after he was elected president in 1988.

Buchanan directly challenged Bush for the GOP nomination as Bush sought a second term in 1992. Bush already was losing popularity because of an economic downturn on his watch. Buchanan, 53, immediately went on the attack and blamed Bush for the nation's woes. He said Bush had abandoned white working-class Americans as he campaigned in the first-in-the-nation Republican primary election in New Hampshire.

Journalist Jeff Greenfield described Buchanan as coming across as

> cheerfully pugnacious conservative who had spent his adult life shuffling between the political world—speechwriter for Richard Nixon, communications director for Ronald Reagan—and the media, where he wrote columns and was a frequent face on TV shows ranging from the *McLaughlin Group* to *Crossfire* to *The Capital Gang*. ... Go back to it now and what's striking is how much his message, delivered on December 10, 1991, in Concord offered a remarkable preview not so much of that year's race, but of what would drive the appeal of Donald Trump in 2016.[21]

Buchanan condemned the elitism of the political establishment of both major parties and accused the elites of ignoring everyday people. He urged the president to put "Americans first," declared that globalization was hurting the United States, questioned whether the United States should continue to pay for the defense of allies abroad, criticized Israel and its "amen corner" of Jewish supporters in the United States, said immigration was excessive, and argued that "our Western heritage" was being diluted.

Greenfield traced the roots of Trump's 2016 campaign to Buchanan's failed primary run.

> [T]o a remarkable extent, just about all of the themes of Trump's campaign can be found in Buchanan's insurgent primary run a quarter-century ago: the grievances, legitimate and otherwise; the dark portrait of a nation whose culture and sovereignty are threatened from without and within; the sense that the elites of both parties have turned their backs on hard-working, loyal, traditional Americans.[22]

Buchanan also found a receptive audience in calls for Americans to take sides in a "religious war" and a "cultural war" that he said were intensifying in the United States. Buchanan won 37 percent of the vote in the New Hampshire primary in 1992, and he won nearly 23 percent of the ballots and nearly 3 million votes nationwide in all the GOP primaries, carrying no states but throwing a scare into the Bush campaign. Even though he lost the nomination, Buchanan emerged as a populist hero of sorts because of his pugnacity and his stands including opposition to abortion and gay rights. Bush lost that November, in part because Buchanan had undermined him among many conservatives.

Four years later, Buchanan narrowly won the New Hampshire GOP primary with 27 percent in a divided field. Buchanan went further in attempting to lead an anti-establishment movement declaring, "They hear the shouts of the peasants from over the hill. All the knights and barons will be riding into the castle pulling up the drawbridge in a minute. All the peasants are coming with pitchforks." He failed to win the GOP nomination again in 1996 as the party went for Sen. Bob Dole of Kansas, another establishment favorite who lost the 1996 general election to Democratic incumbent Bill Clinton. But Buchanan emerged from the campaign with his reputation reaffirmed as a strong conservative and populist voice.

In 2000, Buchanan won the Reform Party nomination for president but did poorly in the general election, gaining only 445,000 votes, largely because he seemed too strident and extreme.[23]

After his campaigns, he became highly visible as a TV commentator and syndicated columnist although he alienated many people with his streams of invective on television and as the author of several books.

As a conservative TV star, he filled shows such as "Crossfire" and "The McLaughlin Group" with caustic commentary, shaping a TV format that remains prevalent today.

Journalist Tim Alberta describes Buchanan's legacy in *Politico*:

> It's the one element of his legacy to which he attaches some regret, repeatedly citing the poisonous tone of cable news discourse as a culprit in our societal and cultural disunion. He invaded America's living rooms and pioneered the rhetorical combat that would power the cable news age. He defied the establishment by challenging a sitting president of his own party. He captured the fear and frustration of the right by proclaiming a great "culture war" was at hand. ... His radically different prescription, which would underpin three consecutive runs for the presidency: a "new nationalism" that would focus on "forgotten Americans" left behind by bad trade deals, [opposition to] open-border immigration policies and foreign adventurism.[24]

Buchanan's prominence declined in recent years as he was accused of being antisemitic, racially insensitive, and too extreme in other ways, allegations he denied. MSNBC, known for its liberal orientation, fired him in 2012 after a decade as a commentator. The cause was analysis from Buchanan in his book, *Suicide of a Superpower*, especially a chapter called "The End of White America" in which he condemned the "mass invasion" of the United States by poor immigrants.[25]

Yet Pat Buchanan cleared the path and set the precedents for Trump's successful campaign in 2016 and his presidency. Buchanan even used a campaign slogan, "Make America First Again," that Trump echoed with his slogan, "Make America Great Again." In fundamental ways, Trump was Buchanan's political descendant.

Rush Limbaugh: Firebrand, Incendiary, Entertainer

The rise of the mass media during the past 100 years has spawned a snarl of commentators who practiced, coarsened, and helped to contaminate public discourse. Among them were television personalities Sean Hannity, Bill O'Reilly, Tucker Carlson, and Laura Ingraham on the right and iconoclastic firebrands Joe Pyne, Morton Downey Jr., Allen Burke, and Bob Grant. But the most influential was Rush Limbaugh.

Many veteran political strategists were critical of these "talking heads" because they used so much vitriol to get attention and had little or no consistent political philosophy. Frank Donatelli, former White House political director for President Ronald Reagan and a respected conservative strategist for many years, pointed out that the incendiary commentators in many cases "never worked in government and never worked in a campaign."[26] They talked on TV or radio and wrote books or gave speeches without a clear agenda of ideas underpinning their comments. Instead,

Donatelli said, "it was with the idea of riling people up and creating hostility and grievance."[27]

Limbaugh set the pace. He rose to fame during the 1990s because of his popular radio show. He loved to be outrageous and specialized in insults, innuendoes, and attacks. He made them more palatable because he infused them with humor. Limbaugh could be very entertaining, which was his greatest strength as a commentator and shaper of public opinion. And he paved the way for Trump by showing that mockery and harsh attacks were more important than serious policy discussions in building a following. Trump roared into the presidency based on his use of these techniques. Trump awarded Limbaugh the Presidential Medal of Freedom in 2020.

Conservative radio host and former Congressman Joe Walsh described Limbaugh's towering influence on the conservative media.

> He was fearless, irreverent, funny and a great talker. Other talkers soon followed. Limbaugh created the entire industry of conservative talk radio, and he remained the king of the hill. ... His daily three hours on the air became all about attacking and mocking the left, and I grew to not believe a lot of what he was saying. His problems with the truth were my giant red flag.[28]

In 2021, media analyst Paul Farhi analyzed Limbaugh's profound influence.

> Since leaping from a local station in Sacramento to nationally syndicated stardom in 1988, Limbaugh has been the bullhorn behind every important conservative initiative, from the "Contract With America" [a right-wing manifesto by House Republicans in the mid-1990s], to the tea party movement [a hard-line populist surge] of the Obama era to the ascent of Donald Trump.
>
> From his earliest days on the air, Limbaugh trafficked in conspiracy theories, divisiveness, even viciousness ("feminazis" was one of his infamous coinages). He created what Columbia University historian Nicole Hemmer calls a kind of "political entertainment" that partially supplanted traditional conservatism.[29]

Here is a sampling of Limbaugh's comments:[30]

- "Feminism was established so that unattractive ugly broads could have easy access to the mainstream."
- "The N.A.A.C.P. should have riot rehearsal. They should get a liquor store and practice robberies."

- "The N.F.L. all too often looks like a game between the Bloods and the Crips without any weapons. There, I said it."
- "If any race of people should not have guilt about slavery, it's Caucasians."
- "Holocaust? Ninety million Indians? Only four million left? They all have casinos—what's to complain about?"

He also referred to 12-year-old Chelsea Clinton, daughter of President Bill Clinton, as a dog;[31] said the lethal coronavirus was actually the common cold; argued falsely that Biden had stolen the 2020 presidential election from Trump; and spread the false allegation that President Barack Obama wasn't born in the United States, supposedly making him an illegitimate president.[32]

Born on January. 12, 1951, in Cape Girardeau, Missouri, Limbaugh's father was a lawyer, as were his grandfather, brother, and uncle. He dropped out of Southeast Missouri State University after two semesters because he was bored. At age 20, he became a disc jockey at WIXZ in McKeesport, Pennsylvania under the name "Bachelor Jeff." He left after 18 months in 1973 and moved from station to station before landing at WABC, a talk radio AM station in New York City where he became a hit and which remained his flagship station for many years.[33]

"The Rush Limbaugh Show," his radio program, became the most listened-to radio show in the United States, at one point in the 2010s attracting 15.5 million listeners weekly.[34]

To many, the damage he caused was enormous. Former U.S. Rep. Joe Walsh wrote that

> the greatest harm of Limbaugh's legacy [was] the destruction of truth, the manipulation of his audience and the promotion of conspiracies. This area of dishonesty I find most troubling because it is pervasive in the conservative media world and Limbaugh led the way on lies and disinformation for most of his career. ... [B]y so demonizing the left, [he] so contributed to the ugly and dangerous polarization of our politics today. And by trafficking in so many lies and conspiracy theories, [he] helped ensure that a sizable segment of the American voting population no longer believes in basic truths. It will take years to undo this.[35]

Conservative commentator Charles Sykes, a veteran talk-radio host, wrote that Limbaugh for a while made conservative ideas more popular, such as tax cuts and less regulation.

But his legacy is double edged. Limbaugh pioneered the rise of the outrage/entertainment wing to dominance in the GOP, a project that culminated in Trump's presidency and a political culture that is driven less by facts and substance than by snark, sophistry, and alternative realities.

While his friends described him as gracious and generous, Limbaugh also cultivated an insensitivity that normalized cruelty, racism, and misogyny.[36]

In 2020, Limbaugh announced he had late-stage lung cancer. He died of the disease in February 2021 at age 70.

Sean Hannity: Trump Cheerleader

Sean Hannity emerged in 2016 as a leading shaper and reinforcer of conservative opinion and defender of Donald Trump through his radio show and his TV program on Fox News.

Hannity was born on December 30, 1961, in New York City, the only son of first-generation immigrants from Ireland. His father Hugh was an officer in New York City's family court system and his mother Lillian was a corrections officer and court stenographer. Sean Hannity was raised in Franklin Square, a suburban community on Long Island, attended local Catholic schools, and took classes at Adelphi University, New York University, and the University of California at Santa Barbara but didn't graduate from college. He left school to pursue a career in radio.[37]

Hannity worked as an unpaid volunteer host at KCSB, a radio station at the University of California at Santa Barbara college station. In 1989 he claimed that gays were the cause of the AIDS crisis, and he called it a "gay disease." He also criticized a gay host on KCSB and was fired. He was given the opportunity to return but instead parlayed his conservative views into a paid job at WVNN in Alabama in 1990. He moved to WGST in Atlanta in 1992 as his popularity grew in right-wing circles partly because of his bluntness and his insults against liberals, gays, and other groups he disliked.[38]

He became known as a rising star among conservatives including Newt Gingrich, who was then an ambitious conservative leader in Georgia trying to make a name for himself. Hannity moved to different radio stations, and in 2001 his show went into national syndication and aired on 500 stations, greatly increasing his following. By 2020, it was estimated that he had 13.5 million listeners, just short of Rush Limbaugh's total.[39]

In 1996, the fledgling conservative television network Fox News hired Hannity as one of its first prime-time hosts. He ran a popular program for 13 years with liberal commentator Alan Colmes and started his own TV show, "Hannity," on Fox in 2009. By early 2018, he averaged 3.2 million nightly TV viewers and had become a leading conservative voice nationally.

He was an ardent supporter of Trump's presidential campaign in 2016, interviewing Trump repeatedly on his television program. The media star backed Trump's false claims that President Barack Obama had not been born in the United States which if true would have made Obama's election unconstitutional. He also echoed Trump's claims that 2016 Democratic presidential nominee Hillary Clinton's health was failing, and he echoed Trump again in the 2020 campaign by alleging that Democratic nominee Joe Biden was in poor mental and physical health.[40]

Hannity also served privately as an adviser to candidate Trump and to President Trump after he won the White House in 2016. He also wrote several books including *America (and the World) on the Brink* in 2020.

"Hannity and Trump worked hand in hand to tar practically the entire American news media as 'fake.' Both men's hypnotic message was that Fox was the only legit network while everyone else was fraudulent," CNN media analyst Brian Stelter said.[41]

Analyst Jane Eisner added that the Hannity-Trump message shaped "the workings of the federal government" during Trump's presidency. She wrote that,

> By mid-2020, according to Stelter, 20 people had jumped from the [Fox] network to the White House, including a member of the Cabinet and a deputy chief of staff. The pipeline flows in the other direction as well. This isn't just a matter of an administration hiring like-minded acolytes; it meant that the Fox worldview would directly affect American policy and American lives.[42]

Stelter has pointed out that Hannity and other Fox commentators, echoing Trump, dismissed or minimized the threat of the coronavirus and praised Trump's mismanagement of the deadly pandemic and overlooked the economic consequences.

Hannity did all he could to win re-election for Trump in 2020. He made it known that he spoke to Trump regularly on the phone and brought the president on his show for interviews. He spent endless hours on his nightly program praising Trump and deriding Biden as "the weak, the frail, the cognitively struggling Biden." After Biden won, Hannity adopted Trump's bogus arguments that the Democrats stole the election through fraud and corruption.

This post-election period showed how deeply Hannity had burrowed into Trump's world and become a negative force in his own right. Hannity, at the time Fox News' most popular personality, could not let go of his conspiracy theories. In the *Washington Post*, Sarah Ellison and Jeremy Barr wrote:

> For a few weeks, it manifested as the denial shared by his fellow believers in the ex-president's unsupported claims of election fraud. After the inauguration of the new president, Hannity pivoted to the next stage—anger—as he lashed out at ... Biden. More recently, he has displayed something closer to depression, as he engages his viewers in a session of public mourning. "My heart's troubled," he told his on-air colleague Laura Ingraham. "It's aching for my country night now."[43]

As of this writing in late 2023, Hannity's vitriol toward Biden continued unabated.

Hannity used his TV show to give Trump a forum and build his own audience by luring Trump fans. In March 2023, Trump used a long interview with Hannity to descend to new lows by promoting his fake conspiracy theories, claiming that he was being unfairly attacked, arguing that he was becoming a political martyr because his opponents were so afraid of him, viciously hammering his critics, and warning that the United States would be ruined if he was not elected again as president. There was no pushback from Hannity, only praise for Trump.[44]

He had decided, it seemed, that his success as a commentator depended on being popular with Trump conservatives. "Hannity had come to see conservatives as not just a political movement, but a cultural tribe" and his audience was "vanguard of a crusade to restore a fading culture" that once celebrated white men and conservative values, Marc Fisher wrote in the *Washington Post*.[45]

Kellyanne Conway, a former senior White House adviser to Trump, has said, "Donald Trump and Sean Hannity are both disrupters of the status quo. Disrupters project a strength and moxie that fascinates some people and causes envy in others."[46] And a Trump loyalist said, "Sean gets programming and the president gets a platform for his message."[47] It was a synergy that suited each man's purposes to a T.

Tucker Carlson: Unrelenting Attacker and Outrage Peddler

Tucker Carlson made a daring career move in the early 2020s—attempting to become the principal media defender, promoter, and definer of Donald Trump and his poisonous style of conservatism. This continued after Trump was defeated in the 2020 election and after he began another White House campaign for 2024. The gambit succeeded in making Carlson the hottest property in conservative media for a while and greatly expanded his influence, at least in right-wing circles and among Trump followers.

Carlson's worship of Trump apparently was a façade. In text messages in early 2023, revealed in a court case, Carlson called Trump "a demonic force, a destroyer" and said, "I hate him passionately." But these views didn't prevent Carlson from continuing to praise Trump during the commentator's TV shows and lend credence to the former president's bogus claims that the 2020 election was rigged against him and that he really won.[48]

Washington Post media critic Margaret Sullivan wrote:

> Carlson is dangerous because he has a cultlike following who believe his nightly rants ... But it's important to remember what Carson is: nothing more than an outrage machine. What he offers is not political commentary. It's Fox-approved nonsense meant to juice ratings—and it works. ... The millions who tune in to Carlson every night to get their outrage on should remember what their favorite host traffics in: bloviating, demagoguery and unrighteous indignation. And they should remember what he *isn't* obligated to deal in: the truth. Among Carlson gambits that drew Sullivan's ire were taking Russian President Vladimir Putin's side and defending Russia's invasion of Ukraine starting in February 2022, blasting U.S. President Joe Biden for failing to back Putin, and calling Putin morally superior to "permanent Washington."[49]

Carlson's hostility was part of a larger trend that Carlson came to embody. Journalist Matt Bai observed:

> Tremors rocked the political establishment as a parade of celebrities and self-styled reformers—Ross Perot, Jesse Ventura, Arnold Schwarzenegger—moved to exploit the sudden vulnerability of industrial-age parties. Then came Barack Obama's toppling of the Democratic order in 2008—a sign that personality and identity had at last supplanted party machines.[50]

Carlson increasingly resorted to outrageous comments and conspiracy theories, emphasizing attacks on Democrats, liberals, and Trump's adversaries including Biden and House Speaker Nancy Pelosi, D-Calif. His goal was to remain close to Trump as the former president attempted to keep control of the Republican Party as he began his 2024 run for the presidency. Carlson also knew that he was likely to keep his high ratings on Fox if he kept trumpeting Trump, who retained a strong following among viewers of the network.

In fact, this fealty to Trump and the ex-president's often false accusations got Carlson into trouble because he became such a shill for the former president. Critics said he pushed the Trump line and Trump lies rather than contradict him because challenging Trump would have cost Carlson and Fox News viewers.[51] Whatever the journalistic ethics, Carlson's gambits succeeded in a hard-boiled marketing sense.

Carlson's show drew an average of three million viewers a night and he was described as "the most watched host on cable news" in 2021.[52]

After a police officer was convicted of murdering an African American named George Floyd in Minneapolis, Carlson speculated that the jury convicted the cop to avoid mob violence in the streets. This caused outrage among many African American leaders and Democratic officials but increased Carlson's popularity with some Americans who favored strict law and order and defended the police.

Carlson's caustic ferocity was part of a larger media strategy based on negativity. Columnist David Von Drehle wrote in the *Washington Post*:

> The old business model [in the communications business] involved huge audiences with little in common; in the digital age—the era of infinite choices—success lies in limited audiences cemented by shared passion. Among the first to appreciate this radical shift was media mogul Rupert Murdoch and his ruthless Rasputin, Roger Ailes. At a time when the television news business was still dominated by networks offering a sort of anodyne neutrality with a Bos-NY-Wash high liberal gloss, their Fox News Channel set out to feed the nation's passionate Republican base. Their colleagues were shocked and envious at the money this strategy generated, and the rest—alas—is our recent history. At Fox News these days, no one wields the sledgehammer like Tucker Carlson.[53]

All this was surprising in view of Carlson's Establishment roots. He grew up in exclusive La Jolla, California, and attended prep school in Rhode Island. He was the son of wealthy executive and prominent Republican Richard Carlson, and Tucker Carlson always enjoyed a life of privilege. Eventually, he set about stirring up resentful conservatives as one of his main career goals as a commentator. Glib, handsome, and perky, he started on the TV show "Crossfire" on CNN in which he argued the conservative side of issues with a liberal co-host. The show was canceled, and Tucker Carlson then tried to play the consummate right-wing commentator on MSNBC, a liberal-oriented network, but it didn't work out.

Von Drehle said,

> He seems determined not to let that happen again and will say anything—anything—to stoke his small but passionate Fox News primetime audience—around 3 million viewers per day, typically among the largest on cable news but only about half the crowd that watches CBS's "Young Sheldon."

One of Carlson's gambits in the spring of 2021 was to support "white replacement theory"—the idea that Democrats are "importing" migrants of color who will vote Democratic, sink the Republicans politically, and damage the culture of white people.

Carlson argued, according to *Washington Post* writer Greg Sargent, that "liberals and Democrats are scheming to replace virtuous native U.S. voters by importing as many immigrants as possible, ideally from the Third World (because they are 'obedient,' Carlson tells us) to dilute their political agency and extinguish their culture."[54]

States that have experienced a surge of migrants have become "unrecognizable," Carlson said.[55]

He also used attacks on journalists and their news organizations to stir up Trumpers and keep them watching his show. Among his targets have been the *New York Times*, the *Los Angeles Times*, and long-time White House correspondent and TV commentator April Ryan, who is African American.

In the *Washington Post*, Jeremy Barr observed:

> Organizations that call out Carlson risk entering into a never-ending back-and-forth with the host, who often laments efforts to "silence" him and turns criticisms of his show into a night's A-block of programming. After Carlson mocked the [*New York*] *Times*'s statement on his March 10 show [regarding a quarrel he was having with the newspaper about online harassment of women], reading it in a dramatic, sarcastic tone, above an on-screen graphic that read "*New York Times* Knows All About Actual Harassment," the newspaper chose not to respond.[56]

Carlson, at the relatively young age of 52, was attempting to take over Trump's political and theatrical mantles after Trump left the presidency, columnist Frank Bruni wrote in the *New York Times*.

> Moving to fill the empty space created by Trump's ejection from the White House, his banishment from social media and his petulant quasi-hibernation, Carlson is triggering the libs like Trump triggered the libs. He's animating the pundits like Trump animated the pundits.[57]

On April 26, 2021, Carlson condemned mask-wearing to combat the coronavirus, a practice that was recommended by health officials to keep the virus from spreading. Carlson said it was a worthless infringement on liberty and he said requiring children to wear masks should be illegal. He told viewers of his show:

> Your response when you see children wearing masks as they play should be no different from your response to seeing someone beat a kid in Walmart. Call the police immediately. Contact child protective services. Keep calling until someone arrives. ... What you're looking at is abuse. It's child abuse and you are morally obligated to attempt to prevent it.[58]

"Night after night, Carlson stokes resentment," journalist Michael Kranish reported. "He blasts liberals, throttles Republican leaders whom he sees as insufficiently devoted to battling the 'woke' left, and generally sets the parameters for the far-right anti-elitism that defines today's GOP."[59]

"Carlson has used his influence to spread unfounded claims that have been embraced by many Republican leaders," Kranish added. "He has echoed Trump's falsehood that the election was 'rigged.' He promoted the baseless notion that FBI agents were behind the storming of the Capitol."[60]

And although he has described himself as "pretty pro-vaccine," Carlson has questioned the efficacy of vaccination against the coronavirus, saying, "maybe it doesn't work and they're simply not telling you that"—leading President Biden's chief medical adviser Anthony S. Fauci to rebut his "crazy conspiracy theory."[61]

He also loves to insult those with whom he disagrees. When Gen. Mark A. Milley, chairman of the Joint Chiefs of Staff, said he wanted to learn more about white rage and the role that racism plays in America, Carlson called him "a pig" and "stupid."[62]

These were examples of how Carlson used toxic politics to ascend to the top of the conservative commentariat.

Carlson also moved into the isolationist camp in assessing foreign policy, another effort to endear himself with conservatives unhappy with the Washington Establishment. Carlson condemned the Biden administration's support for Ukraine after Russia invaded that country in 2022. The pundit said the United States was wasting its money in supporting Ukraine, which he argued was not worth saving from Russia.

Carlson was in effect siding with the authoritarian, expansionist regime of Vladimir Putin, departing from many years of conservative and Establishment opposition to the Kremlin's territorial designs.

Carlson abruptly left Fox in 2023 to make his way as a conservative thinker, provocateur, and performer at other venues.

Notes

1 Amanda Ripley, "Help Tucker Carlson Help Himself," *Washington Post*, June 13, 2023, A19.
2 John Dickerson, "The Original Attack Dog," *Slate*, August 9, 2016, https://slate.com/news-and-politics/2018/08/james-callender-the-attack-dog-who-took-aim-at-alexander-hamilton-and-thomas-jefferson.html.

3 Thomas Jefferson, "From Thomas Jefferson to James Monroe, 15 July 1802," National Archives: *Founders Online* https://founders.archives.gov/documents/Jefferson/01-38-02-0069.
4 "Sally Hemings and Thomas Jefferson ... Callender's Historic Accusatory Letter," www.rarenewspapers.com/view/593716.
5 Annette Gordon-Reed, *Thomas Jefferson and Sally Hemings: An American Controversy*. Charlottesville, VA: University of Virginia Press, 1997. 59.
6 ibid., 60–1.
7 ibid., 78.
8 Dickerson.
9 "James Thomson Callender," *Thomas Jefferson Encyclopedia*. Monticello Research and Education. https://www.monticello.org/research-education/thomas-jefferson-encyclopedia/james-callender/.
10 The Editors of *Encyclopedia Britannica*, "Charles E. Coughlin," *Encyclopedia Britannica*, October 23, 2022. https://www.britannica.com/biography/Charles-E-Coughlin.
11 Albin Krebs, "Charles Coughlin, 30's 'Radio Priest,'" *New York Times*, October 28, 1979, 44. www.nytimes.com/1979/10/28/archives/charles-coughlin-30s-radio-priest-dies-fiery-sermons-stirred-furor.html.
12 Donald Warren, *Radio Priest: Charles Coughlin, the Father of Hate Radio*. New York: Free Press, 1996, 1–2.
13 ibid.
14 Krebs.
15 Warren, 2.
16 Krebs.
17 ibid.
18 Quoted in Krebs.
19 Quoted in Krebs.
20 Warren, 6–7.
21 Jeff Greenfield, "Trump Is Pat Buchanan With Better Timing," *Politico*, September/October 2016, www.politico.com/magazine/story/2016/09/donald-trump-pat-buchanan-republican-america-first-nativist-214221/.
22 ibid.
23 The Editors of *Encyclopedia Britannica*, "Pat Buchanan," *Encyclopedia Britannica*, March 9, 2023. https://www.britannica.com/biography/Patrick-J-Buchanan/.
24 Tim Alberta, "The Ideas Made It, But I Didn't," *Politico* May/June 2017, www.politico.com/magazine/story/2017/04/22/pat-buchanan-trump-president-history-profile-215042/.
25 ibid.
26 Author's interview with Frank Donatelli, April 6, 2021.
27 ibid.
28 Joe Walsh, "Rush Limbaugh Leaves Behind a Conservative Movement No Longer Interested in Truth. That Alarms Me as a Conservative," *Time*, retrieved February 17, 2021, time.com/5915574/rush-limbaugh-dies-legacy/.
29 Paul Farhi, "The Ailing State of Limbaugh and His Industry," *Washington Post*, February 10, 2021, C1.
30 This and all quotes in this section were quoted in Talmon Joseph Smith, "Rush Limbaugh in His Own Words," *New York Times*, February 7, 2020, updated July 22, 2020, https://www.nytimes.com/2020/02/07/sunday-review/rush-limbaugh-trump-medal.html.
31 Todd Leopold, "Limbaugh Revels in the Crossfire after Fluke Comments," *CNN*, March 8, 2012, https://www.cnn.com/2012/03/05/us/rush-limbaugh-controversy/index.html.

32 Joe Walsh.
33 Ze'ev Chafets interview, *All Right Magazine*, August 3, 2010, 35.
34 Brian Wheeler, "Can Limbaugh Survive Advertiser Boycott?" *BBC News Magazine*, March 5, 2012, www.bbc.co.uk/news/magazine-17263546. Also see Ze'ev Chavets, *Rush Limbaugh: An Army of One*. New York: Sentinel, 2010. See also Katherine Q. Seelye, "Republicans Get a Pep Talk from Rush Limbaugh," *New York Times*, December 12, 1994, A16.
35 Joe Walsh.
36 Charles Sykes, "We're All Living in Rush Limbaugh's World," *Washington Post*, February 18, 2021, A23.
37 Marc Fisher, "The Making of Sean Hannity: How a Long Island Kid Learned to Channel Red-State Rage," *Washington Post*, October 20, 2017, https://www.washingtonpost.com/lifestyle/style/the-making-of-sean-hannity-how-a-long-island-kid-learned-to-channel-red-state-rage/2017/10/09/540cfc38-8821-11e7-961d-2f373b3977ee_story.html.
38 ibid.
39 "Sean Hannity," Biography.com, last updated July 22, 2020, https://www.biography.com/movies-tv/sean-hannity.
40 ibid.
41 Quoted in Jane Eisner, "Fox News's Retreat from Journalism," *Washington Post*, August 30, 2020, B1.
42 Eisner.
43 Sarah Ellison and Jeremy Barr, "Hannity Is the Face of Fox's Identity Crisis," *Washington Post*, February 4, 2021, C1.
44 Dominick Mastrangelo, "Hannity Gets 20 Percent Ratings Boost Thanks to Trump Interview," *The Hill,* March 29, 2023, https://thehill.com/homenews/media/3923554-hannity-gets-20-percent-ratings-boost-thanks-to-trump-interview/.
45 Fisher.
46 ibid.
47 ibid.
48 Dana Milbank, "Trump Makes Suckers of House Republicans. Again," *Washington Post*, March 26, 2023, A25.
49 Margaret Sullivan, "After His Defense of Putin, Fox News Should Say 'Do Svidaniya' to Carlson," *Washington Post*, February 25, 2022, C1.
50 Matt Bai, "What Will History Say about Trump?" *Washington Post*, November 18, 2020, https://www.washingtonpost.com/opinions/2020/11/18/what-will-history-say-about-trump/.
51 Jeremy Barr, "Murky Job Description for Fox's Top Hosts," *Washington Post*, March 21, 2023, C1.
52 Jeremy Barr, "The Bully Pulpit," *Washington Post*, April 16, 2021, C1. Also see Frank Bruni, "The New Trump? Easy. It's Tucker," *New York Times*, May 2, 2021, Sunday Review, 3.
53 David Von Drehle, "Carlson Is Making Bank. Making Sense, Not So Much," *Washington Post*, April 14, 2021, A25.
54 Greg Sargent, "Opinion: The Hidden Scam behind Tucker Carlson and the Right's 'Replacement' Game," *Washington Post*, April 23, 2021, https://www.washingtonpost.com/opinions/2021/04/23/tucker-carlson-replacement-rhetoric-scam/.
55 Ibid.
56 Barr, "The Bully Pulpit."
57 Frank Bruni, "The New Trump? Easy. It's Tucker," *New York Times*, May 2, 2021, Sunday Review, 3.

58 Quoted in Margaret Sullivan, "Mask-Fearing Carlson Needs to Be Muzzled," *Washington Post*, April 28, 2021, C1.
59 Michael Kranish, "How Carlson Became Voice of White Grievance," *Washington Post*, July 15, 2021, A1.
60 ibid.
61 ibid.
62 ibid.

11

PROSELYTIZERS OF DIVISION, ENTREPRENEURS OF POLARIZATION, AND OPERATIVES OF ATTACK

During recent decades, there has been a rise in the prominence and power of professional proselytizers, fiery ideologues and political operators who specialized in riding waves of negativity. They pioneered or perfected various techniques to increase the effectiveness of toxic politics and were widely imitated. Often, they were attack entrepreneurs who made money by specializing in negativity as their business model. Journalist Amanda Ripley calls them "conflict entrepreneurs"—people who exploit and inflame conflict for their own ends.[1]

Entrepreneurs of negativity have been part of American life almost from the start of the Republic and their influence, unfortunately, is growing. This section of the book describes some of the most important among them, shows the themes and techniques in which they specialized, and assesses their impact.

Richard Viguerie: Maestro of Direct Mail

Richard Viguerie pioneered the strategy of using direct mail to promote his ideology and undermine adversaries by alarming and frightening aggrieved Americans. This coarsened American campaigns and showed that negative politics could be financially profitable.

"He was the maestro of direct mail," says historian Rick Perlstein, who has studied modern American conservatism.

> He was the guy who figured out that the bigger the mailing list you had and the more terrifying the letters you sent to this mailing list about

DOI: 10.4324/9781003149095-14

> how liberals were going to, you know, end Western civilization as we know it, the better you could do for politicians. And one of the things that it was so effective for, it was a very stealthy strategy.[2]

Viguerie explained his philosophy of negativity this way:

> You see, in an ideological cause like this, people give money not to win friends, but to defeat enemies. You like to change human nature, but you can't—people are more strongly motivated by negative issues than positive ones. When there are no negatives or enemies, the appeal isn't strong.[3]

Viguerie became a political legend among Republicans after the GOP made substantial gains in the 1978 congressional elections. There were "all these conservative results that no one saw coming," said commentator Dave Davies, "because they didn't realize that this guy, Richard Viguerie, was sending out millions of direct mail pieces that were, you know, basically scaring the bejesus out of these ... rural, conservative folk."[4]

Viguerie pioneered using direct mail as a fund-raising tool. After he showed the way, both conservatives and liberals used the same techniques for their own causes and purposes. Among his sales tricks was developing questionnaires on issues and candidates to give direct-mail recipients a sense of participating in a larger enterprise, even though their opinions carried little or no weight for Viguerie's operation or for the candidates he supported. He also used direct appeals from a candidate's spouse as a fund-raising gambit, and offered donors the chance to enter a drawing in which the winner would spend time with the candidate.[5]

Viguerie once said it was Sen. Joe McCarthy, R-Wis., who inspired him to become a conservative. McCarthy, whose role in negative politics is discussed extensively in a previous chapter, argued that there were dangerous communists in the U.S. government and in other institutions such as the armed forces and the entertainment industry. Viguerie said, "I believed in what McCarthy did. Even when he was inaccurate, he articulated the concern about a very big problem. There are Communists in this world and that is not a figment of a few right-wingers' imaginations."[6]

Born on September 23, 1933, in Golden Acres, Texas, the son of a petrochemical executive and a nurse, Viguerie graduated from the University of Houston in 1957 and took an interest in conservative politics.

In the early sixties, Viguerie worked as a conservative activist for Young Americans for Freedom and played a key role in the ascendancy of the New Right, which updated conservatism for the last quarter of the 20th century and made it more aggressive and caustic. He "had a much grander ideological plan: to use single-issue groups to build a conservative majority that would topple the New Deal coalition" built by liberal President Franklin D. Roosevelt in the 1930s and early 1940s, according to scholar Daniel Scholzman.[7]

Viguerie worked for racist, right-wing Gov. George Wallace of Alabama to help retire Wallace's debt from his unsuccessful presidential campaign in 1972. "George Wallace provided a way station for his supporters, mostly Southerners, on their road to supporting Ronald Reagan and the Republican Party," Schlozman wrote.

> Richard Viguerie was a critical mechanism in that transformation. In exchange for unusually lenient terms—Wallace netted half the proceeds, rather than the usual quarter—the Viguerie Co. received the 3 million names on Wallace's mailing list. Viguerie ultimately raised more than $7 million for Wallace.[8]

Viguerie said he and Wallace

> agreed on about 80% of the important issues, social issues like busing and law and order, and the need for a strong national defense. So we struck a bargain. ... My working for Wallace, although I don't think I realized it at the time, was the beginning of my thinking in terms of coalition politics.[9]

He also helped Wallace run for president in 1976, this time in a bid for the Democratic presidential nomination. Wallace was headed for another defeat when he endorsed fellow Southerner Jimmy Carter, the centrist former governor of Georgia, with Viguerie arguing that his direct-mail operation had shifted the campaign themes to the right. Viguerie emerged even stronger as a rising conservative operative who showed that negative campaigning could work very effectively for candidates on the right.

Direct mail—appealing to individual voters rather than raising money from a few big donors—had the effect of pushing politicians into making more extreme and negative statements. This is what raised the most money directly from voters because, then as now, the harsher statements resonated strongly with die-hards and people who were concerned about their future because of a perceived threat.

In all this, Viguerie was another forerunner of Trump, who also used direct appeals to everyday voters and who angrily attacked the Washington and New York Establishment and the media as unfair to him and "fake."

A *New York Times* analysis of Viguerie's methods found that the elderly were special targets of his alarmist pitches, known in political circles as "fright mail." One official-looking envelope read, "All the Social Security Trust Fund Money is Gone!" Millions of elderly people received the solicitation in 1992, but it was wrong. The trust fund was not "gone." But many people were worried that their retirement money was drying up, and they donated to a group called United Seniors Association, which promised in the solicitation to fight to save Social Security. Viguerie was the chairman of the association, according to the *Times*.[10]

"United Seniors, to which hundreds of thousands of retirees have contributed millions of dollars over the last year, has no lobbyist and its directors are experts in fund-raising, not in the problems of the elderly," the *Times* reported in 1992. "Nearly all its proceeds are used to send out still more letters seeking more donors, usually with language that critics describe as misleadingly frightening."[11]

Sen. Daniel Patrick Moynihan, D-N.Y., chairman of the Senate Subcommittee on Social Security, warned Americans that fright mail "can terrorize, even constitute an assault of sorts, on, say, the 80-year-old widow living alone who doesn't have anyone to tell her it isn't so."[12]

Viguerie and other direct-mail specialists also focused on "wedge" issues that riled people up, such as opposition to busing to desegregate schools, opposition to gun control, support for "law and order," white animosity toward African Americans, and concern about the rising anger and perseverance of the civil rights movement. All this presaged Trump.

Schlozman pointed out that Viguerie and other direct-mail specialists helped create today's toxic political world—

> one where political consulting is now a big business, and where financial self-interest and polarized politics go hand in hand. Today's online fundraising, built around expanding and trading lists, then repeatedly bombarding them with appeals for dollars, largely replicates the model pioneered [by Viguerie and other direct-mail specialists.] They showed how a multitude of small donations can accumulate, and, when directed by a skilled political entrepreneur like Viguerie, reorient American politics.[13]

Mike McCurry, former White House press secretary for President Bill Clinton and a long-time Democratic strategist, agreed that Viguerie's methods were path-breaking because they increased the effectiveness of political attacks. In an interview for this book, McCurry described the process:

> It started with the direct-mail campaigns funded by getting more money from small donors. The language in those fund-raising letters got more combative and histrionic. Now there's not a single national development when you don't get an email designed to raise funds. And

> you should see the language! It's overwhelmingly negative and discourages people from speaking to each other in a reasonable way.[14]

Lee Atwater: Widely Imitated Avatar of Attack

Lee Atwater soared to the top of the political ziggurat by making attack politics the centerpiece of the highly visible campaigns he ran. He argued that often the best way to elect a politician was not to focus on that candidate's positions on the issues or personal values but instead to attack the opposition and reduce an adversary's favorability among voters. Atwater built for himself the image of a creative and charming rogue, and he inspired many GOP operatives to follow his lead. In fact, he influenced a generation of politicians and operatives starting in the 1980s because of a widespread belief that his emphasis on negativity won elections.

I knew Atwater well while I was a political writer and White House correspondent for *U.S. News & World Report*, and I interviewed him many times. A big reason for his success was his larger-than-life personality. He used bluster and irreverence to increase his fame and intimidate his adversaries.

Atwater, a fast-talking South Carolinian who was a runner and fitness buff, relished his image as the bad boy of conservative politics. In his 1991 obituary of Atwater for the *New York Times*, journalist Michael Oreskes wrote:

> While [Atwater] loved to talk in sweeping terms about the shape of the electorate, he was best known for his political street-fighting skills, skills that his critics said included a willingness to distort positions, smear opponents and use racial and ethnic messages.[15]

Atwater "wrote the book on the dirtiest of dirty political tricks," wrote journalist David Zurawik in 2008. He continued:

> [Atwater's] tactics helped Ronald Reagan, George H.W. Bush and George W. Bush get elected president. If you know about the infamous and racist Willie Horton ad used in the 1988 campaign to destroy Democratic candidate Michael Dukakis, then you've seen the handiwork of the late Mr. Atwater. ... What a resume: College Republican leader for Richard Nixon in 1972. Internship under the racist Strom Thurmond [a Republican U.S. senator from South Carolina]. And then, a few state races in South Carolina where he falsely accused one candidate of having psychiatric problems and another of fathering illegitimate children. All lies, of course, and he was proud of it. And then, on to bigger lies: helping Ronald Reagan win the South Carolina primary

> by planting a false story that one of his opponents was "buying the black vote."[16]

One GOP strategist who knew Atwater well said he was more disciplined than his critics realized and carefully thought out his tactics to gain maximum advantage. He specialized in exploiting "wedge issues" that divided people—such as law and order, crime and race—because the rifts he created within the electorate helped GOP candidates. And he was entertaining in the process.

Political consultant Rune Olso called Lee Atwater "the most ruthless political warrior in American politics. To Atwater, politics became a holy war."[17]

Born on February 27, 1951, in Atlanta, Atwater's parents moved the family to a working-class community in rural South Carolina when Lee was a boy. He attended the University of South Carolina and Newberry College and showed an early interest in politics.

Almost from the start, the young strategist's career was marked by creative and aggressive use of dirty tricks and noxious political tactics. In working for South Carolina Republican Sen. Thurmond's re-election in 1978, Atwater, then 27, attacked Democratic candidate Charles "Pug" Ravenel in numerous ways. As described by Olso,

> Lee [Atwater] contacted one of his old friends from the Young Republicans, Roger Stone, who was based in New York. Stone came across an article in a small New York publication "by accident." It was about a local fundraiser hosted by a New York couple for their Harvard classmate, Pug Ravenel. Addressing a crowd of 25 in their apartment, the article states, Ravenel said that if elected to the US Senate, he would like to be "the third Senator from New York." To this day, it is still impossible to determine whether the story is real or if it was planted by Stone to help Atwater's candidate.
>
> Real or not, the story was pure gold. Lee put the wheels in motion, pushing the story around South Carolina and planting the right quotes to keep it growing. After a few rounds in the press, even a group of Democratic state legislators berated Ravenel for his comments. A negative ad was aired. Ravenel vehemently denied having ever made the comment, but no one listened. His negatives jumped from 12 all the way up to 43 percent. Thurmond won the race easily with 56 percent of the vote.[18]

Atwater later said, referring to the large Democratic voter registration advantage in the South at the time, "We had to use guerrilla tactics.

Republicans in the South could not win elections by talking about issues. You had to make the case that the other guy, the other candidate, was a bad guy."[19]

In 1979, Ronald Reagan's campaign hired Atwater to run Reagan's presidential bid in South Carolina. Atwater arranged for the state to hold a GOP primary election on March 8, 1980, instead of a convention, thinking that Reagan would have a better chance of winning that way over John Connally, the former Democratic governor of Texas who had turned Republican, and veteran Republican insider George H.W. Bush.

Atwater ran negative ads against Bush arguing that he was too liberal for South Carolina. Olso reported:

> As always, Atwater had something up his sleeve. He had convinced his old pal Dick Greer to work with Bush's campaign manager in the state, for the purpose of subterfuge. So, there wasn't much mystery when an internal memo "suddenly" leaked from the Bush campaign just weeks before the primary. It stated that Connally had endorsed gay rights—a very controversial stand at the time in conservative South Carolina—and that Connally [was] engineering a plan to buy black votes. Connally called the Bush memo "a typical scurrilous, unfounded allegation" and shot back with some dirty allegations of his own.
>
> To the outside world, the primary contest started looking like a mud-slinging contest between Connally and Bush, while Atwater's candidate was keeping his distance. ... Through savvy tactics and dirty tricks, Atwater had pitted the Bush and Connally campaigns against each other, while his own candidate rose above it all—to a clear lead in the polls.[20]

Reagan won the state overwhelmingly.

Atwater was becoming a hot political commodity. Working for Reagan's national re-election campaign in 1984 against Democratic nominee Walter Mondale, he wrote an internal strategy memo that spelled out the GOP "wedge issue" strategy on cultural issues that would dominate the party's approach for a generation. He suggested that the way for Reagan and the GOP to win the South was to "drive a wedge between the liberal Democrats and the traditional southern Democrats." He argued that the traditional Democrats were really "populist voters" with many anti-establishment attitudes: "They are anti-Big Government, anti-Big Business, and anti-Big Labor. They are also hostile to the media, to the rich and to the poor."[21]

This was the strategy that proved so effective against Mondale, and Reagan won a smashing re-election victory.

In a series of interviews with me after he had achieved national success and fame, Atwater outlined some of his tactics. Atwater told me that during his early years in GOP politics he would stage beer parties in the woods far from polling places on Election Day and invite Black male voters, likely Democrats, with the goal of keeping them away from the polls.

He told me he got to know the views and concerns of working-class men by going to NASCAR rallies and talking to the attendees—putting a large bloc of racing-car enthusiasts, naturally conservative and skeptical of elites and authority, on the political map.

He claimed he would attend "dwarf-throwing contests" in backwoods areas of South Carolina where a burly man would grasp a smaller man by the belt and heave him as far as possible as part of a bizarre competition with other "throwers." It was a strange form of fun as far as I was concerned but Atwater said it gave him insights into conservative Southern male working-class culture.

In a notorious 1981 interview with a political scientist that came to light much later, Atwater shocked friends and enemies alike with his bluntness in explaining how Republicans had appealed to racists.[22]

> You start out in 1954 by saying, "Nigger, nigger, nigger." By 1968 you can't say "nigger"—that hurts you, backfires. So you say stuff like, uh, forced busing, states' rights, and all that stuff, and you're getting so abstract. Now, you're talking about cutting taxes, and all these things you're talking about are totally economic things and a byproduct of them is, blacks get hurt worse than whites. … "We want to cut this," is much more abstract than even the busing thing, uh, and a hell of a lot more abstract than "Nigger, nigger."[23]

On the personal side, Atwater was a talented musician, good enough to play guitar with famed guitarist and singer B.B. King at one of George H.W. Bush's inaugural balls. Atwater relished how far he had come, a country boy rising from humble beginnings to the pinnacle of politics, combining an instinct for the jugular with audacity, savvy, and endless energy. He couldn't sit still at meetings, and he was known to bounce his knees rapidly when he was agitated or impatient.

"My entire adult life, I've had exactly one job, which is managing campaigns," he said in 1989, the day George H.W. Bush named him chairman of the Republican party. "I really had two goals in life; one to manage a Presidential campaign and to be chairman of my party."[24]

Atwater knew how to read people, and one of them was George W. Bush, the eldest son of then-Vice President George H.W. Bush as the latter was building his campaign for the 1988 presidential election.

The elder Bush hired Atwater, then 33, who had risen to become a key political operative for President Ronald Reagan, as Bush's campaign manager for 1988. But the big-talking young man at first faced skepticism from others in the campaign.

Bush convened a meeting of his inner circle at Camp David and Atwater began explaining the importance of the Super Tuesday primaries in March 1988 when 17 states would be voting for a Republican nominee.[25]

Dubya, then an oil man in Texas who was serving as a troubleshooter for his father's campaign, interrupted. "How do we know we can trust you?" he said.

"Are you serious?" Atwater responded.

"I'm damn serious," Dubya said. "In our family, if you go to war, we want you completely on our side."

Atwater replied, "If you're so worried about my loyalty, then why don't you come in the office and watch me, and the first time I'm disloyal see to it that I get run off."

Dubya later told friends, quoting Lyndon Johnson: "I'd rather have him inside the tent pissing out than outside the tent pissing in."

The arrangement worked well for both of them—Atwater gained an ally in the candidate's family and George W got to learn Atwater's tricks of the trade, notably his ideas about attack politics.

Atwater and George H.W. Bush had a strange relationship. In their book about the 1988 campaign Peter Goldman, Tom Mathews, and a *Newsweek* team described the dynamic between the two men:

> On the face of it, he and Bush made a dissonant pair, a Willie Nelson duet with Rudy Vallee. Atwater was a Johnny Reb among Yankees, an alley fighter in a Marquess of Queensberry campaign. He came with a reputation as, charitably put, the Peck's Bad Boy of American politics; his hero was Richard Nixon, and his specialty in his intermittent graduate studies was the theory and practice of negative campaigning.[26]

Atwater used his attack skills most effectively and memorably in George H.W. Bush's successful campaign against Democratic nominee Michael Dukakis in 1988. Asked at the start of that campaign to describe his strategy, Atwater replied, "I'm going to scrape the bark off of Michael Dukakis."[27]

He succeeded.

Atwater was closely associated with publicizing the case of Willie Horton, an African American convicted murderer who was given a weekend furlough from the Massachusetts correction system under Dukakis, governor of the state at the time. During his furlough, Horton raped a white woman and stabbed her husband. After the issue was tested in focus groups and left voters upset and aghast, Bush condemned Horton's release and said Dukakis was soft on crime. Critics charged that Bush was trying to scare white voters into thinking that Dukakis would allow dangerous Black criminals to run loose.

The National Security Political Action Committee used the case of Horton in a televised political ad attacking Dukakis; most observers probably assumed the ad was made by the Bush campaign, but Atwater denied this. The ad identified Horton by name and showed a photo of him. The announcer said Governor Dukakis was responsible for Horton's release on "weekend passes" and declared that Dukakis was soft on crime.[28]

Bush's campaign ran its own TV ad about Dukakis and the prison furlough program a few weeks later. It didn't mention Horton but showed men walking through a revolving door, depicting what the announcer said were convicted felons who entered prison and were quickly furloughed by Dukakis. Since so many Americans had seen the alarming PAC ad or were aware of media coverage of this commercial, the Bush campaign's spot served as a compelling reminder of the Willie Horton issue.[29]

The Bush campaign, guided by Atwater, didn't allow the Dukakis bashing to end there. The Democratic nominee's alleged lack of patriotism was another Bush theme. The GOP candidate and his surrogates pointed out that Dukakis had vetoed a bill from the Massachusetts Legislature that required public-school students in the state to recite the Pledge of Allegiance. Dukakis argued that the mandate was unconstitutional. Bush accused Dukakis of being un-American.[30]

Bush, at Atwater's urging, also condemned Dukakis for being weak on national defense. Dukakis tried to counter the damage by riding in an M-1 tank at a military base. Atwater pounced. He and Bush media adviser Roger Ailes arranged for the image of Dukakis in the tank to be featured in a Bush TV commercial that showed Dukakis, wearing an oversized tank helmet and poking his head out of the vehicle with a goofy grin on his face. Many critics said the Democratic nominee reminded them of Snoopy in the "Peanuts" comic strip. All this made Dukakis look foolish and inept.[31]

Atwater and his team also attacked Dukakis's environmental record, supposedly one of his strong points. The Bush campaign ran an ad showing the pollution in Boston harbor. "Bush's advertising team shot an ad in Boston Harbor, showing the pollution-filled waters in the Massachusetts governor's capital city," Swint observed. "The ad was meant to dent his credibility as a candidate and to sow doubt as to the veracity of his message and his leadership. Mission accomplished."[32]

Dukakis, unsure how to fight back, lost an 18-point lead because of Bush's onslaught. Bush won the election overwhelmingly. And Atwater established his reputation nationally as a master practitioner of attack politics.

After collapsing from a brain tumor in 1990, Atwater was told he did not have long to live, and he experienced a spiritual awakening. He began to express regrets for the way he had treated opponents. Atwater apologized to Tom Turnipseed, a congressional candidate in South Carolina whom he had opposed years earlier in a particularly cruel way. Atwater had embarrassed Turnipseed by saying his psychiatric care amounted to being "hooked up to jumper cables." Atwater conceded on his death bed that this characterization was savage and unfair.

He also apologized to Michael Dukakis. "In 1988, fighting Dukakis, I said that I 'would strip the bark off the little bastard' and 'make Willie Horton his running mate,'" Atwater told *Life* Magazine in one of his final interviews. "I am sorry for both statements: the first for its naked cruelty, the second because it makes me sound racist, which I am not."[33]

Before his death on March 29, 1991, at age 40, Atwater apologized to others he had maligned over the years. But the damage had been done and his regrets could not undo the harm he had caused.

Atwater's tactics are still widely utilized today.

Roger Ailes: Caustic Mastermind and Television Strategist

Roger Ailes was once described as having "two speeds: attack and destroy." This assessment came from none other than Lee Atwater, a fierce practitioner of attack politics in his own right who worked with Ailes on George H.W. Bush's successful presidential campaign in 1988.[34]

Ailes was a TV producer and a political consultant who created and then directed the Fox News network, a powerful voice for conservatives and Republicans starting in 1996.

He was known for pugnacity, tenacity, conservatism, and showmanship. As Clyde Haberman described Ailes in the *New York Times*:

> As the [Fox] network's chairman and chief executive, Mr. Ailes was widely feared, particularly by conservative politicians who sought his favor. He cultivated a swaggering persona, accentuated by bursts of obscenity-laced anger. Once, he became so enraged that he punched a hole in the wall of a control room.[35]

He boasted about it during an interview with a biographer. "It was just a drywall, and luckily I didn't hit any beams. But somebody put a frame around the hole and wrote, 'Don't mess with Roger Ailes.'"[36]

He told the *New Yorker*: "I don't ignore anything. Somebody gets in my face, I get in their face."[37]

While conceding his creativity and drive, political scientist Kerwin Swint argued that there also was a dark side to Ailes, especially during his pre-Fox years as a political consultant because he

> too often used his talents to demean his adversaries, to camouflage his clients' intentions, and to obfuscate the truth. ... [I]n this author's opinion, he has engineered some of the most duplicitous, misleading, and occasionally vitriolic and mean-spirited, political campaigns in American history.[38]

Ailes told me during his successful 1988 presidential campaign for George H.W. Bush that other consultants said they lived for their candidate, but he would die for his.[39] I think he was joking. But Ailes believed that politics was "war."[40]

Ailes was born on May 15, 1940, in Warren, Ohio. His father Robert was a foreman at an electric company and his mother Donna was a homemaker who also embroidered handkerchiefs for sale to bring extra money to the family. Ailes biographers say his childhood was difficult—his father was abusive and young Roger had hemophilia and nearly bled to death more than once.[41] He felt the need to prove his toughness, got into fistfights, and dug ditches to make money.

Ailes attended Ohio University in Athens, graduating in 1962, and he developed an interest in the media while working for the campus radio station.

He served as a production assistant on "The Mike Douglas Show" in Cleveland and became executive producer of this talk/variety show at age 28.[42]

Ailes met Richard Nixon on the show in 1968 as Nixon began his second presidential campaign after his bitter loss to John F. Kennedy in 1960. During a conversation with Ailes, Nixon dismissed television as a "gimmick," but Ailes pushed back. "Television is not a gimmick," he told the eventual 1968 Republican presidential nominee, "and if you think it is, you'll lose again." Nixon thought it over, recalling his loss to the telegenic Kennedy, and hired Ailes as a media adviser. Ailes helped the Nixon team give their candidate a makeover—pundits called him "the new Nixon"—more likable, engaged, humorous, approachable. The Nixon team, with Ailes's guidance, orchestrated a series of town hall-style forums with carefully selected voters asking predictable and scripted questions and making Nixon look at ease and confident. At the same time, he used the sessions to attack opponents. All in all, it was a good show—an Ailes trademark.

After Nixon won, Ailes opened a business office in New York, and cultivated his reputation as a media whiz and a political brawler. He helped win Senate elections for Republicans Phil Gramm in Texas, Alfonse

D'Amato in New York, and Mitch McConnell in Kentucky. He played a key role in shaping Ronald Reagan's ads in his successful bid for re-election in 1984.

He rose to the top of national politics as media adviser to then-Vice President George H.W. Bush during his successful campaign for president in 1988. Ailes urged Bush to act and speak with more toughness, especially on law and order. As discussed earlier in this chapter, at the instigation of Ailes and campaign strategist Atwater, the Bush campaign blasted Democratic nominee Michael Dukakis for allowing weekend furloughs for convicted felons, which helped to turn the campaign in Bush's direction.

I got to know Ailes during the 1988 Bush campaign, which I covered for *U.S. News & World Report*. He loved to portray himself as a working-class ruffian despite the fact that by then he was wealthy and working for a rich patrician. He also had little use for most journalists, considering them dilettantes and hopelessly liberal. I always felt that we got along because he realized that I have a working-class background, too—rare for national journalists, especially those in the political press corps. He knew I had spent my pre-adolescence in a working-class household in the Hell's Kitchen neighborhood of New York City and he respected this.

This working-class sensibility and resentment toward elites shaped Ailes's creation of the Fox News network. "I've had a broad life experience that doesn't translate into going to the Columbia Journalism School," he once said. "That makes me a lot better journalist than some guys who had to listen to some pathetic professor who had been on the public dole all his life and really doesn't like this country much."[43]

Ailes started Fox News in October 1996--with conservative Australian mogul Rupert Murdoch footing the bill—as an alternative to liberal and centrist media outlets. It worked brilliantly. The network's conservative commentariat eventually included the popular Bill O'Reilly, Sean Hannity, and Tucker Carlson, and Fox's right-wing approach won over millions of viewers and plenty of advertisers.

Ailes, recognizing a kindred soul, began to give Donald Trump a TV platform. Jane Eisner, director of academic affairs at the Columbia School of Journalism, described the dynamic between the two:

> Ailes and Trump ran in the same New York media circles for decades, and each became adept at exploiting their cynical, mutually transactional relationship. By 2012, when Trump was sullying the political arena by waving the racist banner of birtherism, Ailes gave him a weekly call-in segment on the morning "Fox & Friends" show. That, more than "The Apprentice" [Trump's TV show], allowed him to build an adoring audience for his fact-free crusades.[44]

CNN media analyst Brian Stelter argued that "Monday Mornings with Trump" "changed the course of American politics."[45] CNN Media Analyst Stelter also explained much of this in his book *Hoax: Donald Trump, Fox News, and the Dangerous Distortion of Truth.*

"Trump's weekly gig ended when he rode down the Trump Tower escalator to announce his candidacy, but that didn't stop him from maintaining a regular presence on Fox's shows, both news and opinion," Eisner said.[46]

Ailes left Fox in disgrace during 2016 amid allegations of sexual harassment, and he died in 2017 at age 77 of a subdural hematoma after a fall that injured his head.[47]

Fox commentators including Sean Hannity, Tucker Carlson, and Laura Ingraham continued Ailes' alliance with Trump. Eisner wrote, "Beyond elevating an extreme form of tribalism ... Fox News accelerates and amplifies Trump's denigration of truth, disregard for facts and manipulation of a pliable public into believing an alternative reality."[48]

Roger Stone: "Attack, Attack, Attack"

Throughout his career, Richard Nixon was assisted, directly and indirectly, by some talented dirty tricksters and attack operatives such as Roger Stone. And Stone widened his influence far beyond Nixon.

In May 2008, lawyer and TV commentator Jeffrey Toobin analyzed Stone's longstanding impact:

> For nearly forty years, Stone has hovered around Republican and national politics, both near the center and at the periphery. At times, mostly during the Reagan years, he was a political consultant and lobbyist who, in conventional terms, was highly successful, working for such politicians as Bob Dole and Tom Kean. Even then, though, Stone regularly crossed the line between respectability and ignominy, and he has become better known for leading a colorful personal life than for landing big-time clients.[49]

Toobin said Stone relished his image as a "lovable rogue." Stone told Toobin in 2008, "I'm a libertarian and a libertine."

Stone, an amateur body-builder and flamboyant dresser, was a theatrical figure with his close-cropped silver hair and form-fitting, tailor-made suits. He also lived a hedonistic, free-spending lifestyle and was proud of it.

The Associated Press described Stone as "a larger-than-life political character who embraced his reputation as a dirty trickster."

Stone became known as a practitioner of Nixon-style hardball politics, which Toobin defined as "tactical thuggery." Stone was working as a consultant and lobbyist when Donald Trump considered running for president in 2000. Stone served as a counsellor to Trump, who decided against the race that year and was left with a bad impression of Stone. "Roger is a stone-cold loser," Trump said in 2008. "He always tries taking credit for things he never did." But Stone managed to get back into Trump's good graces—so much that President Trump gave Stone a pardon for his crimes committed in support of Trump's presidency, such as lying to federal authorities.

Stone came from a modest background in Lewisboro, New York. Born in 1952, part Italian and part Hungarian, his father dug wells and his mother was a writer for a local newspaper. He developed an interest in conservative politics in his early teens and when he was 13 worked on weekends for conservative icon William F. Buckley, Jr.'s unsuccessful 1965 campaign for New York mayor.

Over the years, Stone was known for his series of "rules" for practicing politics. Among them: "Attack, attack, attack—never defend," and "Admit nothing, deny everything, launch counterattack."[50] He told an interviewer, "Remember, politics is not about uniting people. It's about dividing people. And getting your fifty-one percent." Another rule: "Hate is a stronger motivator than love."[51] Ever the showman, like Donald Trump, his philosophy was: "The only thing worse in politics than being wrong is being boring."[52]

He deeply admired Nixon because of his toughness (and had the image of Nixon's face tattooed on his back)—the same trait he found appealing in Trump much later. Stone once said:

> The reason I'm a Nixonite is because of his indestructibility and resilience. He never quit. His whole career was all built around his personal resentments of elitism. It was the poor-me syndrome. John F. Kennedy's father bought him his House seat, his Senate seat, and the Presidency. No one bought Nixon anything. Nixon resented that. He was very class-conscious. He identified with the people who ate TV dinners, watched Lawrence Welk, and loved their country.[53]

In view of this praise for Nixon, Stone's bond with Trump seems all the more curious and contradictory. Trump is a billionaire whose father helped him get started in business, just as Kennedy's father helped him in politics. Trump always enjoyed the lifestyle of the super-rich, surrounding himself with gold and remaining isolated from everyday life as experienced by the middle class and the working class. All these traits might have alienated Stone. What drew him in, it appears, is Trump's proclivity to attack and to undermine, insult, and humiliate his opponents, which Stone admired.

In any case, Stone's dirty tricks have become widely known and admired by operatives drawn to his creativity and chutzpah. At the age of 19, he adopted the pseudonym James Rainier and made contributions in the name of the Young Socialist Alliance to the campaign of Pete McCloskey, who was challenging Nixon for the Republican presidential nomination in 1972. Stone sent a receipt for the contribution to the *Manchester Union Leader*, a conservative newspaper in New Hampshire, to prove that McCloskey was a left-wing radical. McCloskey was headed nowhere anyway and lost the nomination overwhelmingly to Nixon. But Stone's "socialist" gambit impressed political operatives who respected audacity. Stone went on to co-create the National Conservative Political Action committee, a bulwark of strident conservativism.

Stone worked on Ronald Reagan's unsuccessful presidential campaign in 1976, and for Reagan's winning campaign in 1980. That's when he met Reagan adviser and New York lawyer Roy Cohn, a key figure in the rise of negative politics. (I describe Cohn's negative efforts elsewhere in this book.) Cohn became a role model for Stone.

In 1988, Stone worked as a senior consultant for George H.W. Bush's highly negative and successful campaign against Democratic nominee Michael Dukakis, run by his friend Lee Atwater, another mastermind of negativity. For nearly three decades, he was a consultant for other campaigns and businesses, including GOP presidential campaigns, but was not in the lead role.

In July 2020, Trump commuted the sentence of Stone in a decision that came a few days before Stone was scheduled to begin serving a 40-month prison sentence for lying to Congress, witness tampering, and obstructing a House of Representatives investigation into political irregularities.[54] Trump intervened in a criminal case that was at the heart of congressional and media investigations into whether Trump and his operatives worked with Russia in 2016 to undermine Hillary Clinton's Democratic president campaign and ensure Trump's victory.

Rep. Adam Schiff, D-Calif., chairman of the House Intelligence Committee, called the decision "offensive to the rule of law and principles of justice. ... With this commutation, Trump makes clear that here are two systems of justice in America: one for his criminal friends, and one for everyone else."[55] Stone denied wrongdoing and said the charges were politically motivated to ruin him.

Dick Tuck: Trickster with a Lighter Touch

Dick Tuck was also the progeny of Nixon, in an unusual way. The *New York Times* described him as "a king gremlin of political shenanigans" and the *Washington Post* dubbed him "the political hobgoblin of Richard Nixon for decades."

These nicknames revealed a key element of Tuck's approach to dirty tricks: He exhibited a light touch and a sense of humor that is unusual in the world of politics.

Tuck, short in stature and said to resemble a leprechaun, began his political career in California during the 1950s and was a longtime Democratic strategist and advance man who organized events for candidates. He managed a few successful state and local campaigns and served as an advance man for candidate Robert F. Kennedy in the 1968 Democratic presidential primaries, but was best known for his clever and creative trickery. Tuck quoted Nixon, no stranger to dirty tricks, as saying on White House tapes, "Tuck did that [used trickery] and got away with it ... Shows you what a master Dick Tuck was."

"To connoisseurs of the dark arts of political tricksters, Mr. Tuck was a master of psychological jujitsu," *Times* reporter Robert D. McFadden wrote in his 2018 obituary of Tuck. "By his own accounts, he shadowed and leapfrogged Republican campaigns, planted agents with surprises at whistle-stops, disrupted schedules, started nasty rumors and issued bogus press advisories. ... Mr. Tuck insisted that his own stunts were benign mischief."

Tuck started his mischief against Nixon when he was a student at the University of Southern California, Santa Barbara, in 1950. He volunteered to work in Nixon's Senate campaign that year against Helen Gahagan Douglas even though he secretly supported Douglas. He arranged for a Nixon rally on campus but didn't publicize it. Only 23 people showed up in an auditorium that seated 2,000. Nixon was furious.

In 1956, Tuck embarrassed Nixon again during the Republican National Convention in San Francisco where Nixon was re-nominated as vice president. Tuck arranged for garbage trucks to drive by the convention center bearing large signs reading "Dump Nixon."

In 1958, Tuck angered Sen. William Knowland at a Republican banquet given by Chinese American supporters of Knowland by arranging for the use of fortune cookies with the message, "Knowland for Premier of Formosa." This was a reference to the island, now known as Taiwan, where Chinese nationalists fled after Mao Zedung won the Chinese civil war for the communists after World War II.

In 1962, Nixon ran for governor of California and Tuck was on his case again. At a Nixon rally in Los Angeles' Chinatown, Tuck arranged for operatives to hold up a sign saying, "Welcome Nixon" and asking, in Chinese, "What about the huge loan?" It referred to a loan by entrepreneur Howard Hughes to Nixon's brother Donald that critics were calling an example of corruption. Tuck had intended for the sign to read

"Hughes" not "huge," but it still made the point by raising an embarrassing issue at an event that was supposed to be a showcase for Nixon's political strength. Nixon, after someone translated the sign for him, rushed over, seized the sign, and tore it up. This moment of rage was captured by TV cameras and made Nixon appear vindictive and out of control. It was just what Tuck hoped for.

Tuck said later, "Exposing the real Nixon was always my goal. The message was simple: Do you want a guy like this running your state or nation?"

But while Nixon lost that gubernatorial race in California, Tuck's tricks couldn't prevent him from winning the presidency in 1968 and getting re-elected in 1972. And Nixon tried to learn from Tuck.

H.R. Haldeman, Nixon's White House chief of staff, hired an operative named Donald Segretti for the 1972 re-election campaign to bring a "Dick Tuck sensibility" to the Nixon effort. Segretti was nastier than Tuck, but Nixon fumed that the media showed a double standard by attacking him and his campaign for Segretti stunts that Nixon said were similar to what Tuck had done (see Chapter 3). "The media being, shall we say, not particularly in my corner, just called that Tuck trickery fun and games," Nixon said in a 1983 interview. "And then when Segretti, our so-called 'dirty tricks man,' whom I frankly had never had the opportunity of even meeting—when he tried to practice some of these things on our Democratic opponents, they became high crimes and misdemeanors."

Tuck, summarizing his approach, said he "made a lot of candidates look foolish, usually with a lot of help from the candidates themselves." His humorous touch is still widely admired among political professionals.

Also fueling the rise of corrosive politics over the years were political action committees and organizations outside the major party system and the mainstream media. They included the ultra-conservative fringe group the John Birch Society, and various hard-line conservative Christian organizations associated with evangelical pastor and televangelist the Rev. Jerry Falwell, a phenomenon that has been documented by historian Kristin Kobes du Mez.[56]

Floyd Brown was a prime example of the PAC operatives. He led political action committees that specialized in harsh attacks and was not officially connected to a specific campaign or candidate. This was how Brown built his influence. The imposing 6-foot-6 operative was known in his heyday for bludgeoning Democratic presidential candidates and producing innuendo-filled ads.

Brown, whose father was a sawmill worker, was born on March 10, 1961, and grew up in Washington State where he attended the University of Washington majoring in economics. At age 15, Brown met Ronald Reagan in 1976 while Reagan campaigned for the Republican presidential nomination, and this chat with the engaging GOP candidate triggered Brown's interest in politics.

At his most influential, from the late 1980s to the early 2000s, Brown was able to raise large amounts of money for his independent political action committees. His fund-raising tapered off later because of more stringent federal regulations for independent groups and the rise of stronger Democratic candidates, giving Brown fewer targets. All this diminished Brown's success and prominence. But for years he was the archetype of the independent operative and political entrepreneur who used attacks to make a name for himself.

In 1988, Brown used independent PACs to push the racially divisive Willie Horton ads that depicted Democratic nominee Michael Dukakis as soft on crime. Such PACs benefited at the time from millions of dollars in contributions but had little accountability. That same year, he also founded Citizens United, a group that became active in attacking Democrats. Brown and Citizens United tried to find dirt on Democratic presidential candidate Bill Clinton in 1992, and spread allegations that Clinton was involved in a corrupt real estate deal called Whitewater in Arkansas, where he had been governor. This was never proven. Brown et al. also investigated rumors of Clinton's adulteries, but couldn't find damning evidence. (Special counsel Kenneth Starr did find such material, leading to Clinton's impeachment by the House and acquittal by the Senate.)

Esquire reported that Brown, after gaining fame for the highly negative Willie Horton ads, proceeded to "start political organizations employing the same basic formula: Apocalyptic direct-mail appeals to raise money, innuendo-laden aids to thrash Democrats and outrageous claims to draw mainstream news interest."[57]

In 2004, when President George W. Bush, the son of George H.W. Bush, was seeking re-election, Brown used phony allegations about Democratic presidential nominee John Kerry's military service aboard U.S. "swift boats" during the Vietnam war to portray Kerry as a liar and unpatriotic. Kerry lost the race.

In 2008, Brown tried to undermine Democratic candidate Obama by claiming he was a Muslim and making other false allegations, but his efforts didn't gain traction. Also in 2008, Brown, through the National Campaign Fund that he had co-founded and other groups, accused Obama of corruption and being an extreme liberal. Obama won anyway.

Brown also began using a news and opinion website, WesternJournal.com, to carry his negative messages. "It may not be a household name, but few publications have had the reach, and potentially the influence, in American politics as *The Western Journal*," reported the *New York Times*. "Even the right-wing publication's audience of more than 36 million people, eclipsing many of the nation's largest news organizations, doesn't know much about the company or who's behind it."[58]

The *Times* reported that *The Western Journal* "stokes outrage and curates a narrative in which conservatives and their values are under constant assault." It has carried stories about

> tradition-minded patriots [who] face ceaseless assault by anti-Christian bigots, diseased migrants and race hustlers concocting hate crimes. Danger and outrages loom. A Mexican politician threatens the "takeover" of several American states. Police officers are kicked out of an Arizona Starbucks. Kamala Harris, the Democratic presidential candidate proposes a "$100 million handout for black families."[59]

The outrage and the negativity never end.

Notes

1 Amanda Ripley, "Help Tucker Carlson Help Himself," *Washington Post*, June 13, 2023, A19.
2 Dave Davies, interview with Rick Perlstein, "Fresh Air," wxxinews.org/;post/reaganland/author-revisits-roots-american-conservatism, August 26, 2020.
3 Quoted in Nick Thimmesch, "The Grass-Roots Dollar Chase—Ready on the Right," New York Magazine, 58.
4 Davies interview.
5 Daniel Schlozman, "How SPLC's Co-Founder Morris Dees and the Conservative Richard Viguerie Changed American Politics," *Washington Post*, April 2, 2019, https://www.washingtonpost.com/politics/2019/04/02/how-splcs-cofounder-morris-dees-conservative-richard-viguerie-changed-american-politics/.
6 Quoted in Thimmesch.
7 Schlozman.
8 ibid.
9 Quoted in Schlozman.
10 Erik Eckholm, "Fear in the Mail—A Special Report: Alarmed by Fund-Raiser, The Elderly Give Millions," *New York Times*, November 12, 1992, 1.
11 ibid.
12 Quoted in Eckholm.
13 Schlozman.
14 Author's interview with Mike McCurry, April 23, 2021.
15 Michael Oreskes, "Lee Atwater, Master of Tactics For Bush and G.O.P., Dies at 40," *New York Times*, March 30, 1991, www.nytimes.com/1991/03/30/obituaries/lee-atwater-master-of-tactics-for-bush-and-gop-dies-at-40.html.
16 David Zurawik, "Lee Atwater: The Dark and Dirty Side of GOP Politics," *Baltimore Sun*, November 10, 2008, www.baltimoresun.com/bs-mtblog-142445-lee_atwater_is_evil-story.html.
17 Rune Olso, *Behind the Curtain of Power*. Pittsburgh, PA: Dorrance Publishing, 2021, 18.
18 ibid., 18–19.
19 Quoted in Olso, 19.

20 ibid., 22.
21 Ibid 28–9.
22 As with other chapters, the author has elected to reproduce the quotes in their original uncensored form to preserve the force of their offensive content and language.
23 Quoted in Rick Perlstein, "Exclusive: Lee Atwater's Infamous 1981 Interview on the Southern Strategy," *The Nation*, November 13, 2012, https://www.thenation.com/article/archive/exclusive-lee-atwaters-infamous-1981-interview-southern-strategy/.
24 Quoted in Oreskes.
25 This account is based on Jean Edward Smith, *Bush*. New York: Simon & Schuster, 2016, 47–8.
26 Peter Goldman, Tom Mathews, and the *Newsweek* Special Election Team, *The Quest for the Presidency: The 1988 Campaign*. New York: Simon & Schuster, 1989, 182–3.
27 Quoted in Kerwin Swint, *Mudslingers: The Twenty-Five Dirtiest Political Campaigns of All Time*. New York: Union Square Press, 2008, 154.
28 ibid., 157–8.
29 ibid., 158.
30 ibid., 158–9.
31 Swint, 158–9.
32 Swint, 160.
33 Quoted in Michael Oreskes, "Lee Atwater, Master of Tactics For Bush and G.O.P., Dies at 40," *New York Times*, March 30, 1991, www.nytimes.com/1991/03/30/obituaries/lee-atwater-master-of-tactics-for-bush-and-gop-dies-at-40.html.
34 Clyde Haberman, "Roger Ailes, Who Built Fox News Into an Empire, Dies at 77," *New York Times*, May 18, 2017, https://www.nytimes.com/2017/05/18/business/media/roger-ailes-dead.html.
35 ibid.
36 ibid.
37 Quoted in Haberman.
38 Kerwin Swint, *Dark Genius: The Influential Career of Legendary Political Operative and Fox News Founder Roger Ailes*. New York: Union Square Press, 2008, 1.
39 Author's interview with Roger Ailes, January 1988.
40 Haberman.
41 ibid.
42 Peter Goldman and Tom Mathews, *The Quest for the Presidency: The 1988 Campaign*. New York: Simon & Schuster, 1989, 182.
43 Quoted in Haberman.
44 Jane Eisner, "Fox News's Retreat from Journalism," *Washington Post*, August 30, 2020, B1.
45 Brian Stelter, *Hoax: Donald Trump, Fox News, and the Dangerous Distortion of Truth*. New York: Atria/One Signal, 2020.
46 Eisner.
47 Haberman.
48 Eisner.
49 Jeffrey Toobin, "The Dirty Trickster," *The New Yorker*, June 2, 2008, downloaded June 20, 2023.
50 Quoted in Toobin.
51 Quoted in Toobin.
52 Quoted in Toobin.

53 Quoted in Toobin.
54 Jeffrey Toobin, "The Roger Stone Case Shows Why Trump Is Worse Than Nixon," *The New Yorker,* July 11, 2020, https://www.newyorker.com/news/daily-comment/the-roger-stone-case-shows-why-trump-is-worse-than-nixon.
55 Quoted in ibid.
56 See Kristin Kobes du Mez, *Jesus and John Wayne: How White Evangelicals Corrupted a Faith and Fractured a Nation.* New York: Liveright, 2021. See also Matthew Dallek, *Birchers: How the John Birch Society Radicalized the American Right.* New York: Basic Books, 2023.
57 Charles P. Pierce, "Old RatF*ckers Never Die. They Adapt and Weaponize New Technologies," *Esquire*, August 22, 2019, downloaded June 28, 2023.
58 Daniel Victor, "How a Conservative News Site Thrived on Facebook and Google," *New York Times*, August 22, 2019, https://www.nytimes.com/2019/08/22/us/western-journal-highlights.html.
59 ibid.

CONCLUSION

George Washington, America's first president, warned that his new country was fragile and vulnerable to great harm. "Cunning, ambitious, and unprincipled men will be enabled to subvert the power of the people and to usurp for themselves the reins of government," he said in his farewell address of 1796.[1] He has been proven correct.

"Two of his successors—Richard Nixon and Donald Trump—demonstrate the shocking genius of our first president's foresight," wrote journalists Bob Woodward and Carl Bernstein, who broke the Watergate story.[2] Both Nixon and Trump sought to undermine the country with an unrelenting emphasis on attacking their adversaries and critics and the governing institutions of the country. Woodward and Bernstein continued:

> The heart of Nixon's criminality was his successful subversion of the electoral process—the most fundamental element of American democracy. He accomplished it through a massive campaign of political espionage, sabotage and disinformation that enabled him to literally determine who his opponent would be in the presidential election of 1972. [This was Sen. George McGovern, D-SD, who turned out to be the weak candidate that Nixon and his henchmen expected, losing to Nixon in a landslide. All this was eventually disclosed, along with Nixon's attempted cover-up, and he resigned from office in 1974.]
>
> Donald Trump not only sought to destroy the electoral system through false claims of voter fraud and unprecedented public intimidation of state election officials, but he also then attempted to prevent the

DOI: 10.4324/9781003149095-15

> peaceful transfer of power to his duly elected successor, for the first time in American history.[3]

Woodward and Bernstein condemned "Trump's diabolical instincts"[4] for endangering American democracy and for leading him to attack truth itself.

Polarization and poisoned politics are everywhere today and extend even to the devaluing of facts. In the growing phenomenon of confirmation bias, Americans increasingly seek reinforcement of their views in the media, such as the internet, television, newspapers, radio, and books, rather than open-mindedly assessing contrarian information or broadening their search for truth. One result is that politicians and their operatives are more willing than ever to play upon the fears, prejudices, and hostilities of voters, especially core supporters. It is part of an often successful effort to manipulate voters into believing only what their would-be leaders say and totally distrusting their adversaries.

Caustic politics is becoming a world-wide phenomenon, accelerating the rise of would-be dictators and autocrats such as Russian President Vladimir Putin who controls the flow of information and disinformation in his country. And the problem is getting worse.

Former U.S. President Barack Obama says he failed to understand the dangers of disinformation and toxic politics until he had left office, and he wished he had taken action to limit the trend while he had power. In a speech at Stanford University on April 21, 2022, Obama said he didn't comprehend "how susceptible we had become to lies and conspiracy theories, despite having spent years being a target of disinformation myself"[5] when opponents including Donald Trump claimed falsely that he wasn't born in the United States and therefore was not eligible to be president. Actually, he was born in Hawaii and the criticism was bogus.

Obama particularly blamed social media such as Facebook and Twitter for "turbo-charging some of humanity's worst impulses." He said there has been a

> profound change that's taken place in how we communicate and consume information. ... Today's social media has a grimness to it. We're so fatalistic about the steady stream of bile and vitriol that's on there. But it doesn't have to be that way. In fact, if we're going to succeed it can't be that way.[6]

Among his examples was false information challenging the effectiveness of anti-Covid vaccines which led to deaths and hospitalizations among the unvaccinated. Obama also cited the spread of false information that the 2020 election had been stolen from Trump which unfairly cast doubt on the legitimacy of Joe Biden's presidency. "The sheer proliferation of conflict and the splintering of information and audiences has made democracy more complicated," Obama said.[7]

Obama's solution was to have government somehow create regulations to police falsity and conflict in social media, but he didn't spell out exactly what he had in mind. Until a solution is found, he added, "All we see is a constant feed of content, where useful, factual information and happy diversions flow alongside lies, conspiracy theories, junk science, quackery, racist tracts and misogynist screeds."[8]

As I have discussed throughout this book, virulent politics has been part of America almost from the beginning of the Republic and it has ebbed and flowed over time along with society's divisions. Sometimes this polarization cannot be bridged, and the country descends into opposing camps willing to think and say the worst about each other and sometimes take action against the other side. This politics of resentment, anger, and grievance often runs its course until the warring sides, or at least one of them, become exhausted and the country tires of the struggle or believes it has gone too far. At this point the negative messaging goes out of style and people settle into a more pacific period.

A big problem today is that millions of Americans have come to hate the opposition. As political analyst Lee Drutman has written, "This ... level of hatred—which political scientists call 'negative partisanship'—has reached levels that are not just bad for democracy, but are potentially destructive. And extreme partisan animosity is a prelude to democratic collapse."[9]

MSNBC columnist Michael A. Cohen noted in 2021 that

> The cleavages in American society have become so extreme that where one lives and how one votes increasingly has life and death consequences. And no recent issue better exemplifies this phenomenon than the growing red state/blue state divide over Covid-19 vaccinations. The vaccine fight, rather than an outgrowth of Trump's divisive presidency, is just another example of how polarization is not just transforming American society—it's literally killing people.[10]

Cohen pointed out that voters who cast their ballots for Democratic presidential candidate Biden in 2020 were far more likely to get Covid-19 vaccinations than Trump voters.

> This disconnect is yet another example of America's increasingly fractured politics. Voters are not only choosing candidates based solely on whether they have a "D" or an "R" next to their name, they are making health decisions using the same criteria. ... Republicans and Democrats are today far more likely to view those members of the other party not

> as competitors, but as enemies, holding overwhelmingly unfavorable views of each other. In Washington, partisanship and dysfunction have paralyzed Congress and the federal government.[11]

Republican pollster Frank Luntz noted that political hostility caused millions of Americans to refuse to get vaccinated against the Covid virus, risking their health and the health of those around them.

> We always ask, what will be the last straw? What will be the moment that we lose the ability to communicate and cooperate and get things done? Well, we've reached it. This is it. Now, decisions are being made not because of evidence or facts or statistics, but strictly on political lines. And now people are going to die.[12]

Historian Molly Worthen wrote in 2021 that President Biden

> has been warning us, in his frank and ecumenical way, that Americans have become a bunch of idol worshipers. He's right. We have transformed political hatreds into a form of idolatry. A team of researchers analyzed a range of survey data and concluded that "out-party hate" now seems to shape American voting decisions more than race or religion do. ... Political hatred has become Americans' animating faith, a chief source of existential meaning.[13]

In an interview with me, historian Alvin S. Felzenberg described the contemporary political climate.

> There is a lot of grievance. There is a lot of anger, especially on the right. Many Trump supporters believe they are disrespected and dismissed by cultural elites such as Hollywood and Washington insiders. Trump speaks to these voters. He rides the anger and they vote for him ...They vote for him because they want to see the other side humiliated.[14]

Felzenberg added: "No president ever in the history of this country challenged the election in this country."[15] But this is what Trump did.

Neither major party has managed to dominate American presidential politics for very long in the modern era. Power tends to swing like a pendulum between the Democrats and Republicans. After the 20-year reign of the Democrats under Franklin Roosevelt and Harry Truman from 1933 to 1953, Americans chose the Republicans under Dwight Eisenhower from 1953 to 1961, the Democrats under John F. Kennedy, and Lyndon Johnson from 1961 to 1969; went back to the GOP under

Richard Nixon and his successor Gerald Ford from 1969 to 1977; Democrat Jimmy Carter, 1977 to 1981; Republicans Ronald Reagan and George H.W. Bush from 1981 to 1993; Democrat Bill Clinton 1993–2001; Republican George W. Bush from 2001 to 2009; followed by Democrat Barack Obama from 2009 to 2017; Republican Trump who served as president in 2017–2021; and Democrat Biden, who began his presidency in 2021.

Political analyst Lee Drutman wrote:

> Simultaneously, the swings in power have imparted the lesson that when you're down, the best thing to do is demonize the other side, refuse to compromise, wait for public opinion to tack against the party in power and ride the pendulum back to a majority. ... If all of this seems unsustainable, it should. The current levels of hyper-partisanship are clearly dangerous. It's bad news for a democracy when 60 to 70 percent of people view fellow citizens of the other party as a serious threat. And the more the parties continue to unify their supporters by casting the other party as the enemy, the higher this number will rise.[16]

Conservative writer David French wrote in The *Dispatch* in 2020:

> Think of the multiple dimensions of our divisions. Yes, all the data indicates that our political enmity is skyrocketing. ... In fact, millions of Americans are now in the grips of what some researchers call "lethal mass partisanship," where they justify even actual violence against political opponents.
>
> We decreasingly enjoy even a common popular culture. In 2016 the *New York Times* published a series of television ratings maps that showed that red and blue Americans watch very different shows that feature very different themes and mores.[17]

Referring to the phenomenon of "pre-deliberation judgments," French said,

> In plain English, that means when like-minded people gather, they tend to grow more extreme ... Now do you see why incentives are so aligned toward greater conflict? If you were a partisan, the chances are that you not only have outright enmity for your political opponents, you don't have many (if any) meaningful real-world relationships with those you oppose, and you may even fear that their control of the levels of government will be in the extinction of your liberty and way of life.[18]

Political scientist Alison McQueen told the *Washington Post* that caustic politics can have profoundly harmful effects.

> At its worst, it divides and excludes. It casts one set of people as heroes and saviors and another set of people as beyond the pale and evil. It's good and evil rhetoric, and once you see your opponents as evil or the belligerent side in a war, that seems to legitimize treating them in ways we'd otherwise find very objectionable. When I look at the resurgence of dark, apocalyptic rhetoric among Republican politicians, what it signals to me is that the country is gearing up for a presidential race and that some of the Republicans are willing to use the Trump apocalypse playbook again, because Trump used this in his first presidential campaign to great effect.[19]

This toxic cloud has spread beyond U.S. borders. Political strategist and author Douglas E. Schoen describes the effect:

> Around the world, citizens no longer trust their governments to solve the enormous problems facing them. They no longer have confidence in the institutions of their societies to manage and lead effectively. A profound cynicism and anger prevails at a time in history when nations desperately need public unity and morale. ... The public loss of trust in political and economic institutions has led to unprecedented political instability and economic volatility, from Moscow to Brussels, from Washington to Cairo.[20]

So, What Do We Do about It?

I would suggest that we as a nation, from our top political leaders through the ranks of business and labor and academia and every other walk of life, use the 250th anniversary of the 1776 founding of the United States to set a goal of committing ourselves to a national renewal based on shared values of tolerance, hard work, perseverance, and a commitment to the Founders' original promise of "life, liberty, and the pursuit of happiness" for all. We need to re-learn how to listen to each other and practice mutual respect with a goal of healing the wounds of polarization and creating national unity and finding common ground. And focusing on these goals in 2026, on the occasion of a profoundly important turning point in American history, would be the perfect time to do it.

"It is time to lower the heat," Schoen argued. "Leaders must tone it down: leaders at the top and leaders of all stripes."[21] He was talking about parents, bosses, reporters, columnists, professors, union chiefs, everyone. I agree.

There are some leaders who are ready to move in this direction. One of them is Utah Gov. Spencer Cox, a Republican conservative who took over as chairman of the National Governors Association in 2023. He told an NGA gathering in Atlantic City in July 2023,

> We are facing a toxic debate unlike anything that we've seen since the Civil War, according to political scientists … I think many of us believe that this division can't continue and that we have to find a way to disagree better.[22]

One of his theories is that political and societal leaders need to work harder to identify areas where most Americans agree and pursue these goals, rather than take on issues that divide and anger. Columnist Dan Balz of the *Washington Post* has pointed out that Cox

> seeks not to dampen debate or disagreement but to do it with less bickering, hostility and the kind of anger that is now commonplace. He believes there is an exhausted majority of people who agree on this.[23]

To these ends, he has already refused to use negative advertising that attacks opponents personally and won the office of lieutenant governor and, most recently, governor with his upbeat approach.

Mike McCurry, former White House press secretary for President Clinton, when asked to advise leaders about how to be a good communicator amid the surge in negativity, said:

> Avoid demonizing those on the other side of the debate. I think what is so poisonous in our system right now is the sense that you have to obliterate your adversary in the public realm of communications. Stop and say, "If I knew this person and I was sitting and talking with them, would I talk to them this way?" It seems like the anonymity—and charge and counter charge—has led people to say things that they wouldn't say in polite company. People who have been around a long time ought to take on some leadership, mentor people and say, "Let's try to find ways to be a little more amicable and take more responsibility for the vocabulary that we use."[24]

I am not arguing for the end of all negative politics. Comparing and contrasting opposing viewpoints and candidates is a natural part of our system of government. As Buell and Sigelman pointed out:

> For all of the aspersions cast on negative campaigning and despite the many ailments of the body politic attributed to it, many a scholar

has acknowledged its valuable contribution to free elections. Glen W. Richardson extolled it as "one of democracy's most cherished expressive freedoms." [William G.] Mayer argued that such criticism provides essential information for casting an informed vote. Similarly, [John G.] Geer argued that the practice of democracy requires candidates to go negative, for otherwise, the costs or benefits of electing one of them would not come out.[25]

But in recent years, as noted in this book, the negativity has reached such outrageous and sustained levels that it is distorting the political process and poisoning civil discourse.

Conservative strategist Michael Gerson wrote:

> [S]ignificant actors in our political life have lost something important. They no longer care about the integrity of our constitutional process or accept the existence of a shared public reality. They care only about achieving their preferred political outcomes. This was the motivating spirit behind the Jan. 6 Capitol revolt and is the continuing inspiration of former president Donald Trump's big electoral lie: If American systems and institutions don't deliver the results we seek, burn them down. ... [T]he United States has a significant portion of citizens—a majority of those currently identifying with the GOP—who say they believe the legitimately elected U.S. president is illegitimate. They say they believe, against all the evidence, that progressives led the violent assault on the U.S. Capitol. And in states across the country, these right-wing, authoritarian populists are re-arranging electoral systems to better dispute and overcome future outcomes that displease them.[26]

Gerson's prescription was amorphous, but it would help heal the nation's wounds. He called it "do-gooderism on steroids." He recommended

> avoiding cynicism and attacks on one's political opponents and attempting to bring together those who are willing to accept the differences among us and avoid hate and the culture of contempt and automatic condemnation. Civil healing is possible only with a measure of civic idealism.[27]

The news media have a special responsibility to lower the decibel level and break away from "bothsideism," in which phony arguments are given equal weight with fact-based analysis. Media critic Tom Rosenstiel has written:

> Call it the Unreality Crisis in America. … [Critics have] suggested that the press bears a good deal of blame for the dire status of empiricism in public life. Professional journalism, they say, remains mired in outmoded political stenography—practices such as quoting both sides in controversies and trying to appear neutral, which can distort the truth and create equivalencies between fact and falsehoods.[28]

Rosenstiel pointed out that

> the news media, especially television, goes out of its way to give airtime to people who will mouth extremist views and fantasist absurdities. Whether the intent is to reveal how extreme and polarized politics has become, or the reasons are more cynical—to create even more conflict on air in search of ratings—the phenomenon is a fact. The people we see on television today distort the reality of our elected officials and their views.[29]

I oppose using government such as the Federal Election Commission, the presidency, or Congress to decide what crosses the line in terms of negative politics. The First Amendment's guarantees of freedom of the press and freedom of speech should be respected. The best way to deal with slash-and-burn politics is for the president and other national leaders to shun rancorous, vitriolic discourse and character attacks, and emphasize their own ideas, not go after the other side as their first instinct.

The long-range answer, however, lies with everyday Americans. To change the rancorous, superficial political environment, Americans will need to stop responding positively to extreme negative campaigning—the kind that shuns the truth and distorts reality—by no longer rewarding its practitioners with their votes.

Even though most people seem interested in attacks and criticism—a fact that I pointed out earlier this book—studies show that many people are willing to reject the negative. As researchers Stuart Soroka, Patrick Fournier and Lilach Nir explain:

> Even as the average tendency may be for viewers to be more attentive to and aroused by negative content, there would appear to be a good number of individuals with rather different or perhaps more mutable preferences. One lesson of our analyses is that work on media coverage and news production should not lose sight of these individual-level differences. For those focused on the substance and nature of news content, individual-level variability in negativity biases highlights the possibility for the audience seeking … news coverage that is less systematically negative.[30]

It's time for a concerted effort to find common ground and show respect for each another. It won't be easy because our toxic culture runs so deep. Nor would this approach satisfy the belligerent advocates of rash, extreme, and undemocratic solutions. But it would set us on a brighter path to the future if most Americans concluded that they no longer have to accept the poisoning of their souls and if they reject enmity as a way of life. Our 250th anniversary as a nation in 2026 would be a most appropriate moment in our history to give it a try.

Notes

1 George Washington "Farewell Address" September 17, 1796. Transcript at American Presidency Project, https://www.presidency.ucsb.edu/documents/farewell-address Also quoted in Woodward and Bernstein, "Woodward and Bernstein, Thought Nixon Defined Corruption. Then Came Trump."
2 Bob Woodward and Carl Bernstein, "Woodward and Bernstein, Thought Nixon Defined Corruption. Then Came Trump," *Washington Post*, June 5, 2022, B1.
3 ibid.
4 ibid.
5 Elizabeth Dwoskin and Eugene Scott, "Obama Says Tech Companies Have Made Democracy More Vulnerable," *Washington Post*, April 21, 2022.
6 Quoted in Kari Paul, "'Democracy Will Wither': Barack Obama Outlines Perils of Unregulated Big Tech in Sweeping Speech," *The Guardian*, April 21, 2022, https://www.theguardian.com/us-news/2022/apr/21/obama-stanford-speech-big-tech.
7 ibid.
8 Quoted in Dwoskin and Scott.
9 Lee Drutman, "How Hatred Came To Dominate American Politics," FiveThirtyEight, Octover 5, 2020, https:fivethirtyeight.com/features/how-hatred-negative-partisanship-came-to-dominate-american-politics/?ex_cid=538twitter.
10 Michael A. Cohen, "Happy 4th of July America. Stop Letting Polarization Kill You," July 4, 2021, https://www.msnbc.com/opinion/happy-4th-july-america-stop-letting-polarization-kill-you-n1273068.
11 ibid.
12 Quoted in Dan Diamond, Hannah Knowles, and Tyler Pager, "Conservatives' Vaccine Hesitancy Crystallizes into Hostility," *Washington Post*, July 17, 2021, A5.
13 Molly Worthen, "Is There a Way to Dial Down the Political Hatred?" *New York Times*, June 11, 2021, www.nytimes.com/2021/06/11/opinion-god-religion-politics-partisanship-html?action=click&module=Opinion&pgtype=Homepage.
14 Author's interview with Al Felzenberg, May 11, 2021.
15 Author's interview with Alvin S. Felzenberg, June 9, 2021.
16 Drutman.
17 David French, "Yes, America Could Split Apart," *The Dispatch*, September 20, 2020, frenchpress.thedispatch.com.
18 ibid.
19 Quoted in Ashley Parker, "Much of the 2024 GOP Field Focuses on Dark, Apocalyptic Themes," *Washington Post*, March 17, 2023, https://

www.washingtonpost.com/politics/2023/03/16/republicans-2024-dark-apocalyptic/.

20 Douglas E. Schoen, *The End of Authority: How a Loss of Legitimacy and Broken Trust Are Endangering Our Future.* Lanham, MD: Rowman & Littlefield, 2013, 2–3.

21 ibid.

22 Quoted in Dan Balz, "Utah's Governor Wants Americans to Learn to 'Disagree Better,'" *Washington Post*, July 23, 2023, A2.

23 ibid.

24 Tom Fox, "Former Press Secretary Mike McCurry on How to be a Good Communicator," *Washington Post*, April 2, 2013, https://www.washingtonpost.com/national/on-leadership/former-press-secretary-mike-mccurry-on-how-to-be-a-good-communicator/2013/04/02/bdbe4b5c-9bca-11e2-9a79-eb5280c81c63_story.html.

25 Emmett H. Buell Jr. and Lee Sigelman, *Attack Politics: Negativity in Presidential Campaigns Since 1960.* Lawrence, KS: University Press of Kansas, 2009, 7.

26 Michael Gerson, "Opinion: To Fight the GOP's Antidemocratic Fire, We Need a National Effort at Civil Healing," *Washington Post*, July 2, 2021, A23. https://www.washingtonpost.com/opinions/2021/07/01/american-democracy-civic-healing-fighting-gop/.

27 ibid.

28 Tom Rosenstiel, "What Can Journalists Do about the 'Unreality Crisis?'" American Press Institute, www.americanpressinstitute.org/publications/articles/what-can-journaists-do-about-the-unreality-crisis/.

29 ibid.

30 Stuart Soroka, Patrick Fournier, and Lilach Nir, "Cross-National Evidence of a Negativity Bias in Psychophysiological Reactions to News," PNAS (Proceedings of the National Academy of Sciences of the United States of America), September 17, 2019, https://www.pnas.org/content/116/38/18888.

SELECTED READINGS

Ansolabehere, Stephen and Shanto Iyenar, *Going Negative: How Political Advertisements Shrink & Polarize the Electorate*. New York: The Free Press, 1995.

Bernstein, Carl and Bob Woodward, *All the President's Men*. New York: Touchstone/Simon & Schuster, 1987.

Berry, Jeffrey M. and Sarah Sobieraj, *The Outrage Industry: Political Opinion Media and the New Incivility (Studies in Postwar American Political Development)*. New York: Oxford University Press, 2016.

Boller, Paul, *Presidential Campaigns*. New York: Oxford University Press, 2004.

Brinkley, Alan, *Voices of Protest: Huey Long, Father Coughiln, and the Great Depression*. New York: Vintage Books, 1983.

Brinkley, Douglas, ed., *The Reagan Diaries*. New York: HarperCollins, 2007.

Buell, Emmett H., Jr. and Lee Sigelman, *Attack Politics: Negativity in Presidential Campaigns since 1960*. Lawrence, KS: University Press of Kansas, 2009.

Bush, George, *All the Best, George Bush: My Life in Letters and Other Writings*. New York: Scribner, 1999.

Cannon, Lou, *President Reagan: The Role of a Lifetime*. New York: Public Affairs, 1991.

Carter, Jimmy, *Keeping Faith: Memoirs of a President*. Fayetteville, AR: University of Arkansas Press, 1995.

Carter, Jimmy, *White House Diary*. New York: Farrar, Straus and Giroux, 2010.

Clinton, Bill, *My Life*. New York: Alfred A. Knopf, 2004.

Conason, Joe and Gene Lyons, *The Hunting of the President: The Ten-Year Campaign to Destroy Bill and Hillary Clinton*. New York: Thomas Dunne Books, 2000.

Cronin, Thomas, *On the Presidency: Teacher, Soldier, Shaman, Pol*. Boulder, CO: Paradigm Publishers, 2009.

Dallek, Matthew, *Birchers: How the John Birch Society Radicalized the American Right*. New York: Basic Books, 2023.

Dallek, Robert, *Flawed Giant: Lyndon Johnson and His Times, 1961–1973.* New York: Oxford University Press, 1998.

Dewey, Donald, *The Art of Ill Will: The Story of American Political Cartoons.* New York: New York University Press, 2007.

Dionne, E.J., Jr., *Why Americans Hate Politics.* New York: Touchstone, 1991.

Donald, Aida D., *Lion in the White House: A Life of Theodore Roosevelt.* New York: MJF Books, 2007.

Duffy, Michael and Dan Goodgame, *Marching in Place: The Status Quo Presidency of George Bush.* New York: Simon & Schuster, 1992.

Du Mez, Kristin Kobes, *Jesus and John Wayne: How White Evangelicals Corrupted a Faith and Fractured a Nation.* New York: Liveright Publishing, 2020.

Ferling, John, *Adams vs. Jefferson: The Tumultuous Election of 1800.* New York: Oxford University Press, 2004.

Fitzwater, Marlin, *Call the Briefing! Reagan and Bush, Sam and Helen: A Decade with Presidents and the Press.* New York: Times Books, 1995.

Fleischer, Ari, *Taking Heat: The President, the Press, and My Years in the White House.* New York: William Morrow, 2005.

Goldman, Peter, Tom Mathews, and the *Newsweek* Special Election Team, *The Quest for the Presidency 1988.* New York: Simon & Schuster/Touchstone, 1989.

Goodwin, Doris Kearns, *No Ordinary Time: Franklin and Eleanor Roosevelt: The Home Front in World War II.* New York: Simon & Schuster, 1994.

Gordon-Reed, Annette, *Thomas Jefferson and Sally Hemings: An American Controversy.* Charlottesville, VA: University of Virginia Press, 1997.

Groeling, Tim, *When Politicians Attack! Party Cohesion in the Media.* New York: Cambridge University Press, 2010.

Harris, John F., *The Survivor: Bill Clinton in the White House.* New York: Random House, 2005.

Healy, Gene, *The Cult of the Presidency: America's Dangerous Devotion to Executive Power.* Washington, D.C.: Cato Institute, 2008.

Heidler, David S. and Jeanne T. Heidler, *The Rise of Andrew Jackson: Myth, Manipulation, and the Making of Modern Politics.* New York: Basic Books, 2018.

Heilemann, John and Mark Halperin, *Game Change: Obama and the Clintons, McCain and Palin, and the Race of a Lifetime.* New York: HarperCollins, 2010.

Hemmer, Nicole, *Messengers of the Right: Conservative Media and the Transformation of American Politics.* Philadelphia, PA: University of Pennsylvania Press, 2016.

Hess, Stephen and Milton Kaplan, *The Ungentlemanly Art: A History of American Political Cartoons.* New York: Macmillan, 1975.

Hobfoll, Stevan E., *Tribalism: The Evolutionary Origins of Fear Politics.* London: Palgrave Macmillan, 2018.

Huntington, John S., *Far-Right Vanguard: The Radical Roots of Modern Conservatism.* Philadelphia, PA: University of Pennsylvania Press, 2021.

Jamieson, Kathleen Hall, *Dirty Politics: Deception, Distraction, and Democracy.* New York: Oxford University Press, 1992a.

Jamieson, Kathleen Hall, *Packaging the Presidency: A History and Criticism of Presidential Campaign Advertising*. New York: Oxford University Press, 1992b.

Johnston, David Cay, *The Making of Donald Trump*. Brooklyn, NY: Melville House, 2016.

Kalman, Laura, *Right Star Rising: A New Politics, 1974–1980*. New York: W.W. Norton & Co., 2010.

Kalmoe, Nathan P. and Lilliana Mason, *Radical American Partisanship: Mapping Violent Hostility, Its Causes, and the Consequences for Democracy*. Chicago, IL: University of Chicago Press, 2022.

Kane, Thomas Harnett, *Huey Long's Louisiana Hayride: The American Rehearsal for Dictatorship, 1928–1940*. New York: William Morrow, 1941.

Kantor, Jodi, *The Obamas*. New York: Little Brown, 2012.

Kennedy, David M., *Freedom from Fear: The American People in Depression and War, 1929–1945*. Oxford: Oxford University Press, 2001.

Knott, Stephen E., *The Lost Soul of the American Presidency: The Decline Into Demagoguery and the Prospects for Renewal*. Lawrence, KS: University Press of Kansas, 2020.

Kuhn, Jim, *Ronald Reagan in Private; A Memoir of My Years in the White House*. New York: Sentinel, 2004.

Kurtz, Howard, *Spin Cycle: Inside the Clinton Propaganda Machine*. New York: The Free Press, 1998.

Luntz, Frank, *Words That Work: It's Not What You Say, It's What People Hear*. New York: Hyperion, 2007.

Lynes, Russell, *The Tastemakers: The Shaping of American Popular Taste*. New York: Dover Publications, Inc., 1980.

Matviko, John W., ed., *The American President in Popular Culture*. Westport, CT: Greenwood Press, 2005.

McCullough, David, *Truman*. New York: Simon & Schuster, 1992.

Navasky, Victor S., *The Art of Controversy: Political Cartoons and Their Enduring Power*. New York: Alfred A. Knopf, 2013.

Obama, Barack, *Dreams from My Father: A Story of Race and Inheritance*. New York: Crown, 2007.

Olso, Rune, *Behind the Curtain of Power*. Pittsburgh, PA: Dorrance Publishing Co., 2021.

Parsons, Lynn Hudson, *The Birth of Modern Politics: Andrew Jackson, John Quincy Adams, and the Election of 1828*. New York: Oxford University Press, 2009.

Perlstein, Rick, *Nixonland: The Rise of a President and the Fracturing of America*. New York: Scribner, 2008.

Perlstein, Rick, *Reaganland: America's Right Turn 1976–1980*. New York: Simon & Schuster, 2020.

Peters, Jeremy W., *Insurgency: How Republicans Lost Their Party and Got Everything They Ever Wanted*. New York: Crown, 2022.

Phillips-Fein, Kim, *Invisible Hands: The Businessmen's Crusade Against the New Deal*. New York: W.W. Norton, 2009.

Reagan, Nancy with William Novak. *My Turn: The Memoirs of Nancy Reagan*. New York: Random House, 1989.

Reagan, Ronald, *Ronald Reagan: An American Life*. New York: Simon & Schuster, 1990.

Reedy, George E., *The Twilight of the Presidency*. Cleveland, OH and New York: New American Library/World Publishing Company, 1970.

Roberts, Rebecca Boggs, *Untold Power: The Fascinating Rise and Complex Legacy of First Lady Edith Wilson*. New York: Viking, 2023.

Sabato, Larry J., *Feeding Frenzy: How Attack Journalism Has Transformed American Politics*. New York: The Free Press, 1991.

Schoen, Douglas E., *The End of Authority: How a Loss of Legitimacy and Broken Trust Are Endangering Our Future*. Lanham, MD: Rowman & Littlefield, 2013.

Schweizer, Peter and Rochelle Schweizer, *The Bushes: Portrait of a Dynasty*. New York: Doubleday, 2004.

Skinner, Kiron K., Annelise Anderson, and Martin Anderson, *Reagan: In His Own Hand*. New York: Free Press, 2001.

Smith, Jean Edward, *Bush*. New York: Simon & Schuster, 2016.

Sorensen, Theodore C., *Kennedy*. New York: Harper & Row, 1965.

Stelter, Brian, *Hoax: Donald Trump, Fox News, and the Dangerous Distortion of Truth*. New York: Atria/One Signal, 2020.

Stephanopoulos, George, *All Too Human: A Political Education*. Boston, MA: Little, Brown, 1999.

Swint, Kerwin, *Dark Genius: The Influential Career of Legendary Political Operative and Fox News Founder Roger Ailes*. New York: Union Square Press, 2008a.

Swint, Kerwin, *Mudslingers: The Twenty-Five Dirtiest Political Campaigns of All Time*. New York: Union Square Press, 2008b.

Taylor, Tim, *The Book of Presidents*. New York: Arno Press, 1972.

Troy, Tevi, *What Jefferson Read, Ike Watched, and Obama Tweeted: 200 Years of Popular Culture in the White House*. Washington, D.C.: Regnery Publishing, Inc., 2013.

Truman, Margaret, *Harry S. Truman*. New York: William Morrow & Company, 1973.

Trump, Donald and Tony Schwartz, *Trump: The Art of the Deal*. New York: Ballantine, 2015.

Tye, Larry, *Demagogue: The Life and Long Shadow of Senator Joe McCarthy*. New York: Houghton Mifflin Harcourt, 2020.

Walsh, Kenneth T., *Feeding the Beast: The White House Versus the Press*. New York: Random House, 1996.

Walsh, Kenneth T., *Ronald Reagan: Biography*. New York: Park Lane Press, 1997.

Walsh, Kenneth T., *Prisoners of the White House: The Isolation of America's Presidents and the Crisis of Leadership*. Boulder, CO: Paradigm, 2013.

Walsh, Kenneth T., *Presidential Leadership in Crisis: Defining Moments of the Modern Presidents from Franklin Roosevelt to Donald Trump*. New York: Routledge, 2020.

Warren, Donald, *Radio Priest: Charles Coughlin, the Father of Hate Radio*. New York: Free Press, 1996.

Wicker, Tom, *Shooting Star: The Brief Arc of Joe McCarthy*. New York: Harcourt, 2006.

Williams, T. Harry, *Huey Long*. New York: Vintage, 1981.
Woodward, Bob, *The Choice*. New York: Simon & Schuster, 1996.
Zelizer, Julian E., *Burning Down the House: Newt Gingrich, the Fall of a Speaker, and the Rise of the New Republican Party*. New York: Penguin Press, 2020.

INDEX

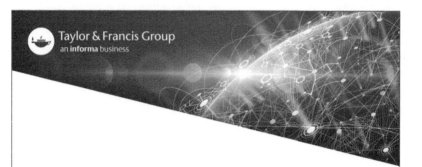

For Product Safety Concerns and Information please contact our EU representative GPSR@taylorandfrancis.com Taylor & Francis Verlag GmbH, Kaufingerstraße 24, 80331 München, Germany